Reimagining Liberation

Reimagining Liberation

Gawani Theology and Hermeneutical Perspectives in the Malawian Context

DONG IN BAEK

WIPF & STOCK · Eugene, Oregon

REIMAGINING LIBERATION
Gawani Theology and Hermeneutical Perspectives in the Malawian Context

Copyright © 2025 Dong In Baek. All rights reserved. Except for brief quotations in critical publications or reviews, no part of this book may be reproduced in any manner without prior written permission from the publisher. Write: Permissions, Wipf and Stock Publishers, 199 W. 8th Ave., Suite 3, Eugene, OR 97401.

Wipf & Stock
An Imprint of Wipf and Stock Publishers
199 W. 8th Ave., Suite 3
Eugene, OR 97401

www.wipfandstock.com

PAPERBACK ISBN: 979-8-3852-5295-4
HARDCOVER ISBN: 979-8-3852-5296-1
EBOOK ISBN: 979-8-3852-5297-8

06/30/25

Scripture quotations are taken from the Holy Bible, New International Version®, NIV®. Copyright © 1973, 1978, 1984, 2011 by Biblica, Inc.™ Used by permission of Zondervan. All rights reserved worldwide. www.zondervan.com.

Contents

Preface | vii

Prologue: Seeds of Solidarity—How Gawani Theology Blooms in Malawi's Shared Landscape | xi

Introduction: Gawani Theology, Grassroots Solidarity, and the Hermeneutics of Communal Care | xvii

1. Malawi Mission Journey and the Emergence of Gawani Theology: The Power of Sharing and Distribution | 1

2. Gawani Theology as a Communal Framework of Faith and Shared Responsibility | 10

3. Viewing the World Through a Worm's Eye: Critical Perspective and Practical Wisdom in Gawani Theology | 19

4. Gawani in Creation and Salvation: An Interdependent Relationship Linking God, Humanity, and Nature | 34

5. A Contemporary Reconsideration of the Kingdom of God Through Liberation Theology and the New Political Theology | 57

6. Gawani Christology: The Son of Human Being and the Restoration of Humanity in the Gospels and Acts | 72

7. Embodying God's Kingdom Through Solidarity with Marginalized Communities | 104

8. Toward a Gawani-Feminist-Black Liberation Ethos: Reimagining Community and Resource-Sharing | 153

9. Shared Horizons: A Thematic Conclusion on Community, Resource Sharing, and Transformative Faith | 229

Epilogue: Where Seeds of Mercy Take Root | 243

Bibliography | 247

Preface

DEAR READER,

You are about to explore *Reimagining Liberation: Gawani Theology and Hermeneutical Perspectives in the Malawian Context*. This volume brings together multiple strands of reflection and research, culminating from long-standing engagements with theology, history, and interfaith dialogue. It also represents a fruitful collaboration that began in March 2023, when I received a concise yet remarkable manuscript from Dr. Joseph Kang, who had served for ten years as a Presbyterian missionary in Malawi. Although his contribution consisted of only about twenty pages, it brimmed with thoughtful biblical exegesis and a resolute focus on the practice of gawani—an ethos of sharing and distributing within communal life. Building on Dr. Kang's insights and drawing from my own broader inquiries, this work expands that preliminary text into an in-depth study of how gawani theology can resonate with both Malawian contexts and global questions of liberation, justice, and faith.

The broader context for this book stretches back to 2011, when I began gathering research materials and shaping ideas for the Nature and Time series (Volume I, Volume II, Volume III). Over these years, I found myself crossing disciplinary boundaries, blending theological concerns with philosophical and sociocultural explorations. Yet it was only in receiving Dr. Kang's text, encapsulating his decade of missionary experience, that I discovered a powerful lens through which to integrate these lines of investigation. Gawani theology, as gleaned from his reflections and my subsequent research, aligns naturally with liberation theologies and various grassroots movements worldwide, yet it remains deeply

Malawian at its core—rooted in everyday acts of sharing that sustain entire communities under adverse economic and political conditions.

Dr. Kang's background as an American Presbyterian missionary in Malawi adds further depth to this study. His daily interactions with local churches, families, and village leaders granted him a vantage point from which he documented not only biblical and doctrinal interpretations, but also the lived experiences of people who strive for dignity and survival under constant watchfulness. His manuscript revealed that faith, culture, and mutual care are intricately woven; in Malawi, distributing seeds or extra food is not mere benevolence but a norm grounded in shared identity. Drawing upon Chichewa vocabulary and scriptural motifs, gawani theology offers a distinctive paradigm that resonates with Christian teachings on neighborly love and the pursuit of liberation.

This book owes its shape to many influences. First and foremost, to the Malawian communities whose stories inform these pages. Their collective resilience offers a tangible example of how trust, resource pooling, and faith blend to form a protective network amid difficult circumstances. Second, to the Korean missionary circles that championed deeper understanding of Malawi's spiritual heritage, fostering cross-cultural learning. And finally, to the theological, historical, and hermeneutical conversations I have participated in over the years—each has widened my perspective on how local ethics and global questions intersect.

The volume itself is structured to highlight both specific cultural insights and their broader applications. Certain chapters delve into the scriptural underpinnings of gawani, tracing how biblical narratives of covenant, hospitality, and communal care find renewed meaning in Malawian contexts. Others situate gawani within the wider tapestry of liberation and contextual theologies, suggesting that its emphasis on shared survival and dignity parallels concerns voiced by minjung theology, Latin American base communities, and feminist or postcolonial hermeneutics. Rather than viewing these as separate discourses, I posit that they converge in their call for a reorientation of power, economics, and communal relationships.

At its core, gawani theology presses us to see faith as actively shaping, and shaped by, day-to-day actions: a congregation deciding how to allocate leftover produce, a group of farmers agreeing to a rotating microloan scheme, or a pastor rearranging Sunday gathering to accommodate communal decision-making. In these domains, theology does not remain a set of abstract principles but becomes a lived pattern—transforming worship, shifting social hierarchies, and giving greater voice to those at the margins. The goal is to highlight how resource-sharing, undergirded by scriptural guidance, can nurture moral clarity and unity.

This work would not exist without the steadfast backing of colleagues, faith communities, and academic mentors who encouraged me to keep crossing boundaries. Their advice challenged me to regard theology as far more than an intellectual pursuit—an outlook reaffirmed each time I encountered new stories of cooperation and persistence from Malawian families. While I have endeavored to integrate scholarly rigor, my sincere wish is that readers will also perceive the heart of this project: a conviction that communal faith, marked by concrete acts of solidarity, remains vital for envisioning a more just society.

I also acknowledge those unnamed individuals in Malawi who welcomed Dr. Kang and others with open arms, showing that genuine hospitality far surpasses mere words. I thank Joe George, copyeditor, pop-culture writer, and English lecturer, whose careful reading and steady edits brought each page into clearer focus. I am equally grateful to Wipf and Stock for their trust and support, which made it possible for this work to reach its readers. Their daily leadership, wisdom, and fortitude have shaped my understanding of how scriptural teachings on sharing and reconciliation take root in tangible ways. May this book, in some measure, honor that legacy and invite others to do likewise in their own contexts.

As you engage these chapters, I invite you to consider gawani's implications for your own spheres—be they parishes, universities, or local communities. The questions it poses—about how we distribute resources, share authority, and enact care—carry significance for communities far beyond Malawi. If this text sparks fresh thinking on how theology and communal collaboration might be integrated, it will have fulfilled its purpose.

Thank you for embarking on this journey through *Reimagining Liberation: Gawani Theology and Hermeneutical Perspectives in the Malawian Context*. May it open conversations, inspire practical changes, and ultimately encourage us to see that theology can be lived out wherever people gather to share, uphold each other's dignity, and strive for a broader vision of freedom.

Yours with gratitude,

Dong In Baek
3/31/2025

Prologue

*Seeds of Solidarity—How Gawani Theology
Blooms in Malawi's Shared Landscape*

Contemporary theological discussions about gawani theology bloom from a landscape where neighbors sought each other's hands during heavy watchfulness, where identification checks lingered at every corner, and where trust was a delicate flame. In those Malawian households burdened by Hastings Banda's policies, families discovered that survival meant standing shoulder to shoulder: extra maize quietly given, a few coins slipped into another's palm. Like a secret chord, gawani— "to share"—tuned their daily rhythms with an ethic of mutual belonging.

Within that mosaic, the threads of cooperation were not confined to one village or congregation; instead, they wove through countless interactions—shreds of produce, fragments of savings, solemn words of comfort. No one thrived in isolation. The acts of exchanging seeds or giving away handfuls of grain shaped an understanding of well-being as something that grows whenever the community nurtures it. This communal leaning, once perceived as mere kindness, emerged as a steady compass guiding moral life.

Turning to the biblical narratives, gawani theology reminds us that faith is rarely a private whisper. Gospel texts show how material wealth becomes an isolating fortress if not opened for others. In the eyes of gawani thinkers, redemption itself wears a physical form: money offered at the right time, an empathetic gesture, spiritual convictions braided into everyday duties. It is not enough to hold possessions lightly; one must be ready to let them flow to others—because in that giving, they become a sign of living faith.

This perspective carries over into care for the earth. Some read Genesis as an invitation to safeguard the land for generations yet to come. In Malawian settings, farmland and gardens are more than static properties; they breathe with the stories of families who work them and feed entire communities. Gawani theology underscores that caring for the soil cannot be pried apart from caring for neighbors, because the health of the land and the health of the people rise or wither together.

A worm's eye vantage casts light on those who typically walk in shadows. Gawani-oriented discussions favor hidden places—small gatherings, church corners, quiet markets—where humble acts of sharing reveal deeper truths about resilience. These scenes challenge assumptions that poverty means helplessness. Instead, they reveal a gracious resourcefulness. Whether the item exchanged is a leftover vegetable or a shared bus fare, it can become an anchor of solidarity in a system that otherwise rewards isolation.

Such sharing resonates with liberation themes that behold power in the margins. In the exodus story, a divine voice answers cries from those shackled by oppressive forces, while in the Gospels, Jesus stands with those pushed aside. Translating this into modern Malawi, gawani theology reminds congregations that identification cards or forced loyalty pledges often corrode communal unity. But by weaving support into church life—borrowing, distributing, encouraging—they stand up to systems that would scatter them.

Others in Malawi link gawani to ubuntu: "I am because we are." This call speaks to a moral duty of distributing not just surplus items but also time and energy. Whenever a neighbor's roof leaks or a stranger travels with empty hands, the gawani spirit prompts an active generosity that resonates with biblical ideals. This ethos takes root in small tasks—pounding grain side by side, sharing leftover seeds for replanting. Traditional understanding and Christian ethics merge in a tapestry of everyday goodness.

Gawani likewise converses with the voices of Black liberation theology, feminist theology, and more—those who insist that any genuine talk of justice must confront the policies under which people labor. Black liberation theologians point out how religion must not close its eyes to oppression; feminist perspectives highlight how unacknowledged burdens fall mostly on women. Gawani is unafraid to gather these different notes into a single score, calling for a shift in how society views cooperation and responsibility.

In the pages of the Gospels and Acts, some gawani interpreters see Jesus naming himself "Son of Human Being" in a way that embodies camaraderie and redemption. This phrasing portrays Jesus as standing alongside those bearing life's heavier yoke. Gawani looks at Malawian families supporting one another under governmental suspicion and sees Jesus walking that same tightrope: offering relief, challenging exploitative habits, defining faith by action. It is a bold stance asserting that belief must confront the structures harming daily life.

The communal outlook of Acts—believers holding "all things in common"—becomes a blueprint for gawani's approach. Instead of viewing it as an archaic model, gawani frames it as a living invitation to keep reexamining how churches use tithes, manage construction projects, or handle political engagement. Hoarding resources among a few starves the broader group. Thus, gawani demands that the church's internal culture reflect openness, from budgeting to leadership, urging transparent, shared practices that uphold the dignity of all.

Malawian anthropological insights around rituals like *nyau* further enrich gawani theology. These cultural practices, often misread by outsiders, speak of solidarity that arcs beyond mere economic exchange into the spiritual memory of a people. Everyday gestures, stories, and ceremonies become the backbone of a community's capacity to endure. Gawani seizes on such traditions and interprets them through Christian teachings, forging a spiritual movement that breathes through the dust of real roads, real fields.

Local mission strategies that once carried a Western imprint are slowly being reshaped by this gawani ethic. Those who come from afar are encouraged to wait, to listen to the hum of local needs and initiatives. Rather than imposing top-down schemes, they can fortify existing social bonds. This approach calls for collaboration, a readiness to learn, and humility in the face of deep cultural wisdom. It is a posture that recognizes that local patterns of mutual assistance often hold the key to lasting impact.

Discussions around caring for creation also find renewed vigor when filtered through gawani's lens. Topsoil erosion, inadequate water supplies, and the disappearance of native flora pose acute problems for agricultural communities. Yet, a congregation that recalls scriptural mandates to be stewards of the land can embrace creative, community-led approaches to sustainability. Seed sharing or farm tool exchanges thus become extensions of a belief that the earth too belongs to the fellowship of neighbors.

Comparisons with minjung theology highlight how everyday people, often excluded from official narratives, become protagonists of their own story. Just as minjung rose in a South Korean context of political upheaval, so too does gawani bloom where families wrestle with limited farmland or uncertain incomes. Both theological streams contend that interpretation of Scripture must arise from those who, in the world's eyes, stand at the margins, believing that their perspective unveils a deeper moral compass.

The kingdom of God, under gawani's reevaluation, emerges not as a distant horizon but as the moment in which we dare to share resources in defiance of oppressive norms. Whenever a local church chooses to pool finances for communal bread, or neighbors decide to pay one another's school fees rather than wait for an elusive government fix, they enact the kingdom with each choice. Such daily acts illustrate that discipleship thrives in the details of economic practice, not merely in lofty sermons or pious words.

Some theological voices fold this perspective into Christology, declaring that Jesus is found in the face of the ones who share. If the Incarnation testifies to God's solidarity with humanity, then gawani upholds that Christ continues to appear wherever people open their hands to each other. Such a reading insists that Son of Human Being is not only an identity Jesus once claimed but also an ethic for us to embody now—dismantling fear and forging communities of trust.

Feminist theology brings fresh questions to gawani: tasks like cooking for large gatherings or caring for children all day often weigh on women. Hence, gawani-oriented proposals must ensure women's leadership is no mere afterthought. In this synergy, a truly inclusive communal ethic recognizes that if we laud shared labor but ignore gender disparities, we remain blind to half the truth. Embracing gawani means building structures that see and honor women's contributions as a core element of shared life.

Analogous reflections follow when we look at racial or ethnic inequalities. Gawani theology reminds believers that no real communal economy can flourish if racial barriers or cultural discrimination remain intact. Conversations with Black-led churches in other nations suggest that resource redistribution is intimately tied to confronting prejudice. Across continents, gawani might find resonance among congregations searching for ways to nurture fellowship beyond superficial diversity statements.

On the hermeneutical front, gawani aligns with Gadamer's concept of dialogical understanding. By inviting local elders, visiting mission workers, and Bible scholars into genuine conversation, new meanings surface. Interpreters can let biblical texts speak to the real conditions in the market stalls and farmland, while local experiences shape how we comprehend the scriptural call to "love your neighbor." This circular reading fosters a humility that acknowledges the text remains alive in the interplay of varied voices.

Church members who welcome gawani theology often press for structural overhaul, from collectively governed savings programs to demands for open local council meetings. After all, it is hard to maintain relational unity if external power structures block the community from genuine self-determination. Over time, alliances formed at the household level can stretch into movements that stand firm, even against repressive edicts. As history teaches, small seeds of solidarity can thrive in the stoniest grounds.

In so shaping daily life, gawani theology reshapes the meaning of mission. Outreach flows from the ongoing presence of moral and material support, rather than from sporadic charity or detached preaching. Western agencies, too, find themselves challenged to adapt once they realize that local knowledge has guided Malawians through storms for generations. In a region prone to cycles of scarcity, such an approach stands as a living testament that solutions often dwell within, awaiting recognition and uplift.

Some question whether gawani's tilt toward cooperation underestimates the need for direct confrontation against formidable powers. Proponents acknowledge that not every conflict dissolves through quiet consensus. When exploitative measures intensify, communities must, at times, collectively oppose them. Yet, the readiness to unify for resistance is fortified by the very networks gawani fosters. Resource-sharing paves the way for unified protest—no one stands alone because they have woven themselves into a supportive net.

Others wonder if this emphasis on collective giving will survive quieter seasons, when threats recede. Gawani advocates say yes, for its essence is neither crisis-driven nor fleeting. Once the habit of solidarity takes root, it shapes how people greet each new day. Through cultural stories, worship gatherings, and repeated acts of kindness, gawani remains an undercurrent that counters apathy, reminding believers that every new morning holds the chance to care for one another anew.

In wider theological dialogues, gawani exemplifies a grassroots approach applicable to global issues like climate change, forced displacement, or precarious labor markets. Malawian experiences speak to others wrestling with parallel injustices. Whether in a Latin American shantytown or a Southeast Asian fishing village, a theology of shared life can translate local resilience into broader hope. Enculturation specialists foresee gawani forging cross-cultural bonds—a bridging of hearts as much as of ideas.

Observing the ecumenical dimension, some dream that gawani might unify various denominations around purposeful action. Joint projects—building simple mills, organizing farmland cooperatives—offer an uncontroversial yet profound ground for partnership. In striving side by side for the common good, theological differences might find new perspectives, as the synergy of love supplants abstract debate. Gawani, then, becomes a signpost of how unity in service can illuminate deeper reconciliation.

Finally, the pages ahead chronicle cases where gawani changed how churches allocated budgets, set up microloans, or evangelized in subtle but robust ways. These examples illustrate that the theology of shared life and resource distribution is no airy theory but a workable design for ministry. For those seeking ways to heal oppression, or to face economic pressures with grace, gawani offers a tapestry of local tradition, scriptural reflection, and unwavering compassion.

So, for all who ponder how a faith community might answer authoritarian edicts or persistent inequities, these chapters narrate the drama of neighborly trust outlasting intimidation. Malawian knowledge, biblical insight, and communal determination collaborate in forging paths to liberation, demonstrating that hope grows through the everyday gestures people make for one another.

In this synergy—where gawani converses with liberation theologies and fresh interpretive frameworks, the call to love one's neighbor emerges as vividly practical. Malawi's circumstances—scarcity, government oversight, unwavering watchfulness—become the proving ground for biblical commitments. The bond of solidarity and trust, even under tension, endures.

Thus, these pages beckon readers to a realm where offering produce or bus fare is laden with significance. Here, theology seamlessly intersects with daily motions, and the economy of resources evolves into a moral tapestry. Gazing upon Malawi's communal ethos, gawani reimagines the shape of relationship and shared calling, revealing that liberation arrives through a corridor of collective footsteps, carrying each other forward.

Introduction

Gawani Theology, Grassroots Solidarity, and the Hermeneutics of Communal Care

Contemporary theological discussions often grapple with how faith communities can enact tangible care for neighbors under conditions of economic adversity and political constraint. These discussions stretch across various contexts, addressing both the micro-level interactions of individual believers and the macro-level structures that guide resource distribution. This volume intervenes in that discourse by highlighting gawani theology, a conceptual framework deeply rooted in Malawian contexts where culturally embedded sharing practices intersect with state-imposed surveillance. Rather than depicting gawani theology as a mere artifact of local custom, the text presents it as an integrative lens. Through that lens, moral collaboration and communal spirituality align to form a holistic framework of mutual care. By foregrounding how religious identity, social support, and practical resilience intertwine, the volume suggests that gawani theology transcends standard approaches to mission or charity. It advances the view that faith communities can embody consistent and proactive attention to one another's needs, even under coercive regimes. Consequently, readers are invited to consider how local strategies of distribution can ground a broader theological perspective, one that privileges relational ties over top-down models of benevolence and aligns worship with daily acts of giving.

Dr. Joseph Kang's extended sojourn in Malawi, alongside his spouse, Hannah, becomes a foundational narrative that illustrates how gawani theology took shape in a climate of political tension. In a setting marked by President Hastings Banda's one-party rule, citizens faced relentless scrutiny from the Malawi Young Pioneers, while market visits and simple travel required displaying loyalty through official party identification. Despite these hostile conditions, local Malawian families regularly forged practical alliances. They quietly pooled leftover food, offered bus fare, and provided safe lodging to neighbors who faced eviction or intimidation. Through firsthand observation of these everyday acts, Dr. Kang discerned the centrality of a Chichewa term "gawa," which goes beyond sporadic charitable acts to signify an enduring ethic of distribution and care. The subtle but pervasive influence of this ethic led Kang to formulate gawani theology as a tool for recognizing how the moral obligations underlying neighborly support can serve as a cornerstone for theological reflection. Crucially, this approach resists portraying impoverished communities as passive recipients, proposing instead that their resourcefulness and commitment to shared responsibility can inform—and even reshape—traditional theological frameworks that have too often been preoccupied with top-down efforts at "help" or "development."

Under gawani theology, resource-sharing occupies the center of a broader conversation about how spiritual convictions and cultural norms reinforce one another. Although the theology has local roots, its implications extend to global questions of how faith groups address structural poverty, political oppression, and social marginalization. Gawani theology contends that solidarity does not unfold as an optional kindness but as a defining characteristic of communal life, tying economic interdependence to religious devotion. The text emphasizes that leftover produce, informal counseling, and shared labor become more than utilitarian survival tactics. Instead, they represent a cohesive moral practice built around sustaining each other's well-being. This integrative mindset challenges models of external "rescue" that treat local communities as incapable of self-guided organization. By focusing on the internal dynamics of resource-sharing, gawani theology illustrates how neighbors, connected through long-standing cultural ties, develop collective resilience. These daily habits of distribution do not merely respond to immediate crises; they generate a consistent framework that binds spiritual identity to moral obligation, thereby dislodging the assumption that impoverished people exist in a constant state of helplessness.

A recurring cultural motif is the idea of "ubale," highlighting how Chewa society conceives of interconnected responsibilities that merge sacred and communal dimensions. Far from understanding faith as isolated doctrine or personal practice, Chewa traditions show that worship, ancestry, and neighborly care interlock in cohesive ways. Rituals such as *nyau*, marked by dances that honor departed forebears, reaffirm a societal principle that transcends individual mortality and anchors collective belonging. Gawani theology underscores that these cultural enactments are not tangential to understanding Christian mission; rather, they clarify how spiritual life permeates everyday relations. By drawing on local symbolism, gawani theology proposes an embedded approach to theology—one that arises directly from how communities navigate threats of eviction or loss. The ensuing perspective treats every moment of shared labor, shelter, or counsel as part of an unfolding spiritual testimony. Consequently, the theology not only aligns with broader communal theologies but also exemplifies a context-attuned approach that honors indigenous knowledge and ritual without erasing its Christian commitment.

The worm's eye viewpoint expands upon these local dynamics by advocating a bottom-up mode of inquiry. Instead of starting with institutional doctrines or official histories, this vantage privileges the testimonies of individuals living in precarious conditions—laborers, displaced families, or those silenced by governmental strictures. By doing so, the text presents gawani theology as part of an ongoing conversation about whose experiences matter in theological reflection. This approach seeks to correct an established pattern in which academic or institutional voices overshadow the lived realities of marginalized populations. Drawing on Gadamer's notion of dialogue, gawani theology embodies a willingness to learn from those at society's edges, illustrating how theological claims become more grounded when they emerge in conversation with everyday struggles. Through this method, the interplay between local stories and biblical mandates produces a more accountable and participatory framework of faith. Rather than relegating the poor to the status of illustrations or passive figures, the worm's eye lens insists that meaningful religious discourse must be influenced by and remain answerable to the realities of those who occupy the fragile margins of power.

The text then weaves in biblical accounts, especially from Genesis and Exodus, to underscore how care for creation and the pursuit of social justice converge. In the gawani reading, Genesis portrays human beings not as supreme rulers over nature but as custodians responsible for sustaining the earth's capacity to support life. This insistence on stewardship resonates with the exodus story, where liberation from bondage underscores God's active opposition to exploitation. Gawani theology contends that ecological welfare and human dignity belong to the same moral tapestry, arguing that economic systems benefiting a few while harming the environment run contrary to the vision of shared flourishing set forth in Scripture. Moreover, the approach posits that ignoring environmental degradation often harms the most vulnerable communities first. In that sense, a gawani-informed ethic would entail reevaluating agricultural practices, land use, and environmental policies to align with a covenant-based commitment that extends to all creation. This interconnection of creation care and human emancipation strengthens the conviction that a faith perspective must challenge extractive structures, thereby highlighting the shared responsibilities of believers toward both their neighbors and the broader ecological context.

Central to the volume's exploration is the theme of the kingdom of God, reframed through the lens of liberation theology, the new political theology, and gawani itself. Historically, many Christian communities have treated the kingdom as a distant or purely spiritual realm, anticipating its eventual arrival while overlooking present inequities. Liberation theology disrupts that assumption by insisting on the kingdom's immediate implications—namely, that true alignment with God's reign requires standing against oppressive authorities and advocating for the marginalized. Kang's gawani vision connects these broad liberationist aspirations to localized cultural norms in Malawi, illustrating how communal self-giving works as an antidote to corruption and poverty. The volume argues that when believers interpret the kingdom as an active reality, they embark on a shared social project, forging alliances that mirror biblical values of hospitality and inclusion. Rather than seeing Malawi's approach to neighborly care as an exception, gawani theology suggests it is an illustrative case, revealing how religious communities worldwide might harness their local traditions to advance the kingdom's transformative ethos.

Christology also plays a significant role, particularly through the "Son of Human Being" designation in the Gospels and Acts. The text amplifies Kang's argument that Jesus's self-identification underlines the importance of restoring dignity to those systematically diminished by structural forces. Gawani theology fuses this christological perspective with the tangible concerns of marginalized groups, suggesting that the incarnational mission involves direct participation in healing social rifts and reversing exploitative practices. The phrase "Son of Human Being" becomes more than a remote theological concept; it signals a commitment to inclusive fellowship that unseats hierarchical relationships. By binding the theological domain to everyday realities, gawani theology echoes liberationist thinkers who argue that faith remains incomplete if it remains confined to inward devotion. In practical terms, this viewpoint invites believers to reinterpret discipleship as a dynamic engagement with social, economic, and cultural barriers. The result is a Christology that both affirms spiritual reverence and mandates structural transformation, simultaneously drawing on biblical exegesis and local testimonies of tenacious cooperation.

The notion of solidarity likewise emerges as a core principle, particularly in the volume's assessment of how faith communities might manifest God's kingdom among the marginalized. Examining Luke's accounts of the wealthy official and Zacchaeus reveals a pattern in which possessions and social power can either entrench exclusion or foster reparation. Gawani theology resonates with minjung theology, liberation theology, and similar frameworks that highlight the tangible implications of belief in contexts of inequity. Under these approaches, conversion is not solely personal repentance but also a decision to rectify or redistribute resources and power. By emphasizing these structural elements, the text compels readers to think about how local congregations can become platforms for ongoing economic realignment, confronting issues such as tenant displacement, wage theft, or nepotistic favor. This broadened understanding of solidarity encourages communities to move beyond short-lived benevolence activities and toward more sustained forms of commitment, in which faith identity translates into deliberate, collective strategies for inclusion.

Another thematic layer involves the intersection of feminist and Black liberation perspectives with gawani theology. Feminist critics stress how ecclesiastical practices often undervalue or sideline women, who bear critical responsibilities in sustaining family and congregational life. Black liberation approaches, rooted in critiques of structural racism, add further clarity by examining how racial hierarchies distort the economic and social opportunities of certain groups. The text contends that a comprehensive approach to justice requires an awareness of these overlapping challenges, so that communities do not address one form of oppression while tacitly ignoring others. Gawani theology enriches this conversation by underscoring the shared ethic of distribution and reciprocity; feminist and Black liberation viewpoints demonstrate that no distribution can be equitable without reckoning with who wields authority and who is consistently overlooked. By integrating these currents, the volume urges congregations to design leadership structures, budgeting processes, and worship practices that acknowledge and work against multiple axes of exclusion.

The emphasis on resource-sharing returns frequently, as the text details how churches might develop robust forms of common ownership. Gawani theology encourages participants to conceive of giving not merely as an individual act but as a collective dynamic that sustains communal welfare. Congregations might experiment with transparent finances, rotating governance committees, or alliances with local cooperatives to prevent wealth from pooling in the hands of a few. Feminist concerns spotlight whether women's contributions and leadership receive equal consideration, ensuring that the push for economic fairness includes recognition of underappreciated forms of labor—such as caregiving and administrative tasks that uphold congregational life. This integrated perspective aims to produce a church culture where decision-making power is shared, budgets reflect communal ethics, and resource allocation is considered a core element of the faith journey rather than a peripheral or optional concern.

Local cultural practices and symbols, such as Chewa dances or clan-based solidarity rituals, emerge as important catalysts for collective identity. Gawani theology argues that rather than discarding such rituals as folk traditions, the church should recognize their integral role in forming cohesive societies. These acts, which blend spiritual reverence and community-building, serve as tangible expressions of the ethic that informs communal life. By grafting worship onto existing cultural scaffolding, congregations create a theology that is both reverential and grounded in lived reality. This stands in contrast to models that either import foreign worship styles wholesale or treat local practices as incompatible with Christian doctrine. Instead, gawani theology shows that these rituals, when aligned with the broader call to love neighbor and share resources, can deepen communal bonds. The approach thus provides an example of a culturally contextualized faith practice that neither romanticizes tradition nor dismisses it.

A major question the text poses is whether religion should remain a private affair or actively engage political and social structures. By examining stories like Zacchaeus's pledge to redistribute wealth, gawani theology and its affiliated models emphasize that spiritual renewal necessarily entails renegotiating one's role in broader systems. This reorientation can include lobbying for tenant protections, advocating fair wages, or supplying safe havens for those fleeing violence—practical outworkings of worship that link devotion to public stewardship. Such an approach contests any theological stance that confines faith to personal beliefs or rites, proposing instead that acts of justice are integral to the church's moral life. In so doing, gawani theology aligns with other liberationist traditions, which have long maintained that without concrete social transformation, religious claims risk becoming hollow pronouncements disconnected from the material struggles of daily existence.

Across the chapters, readers repeatedly see how seemingly minor gestures—like sharing leftover crops or carpooling to political demonstrations—can accumulate into a pattern of deliberate community building. Gawani theology maintains that these grassroots initiatives, though easily overlooked, forge the social architecture needed for broader reforms. Over time, consistent participation in cooperative networks fosters trust, enabling believers to tackle systemic challenges with a united front. When authoritarian regimes clamp down on freedoms or economic hardships intensify, these preexisting connections enable communities to respond swiftly and collectively, mitigating the harm endured by isolated families. By situating these grassroots actions within a covenant ethic that unites human, divine, and environmental wellbeing, the text shows that resilience emerges when local collaboration aligns with biblical calls to mutual care. As a result, gawani theology frames daily acts of sharing not as ad hoc survival strategies but as embodiments of faith's deeper moral impetus.

Collectively, the volume sets out a vision where theological understanding emerges from the confluence of everyday practice, scriptural tradition, and cultural belonging. It contends that gawani theology, anchored in Malawi but adaptable to other contexts, exemplifies an approach that transcends purely abstract or sporadic conceptions of compassion. By articulating how leftover produce, ancestral reverence, or communal governance reflect a unifying ethic, the text encourages leaders, researchers, and worshippers to adopt comparable frameworks in their own settings. Ultimately, the argument is that genuine ministry thrives when local expertise, biblical perspectives, and communal solidarity intersect in systematic yet flexible forms of support. When communities embed sharing, accountability, and cooperation into their core religious activities, they not only sustain themselves through crises but also articulate a credible witness of faith in action. This culminating perspective merges scriptural imperatives with everyday relational practices, opening fresh avenues for how theology can reshape—and be reshaped by—the communities it aims to serve.

1.

Malawi Mission Journey and the Emergence of Gawani Theology

The Power of Sharing and Distribution

Dr. Joseph Kang and his spouse Hannah undertook an extended missionary venture in Malawi that deliberately transcended the boundaries of standard evangelistic practice.[1] Over the course of their involvement, they observed and participated in the everyday lives of Malawian families who were struggling under the watchful eye of President Hastings Banda's one-party rule. Under Banda, the Malawi Young Pioneers (MYP) enforced pervasive surveillance and regularly compelled individuals to swear loyalty to the Malawi Congress Party (MCP), generating an atmosphere of constant apprehension.[2] Citizens often found

---

1. Kang, *Theology of Gawani*, 1. Kang underscores that his fieldwork revealed how Malawian sociopolitical conditions demanded innovative approaches to mission. Dr. Kang, born in 1945 in Boryeong, studied theology at Hanshin University before undertaking doctoral work in New Testament at San Francisco Theological Seminary. He served as a chaplain in the Korean Army, pastored congregations in Korea and the United States, and taught at Zomba Theological College and the University of Malawi under the Presbyterian Church (USA). Later, he taught at Hanshin University and a Lutheran seminary in Russia. Now retired from overseas service, he devotes himself to writing and translation, especially on gawani theology, shaped by his experiences in Malawi.

2. McCracken, *History of Malawi*, 2. McCracken explains how Hastings Banda's centralized power touched nearly every aspect of societal life.

themselves subjected to extensive public checks at local markets; those lacking MCP identification cards were sometimes denied entry or pressured to purchase a short-term pass.[3] Despite these restrictive measures, however, many local inhabitants established unspoken coalitions of mutual support, demonstrating resourcefulness through their capacity to share limited provisions and offer social shelter to neighbors in distress.

Amid this politically fraught environment, Dr. Kang discerned that a specific Chichewa notion called "gawa" described how Malawians divided goods and responsibilities among one another.[4] Over time, Kang developed these observations into what he termed "gawani theology," an interpretive framework that underscores sharing and distributing as moral imperatives. In Kang's view, gawani constitutes a cultural ethic whereby individuals are not merely charitable but embrace a long-term commitment to sustaining communal well-being.[5] This model pivoted away from presuming that impoverished communities required external "rescue." Instead, it proposed that local people could forge resilience by channeling existing structures of collaboration. In practice, families that had been evicted for failing to comply with MYP mandates benefited from neighbors who supplied them with leftover produce, bus fare, or even spiritual counsel, thereby counterbalancing the fear introduced by Banda's regime.[6]

1.1. ENFORCED LOYALTY AND THE EMERGENCE OF BOTTOM-UP ALLIANCES

State enforcement of loyalty pledges in the form of forced MYP membership or conspicuously displayed MCP identification frequently led to harsh penalties for those who hesitated to comply. In some cases, individuals who attempted to return MYP uniforms were immediately

---

3. McCracken, *History of Malawi*, 317. Citizens lacking the mandated identification often improvised covert support systems, illustrating the complexity of surviving under Banda's one-party administration.

4. Vermeullen, *Dictionary*, 14. Vermeullen provides linguistic background, detailing how gawa signifies dividing or distributing.

5. Kang, *Theology of Gawani*, 2. Kang notes that everyday sharing under adverse conditions became a linchpin of communal endurance.

6. Kang, *Theology of Gawani*, 4. Kang recounts specific households who, despite their own shortages, shared produce to prevent neighbors from slipping into famine.

incarcerated without trial.[7] This ironfisted approach aimed to break local solidarity, replace trust with fear, and redirect communal allegiances to the president. Yet, ironically, it sometimes generated the opposite effect. Many Malawians became more attuned to each other's struggles and spontaneously cultivated protective networks. Dr. Kang recorded the story of one young man whose father was arrested for returning an MYP uniform; within a matter of days, their family lost all formal housing privileges. Although they were effectively homeless and living in a cramped mud structure behind a Presbyterian church, fellow parishioners consistently donated leftover food to help them survive.[8]

For Dr. Kang, witnessing these grassroots acts of generosity underscored the importance of what he later described as a "shared spiritual and socioeconomic ethos." Gawani theology took shape as a realization that local capacity for self-organization—rooted in everyday acts of dividing limited resources—directly interacted with biblical understandings of solidarity and community. Echoing Jean-Marc Ela's premise that African theologies emerge most genuinely "under the tree," that is, from concrete communal experiences, Dr. Kang urged that theological discourse must engage the lived realities of those facing political oppression.[9] This grounding challenged abstract mission strategies that sometimes failed to appreciate local culture. Instead, it advanced an approach that integrated agricultural tasks, neighborhood gatherings, and worship contexts into a unified ethic of "interdependence and wholeness of life."[10]

1.2. GAWANI THEOLOGY AND BIBLICAL RESONANCES

The impetus for gawani theology aligns with particular biblical motifs emphasizing collective care. Dr. Kang often related gawani to the theme of "the afflicted and the hungry," drawing from passages such as Exod 3:7–10, where God is depicted as recognizing and intervening on behalf

---

7. McCracken, *History*, 419. Arrests for rejecting MYP positions frequently bypassed legal protocol, undercutting any semblance of judicial process.

8. Kang, *Theology of Gawani*, 8. Kang records how homeless families found refuge through local churches, highlighting how moral commitment overrode fear.

9. Ela, *Cri de l'homme*, 9. Ela posits that genuine African theology emerges from social reality rather than academic abstraction.

10. Kang, *Theology of Gawani*, 7. Spiritual convictions and daily activities—such as cooking and cultivating—were interwoven into a single communal ethic.

of the oppressed.¹¹ Additionally, he underscored how Jesus's proclamation of God's reign entailed reconciling marginalized groups and addressing tangible needs. Kang contended that the incarnation implies divine participation in human suffering, suggesting that gawani embodies a practical echo of grace among those confronting resource scarcity. Accordingly, handing over a portion of one's remaining maize is more than an act of momentary kindness—it represents a lived confession of faith that acknowledges the neighbor's vulnerability as part of one's own.

In line with Dietrich Bonhoeffer's perspective, shared life is not constructed by rigid hierarchical dictates but emerges where each person accepts a measure of responsibility for the other.¹² Kang illustrated how Malawian families, drawing on local traditions of reciprocity, frequently blurred the lines between worship and daily livelihood. Some congregations, for instance, designated official "gawani Sundays," where believers brought surplus produce to the church for communal distribution after worship. Such practices were not strictly philanthropic gestures but functioned as communal affirmations that no one should face starvation in silence. Moreover, by incorporating these rituals into the structure of worship, believers merged theological reflection with social action, reducing the gap that sometimes divides religious services from real-world hardships.

1.3. DIALOGUE-CENTERED MISSION IN AN AUTHORITARIAN CONTEXT

Paulo Freire's reflection on dialogue-based education provides a supplementary viewpoint on how gawani theology counters authoritarian practices.¹³ Freire argues that without genuine dialogue, external interventions—particularly from missionary organizations—risk diminishing local agency. Dr. Kang echoed this concern, noting that well-intentioned but top-down mission programs can effectively overshadow indigenous knowledge and inadvertently relegate community members to passive

---

11. Kang, *Theology of Gawani*, 7. Kang draws parallels between Old Testament accounts of oppression and Malawi's political climate, suggesting that gawani is a tangible embodiment of empathy.

12. Bonhoeffer and Wells, *Life Together*, 84. Bonhoeffer articulates the communal dimension of faith, paralleling gawani's interdependent perspective.

13. Freire, *Pedagogy of the Oppressed*, 2018, 30. Freire maintains that meaningful transformation hinges on collaborative dialogue rather than imposition.

roles. Gawani theology instead proposes that holistic transformation begins when missionaries become learners, intentionally deferring to local insight on farming, social ties, and the distribution of meager resources. This posture reshapes the missionary-community relationship from teacher-student to cocollaborators who share both the burdens and the breakthroughs of daily living.[14]

MYP intimidation, paradoxically, often intensified the impetus for dialogue. In the face of forced pledges, entire villages recognized that fragmenting into isolated units would render them even more vulnerable. Hence, clandestine gatherings after dark or discrete communal meetings on Sunday afternoons allowed them to strategize collectively. They examined ways to redirect small funds to cover a neighbor's rent, or to smuggle leftover vegetables to those with imprisoned family members. Dr. Kang recorded that such alliances, while rarely visible to outside observers, underscored the community's capacity to generate organic solutions despite oppressive constraints.[15] This concealed web of reciprocity emerged as a genuine grassroots bulwark against the state's attempt to monopolize control. In theological terms, it illustrated a theology under threat, wherein faith commitments interfaced with real survival strategies.

1.4. PRACTICAL EXPRESSIONS OF GAWANI: MEALS, SEEDS, AND MICROECONOMICS

One consistent manifestation of gawani theology involved rotating meal plans in villages, especially during the lean season. Families with even minor surpluses contributed items such as dried beans, cassava, or newly harvested vegetables, which were then centrally cooked and portioned out to those most lacking. Dr. Kang observed that this system was not formalized by any government decree; rather, it functioned as an unwritten understanding.[16] In effect, these distribution circuits decreased the overall sense of desperation, discouraging people from resorting to theft or confronting the MYP out of desperation. Instead, the act of preparing

---

14. Kang, *Theology of Gawani*, 11. The "co-learning model" positions missionaries and local leaders as partners rather than hierarchical counterparts.

15. Kang, *Theology of Gawani*, 4. Kang chronicles clandestine gatherings where leftover produce was discreetly pooled, demonstrating resilience in the face of oppression.

16. Kang, *Theology of Gawani*, 7. The "common pot" custom exemplifies the bedrock principle that daily bread belongs to the entire collective, not solely to those with temporary surpluses.

a communal pot reaffirmed the principle that each participant was responsible for collective survival.

Moreover, certain local churches supplemented gawani theology with microeconomic initiatives. Drawing on Kang's suggestion, they pooled minimal financial resources—collected from weekly offerings or from church-based cooperatives—and distributed small loans to families in jeopardy of losing farmland due to MYP encroachment. While these loans were modest, they often financed essential seeds, enabling small-scale farmers to plant additional crops for the next season. Loan recipients, in turn, were encouraged to pay forward any successful yields by contributing extra produce to neighboring families.[17] This cyclical pattern not only protected farmland from forced state acquisition but also broadened the idea that faith communities could demonstrate practical solidarity, thereby fortifying village-level resilience. Such measures highlight gawani theology's emphasis on self-determination, bridging personal faith and economic realities in an ongoing interplay of "love in practice."[18]

1.5. CHALLENGES, TENSIONS, AND THE NEED FOR MORAL VIGILANCE

Despite its constructive impact, gawani theology did not simplify or romanticize communal life. Dr. Kang warned that certain MYP officers, or local elites beholden to them, might exploit the community's trust, insisting that shared resources be directed toward unapproved projects.[19] He also documented instances where a portion of the community resisted open sharing, fearing that publicly visible acts of cooperation might invite official scrutiny. Some families therefore opted to practice gawani in secrecy, only confiding in a small circle of trusted allies. This cautious approach highlights that gawani theology evolves within intricate power dynamics, requiring persistent ethical discernment to prevent manipulation or misuse.

---

17. Kang, *Theology of Gawani*, 11. Small-scale seed loans often facilitated the next planting season, offering a grassroots microeconomic buffer against the looming threat of MYP confiscation.

18. Bonhoeffer and Wells, *Life Together*, 87. Bonhoeffer contends that communion deepens when believers engage in practical acts of care, a principle mirrored in gawani practices.

19. Kang, *Theology of Gawani*, 2. Kang warns that manipulative figures can still exploit the community's trust, underscoring the necessity of vigilance.

Furthermore, while the rotating meal or seed loan practices helped mitigate immediate crises, they did not immediately dismantle the structural injustices entrenched in the one-party system. Kang recognized that local resourcefulness could only extend so far without broader social and political transformation.[20] He thus advocated for strategic partnerships with nongovernmental organizations and denominational agencies, proposing that outward alliances might complement grassroots initiatives without overriding them. The ultimate aim was to ensure that gawani theology remained both context sensitive and open to external networks of support—particularly in addressing large-scale challenges such as protracted drought or economic embargoes.

1.6. THEOLOGICAL IMPLICATIONS BEYOND MALAWI

Although gawani theology took shape under Malawi's particular political strains, Dr. Kang argued that this framework transcends local boundaries. In global mission discourse, the model provides a case study of how indigenous ethics of interdependence can disrupt standard top-down paradigms. For communities facing economic inequity or environmental depletion, the concept of dividing and sharing calls for reevaluating whether development strategies inadvertently eclipse local knowledge. Dr. Kang maintained that gawani theology, by emphasizing each community's agency, could inform a broader conversation on collaborative mission, especially in contexts of political instability.[21]

Within theological scholarship, it intersects with Bonhoeffer's insistence that real fellowship arises through concrete, mutual responsibility rather than distant paternalism.[22] It also affirms Paulo Freire's contention that "dialogue cannot exist without humility," cautioning outside agents not to undermine the autonomy of those they intend to help.[23] In Dr. Kang's assessment, gawani theology thus unfolds as an applied theology, bridging biblical perspectives on compassion with everyday negotiations

---

20. Kang, *Theology of Gawani*, 8. Kang acknowledges that local resource sharing can mitigate emergencies but does not alone overhaul a repressive regime.

21. Kang, *Theology of Gawani*, 11. Partnerships with regional and international entities, when approached respectfully, can expand the impact of gawani-based collaboration.

22. Bonhoeffer and Wells, *Life Together*, 90.

23. Freire, *Pedagogy of the Oppressed*, 2018, 37.

of resource scarcity, forging a synergy that fosters resilience against authoritarian constraints.

1.7. CONCLUSION: COMMUNAL FAITH, LOCAL STRATEGIES, AND ENDURING NETWORKS

Dr. Kang's experiences in Malawi demonstrate that small yet determined acts of resource sharing can evolve into a structured moral framework with potential to counter political intimidation. Rural families faced with sudden evictions did not resort solely to outside aid; they drew on long-standing traditions of collaboration, forging hidden networks that supplied food, lodging, or seed loans. Such collective endeavors formed a tangible manifestation of loving one's neighbor, tying personal convictions to strategic community action. Gawani theology, grounded in the Chichewa ethic of dividing and distributing, articulates how local customs can align with biblical mandates to foster resilience under authoritarian pressures.

By establishing that every neighbor is collectively responsible, gawani theology offers a communal alternative to models of mission or development that treat communities as passive beneficiaries. Malawian churches embracing this approach integrated Sunday worship, meal rotation, and microeconomic support into a unified practice of neighborly care. Far from being an isolated ritual, resource distribution became a spiritual act that mirrored the church's broader calling. In conversation with liberation theology and Bonhoeffer's emphasis on shared accountability, these practices rooted faith in ongoing social commitments rather than in short-term charity.

Paulo Freire's emphasis on dialogue and colearning finds a parallel in gawani theology. Dr. Kang's mission did not revolve around one-directional teaching; he instead realized that local know-how—cultivating leftover maize, reorganizing farmland, and mobilizing neighborly solidarity—provided the essential framework for building trust. Such reciprocal learning shifted the missionary role from that of an authoritative giver to that of a collaborator who learns from local experts. In an environment marked by constant surveillance, these small alliances mattered deeply, confirming that moral strength arises when communities shape their own survival strategies.

Local churches and neighborhood councils also expanded gawani's influence by forming subtle support networks. Families who faced arrests or forced relocations frequently discovered that neighbors could step in with leftover produce or minimal rent assistance. While these gestures did not overthrow Malawi's one-party system, they offered practical demonstrations of mutual protection in the short term. Over time, this organic cooperation pointed beyond daily solutions to a vision of social life capable of outlasting a repressive regime.

At the theological level, gawani stands for a consistent ethic where worship, daily chores, and political realities interconnect. Dr. Kang observed that many Malawian believers seamlessly combined agricultural labor, Sunday prayers, and charitable practices. Interpreting these elements as part of a single covenant ethic, gawani theology bridged the gap between spiritual devotion and material welfare. Community meal plans, seed exchanges, and covert gatherings after dark emerged as outward signs of an inward unity, confirming that faith communities can thrive where standard mission tactics might falter.

Concerns remain that such local solidarity, while beneficial in times of crisis, might be co-opted or disrupted by vested interests. Dr. Kang admitted that authoritarian offices occasionally sought to twist communal loyalty for their own ends. Yet the fact that gawani persisted, often in the background, underlines its potential to adapt to changing pressures. In practical terms, Malawian families did not abandon cooperative values when faced with intimidation; instead, they refined them, operating discreetly when needed. This indicates that gawani theology, though tethered to one historical context, presents a flexible structure relevant for other communities wrestling with similar threats to freedom.

Ultimately, gawani theology stresses that the dividing and sharing of limited resources can become a moral bedrock for faith communities under strain. Local knowledge, shaped by tradition and tested in real adversities, stands at the core of a socially grounded mission. Dr. Kang's fieldwork and subsequent reflections affirm that resource sharing, while modest, holds a transformative capacity. Families who share leftover produce do more than alleviate hunger; they model how collective life, infused with biblical imperatives, can endure even where political oppression looms. This perspective underscores that in many settings worldwide, an ethic of communal responsibility—rooted in daily practice and shaped by shared worship—offers a sturdy foundation for hope.

2.

Gawani Theology as a Communal Framework of Faith and Shared Responsibility

Gawani theology takes its name from the Chichewa word "gawani," signifying "to share" or "to distribute," especially within closely bonded communities such as extended families or neighbors. This concept not only describes the act of distributing resources in a narrow material sense but also conveys a deeper moral and spiritual responsibility to uphold communal well-being. Such an ethos strongly parallels the southern African notion of "ubuntu," widely rendered as "I am because we are," in which a person's identity, dignity, and moral obligations are realized through the intersubjective dimension of community.[1]

Yet, unlike certain theoretical models that focus on communitarian ideals in abstraction, gawani theology explicitly grounds itself in the lived experiences of Malawian individuals. It draws profound inspiration from the historical accounts of Charles Madukani, whose narratives highlight

---

1. Ubuntu, often rendered "I am because we are," is anchored in African communal philosophy. Desmond Tutu points out that the absence of ubuntu played a tragic role in conflicts such as the genocide in Rwanda. He further notes that resentments and a deficit of communal reconciliation eroded public trust in places like the Belgian Congo. Tutu, *No Future*, 31–32, 35.

how communities survive—and even flourish—amid extreme poverty and oppression, provided they collectively embrace "umodzi."[2] According to the tradition in question, Malawians have repeatedly mobilized these communal strategies during times of political turmoil, particularly under dictatorships, by pooling resources, exchanging labor, and sharing not merely possessions but also hope. In this sense, gawani theology is not an abstract notion of communal love, but a codification of age-old African survival methods that sustain both moral and socioeconomic harmony.

The concept of "ubale" ("relationship" in Chewa) becomes central in illuminating the theological contours of gawani.[3] Chewa society, as explained by anthropologists and local scholars, emphasizes reciprocal obligations that extend beyond the tangible—reaching into ancestral veneration and divine worship. The Chewa hold that God fashioned the first ancestors and endowed them with the extraordinary capacity to convey life to successive generations, creating ongoing linkages that call for reverence toward both the living and the departed. Such a worldview underscores that no human being stands alone; rather, every individual's existence unfolds within overlapping spheres of relationship, be it family, ancestors, or the divine.

2.1. SYMBOLISM OF *NYAU* AND SHARED ANCESTRAL BONDS

Within this Chewa cosmology, a prime illustration of communal ritual is the *nyau* dance, often performed to ensure that a deceased person's spirit transitions smoothly into "mizimu," the ancestral spirit domain.[4]

---

2. Charles Madukani's accounts of Malawian communities surviving political oppression and economic hardship highlight umodzi, a Chewa expression referring to "unity" or "oneness" for collective survival. Phiri, *Women, Presbyterianism and Patriarchy*, 12. Phiri provides ethnographic data on how family solidarity in Chewa society enabled people to help one another during crises.

3. Chewa religion upholds that God (Chauta) endowed the first ancestors with life-giving power, forming the basis of relational obligations across generations. See van Breugel, *Chewa Traditional Religion*, 28. This perspective underscores that every lineage not only inherits physical traits but also spiritual responsibilities.

4. The *nyau* ritual, which fosters communal empathy across the boundary of death, exemplifies how the living invokes mizimu or ancestral spirits. See van Breugel, *Chewa Traditional Religion*, 40. The practice indicates that Chewa society perceives moral obligation as transcending mortal existence, resonating with gawani theology's ethic of enduring solidarity.

Oral histories and genealogical myths suggest that ancestors took special delight in these dances during life, and by reenacting *nyau*, the living reaffirm an enduring bond that is believed to persist beyond physical death. Far from being an archaic performance, the dance exemplifies the Chewa conviction that empathy, sympathy, and mutual care remain vital even in confronting mortality. This resonates with gawani theology's broader call to see sharing not merely as an economic transaction but a sacred, relational practice bridging human, ancestral, and divine realms.

Nyau also signifies how gawani theology welcomes cultural expressions of identity into the theological fold. If the gospel message is to be truly incarnational, advocates of gawani theology argue, it must take root in the tangible symbols and actions that already anchor communal identity in places like Malawi. The sharing that gawani theology espouses thus shifts from rhetorical principle to an experiential phenomenon marked by ritual, story, and habit. Such emphasis on rootedness in local patterns—be they dances, songs, or clan-based solidarity—distinguishes gawani from more generalized communal theologies.

2.2. BIBLICAL FOUNDATIONS AND CONTEMPORARY CHALLENGES

Scripturally, gawani theology resonates with teachings that highlight mutual care and sacrificial love. In particular, the New Testament repeatedly addresses themes of bearing one another's burdens, calls to stewardship, and genuine hospitality for the stranger. Gawani adds an African communal lens, insisting that Christian ethics must move beyond private charity to incorporate structural solidarity. This stance implies that the church is called to be a kin group in which resources, joys, and sorrows are openly shared, echoing Acts 2:44's portrayal of early believers who "had all things in common." Boff and Boff, theologians of liberation, emphasize that such textual grounding should be tested against concrete social realities—namely, how effectively a local church responds to poverty, marginalization, and institutional injustice.[5] From the vantage of gawani theology, the measure of faithfulness is found in practical,

---

5. Leonardo and Clodovis Boff emphasize that the test of genuine liberation theology is in its engagement with lived realities: "No theology is valid that fails to address systemic injustice at its roots." Boff and Boff, *Introducing Liberation Theology*, 7. The synergy with gawani arises in confronting economic disparity through communal ownership and sharing. See Boff and Boff, *Introducing Liberation Theology*, 29.

communal transformation that sees every neighbor as part of one's extended household.

Modern contexts, however, present additional complexities. Rapid urbanization in southern Africa, ecological degradation, and the dominance of global consumer culture have disrupted many forms of local sharing once integral to communal structures. If gawani theology remains relevant, it must grapple with how to adapt those local traditions in an era of resource scarcity and intensifying class disparities. Some Malawian theologians propose networks of base communities that intentionally practice shared agriculture, cooperative economics, and collaborative child rearing. But they also note the challenges of sustaining this model when younger generations relocate to cities. To sustain gawani as a living principle, not a nostalgic ideal, these theologians argue, the church must integrate new forms of activism and policy advocacy.

2.3. INTEGRATION WITH OTHER CONTEXTUAL THEOLOGIES

Beyond Malawi, gawani theology establishes affinities with other contextual or liberation-oriented theological streams. For instance, Latin American liberation theology, exemplified by Gustavo Gutiérrez, systematically underscores the "preferential option for the poor" as the hermeneutical key for biblical interpretation.[6] Gawani theology shares this emphasis but foregrounds Chichewa or Chewa cultural distinctives: synergy emerges when local sharing models meet systematic critiques of oppressive social structures, enabling communities to see how localized acts of solidarity can support broader transformations. Similarly, minjung theology in Korea accentuates the lived experiences of the disenfranchised as central to theological reflection, an approach gawani theology could align with, given its conviction that genuine theology must lift up the voices and experiences of those subjugated by historical and political forces.

Feminist theology also finds a valuable conversation partner in gawani theology, given that many of the burdens of gawani—the daily tasks of sharing food, water, and spiritual care—traditionally fall on women's

---

6. Gustavo Gutiérrez's notion of "preferential option for the poor" underscores that community-based praxis should inform biblical reading, paralleling gawani's view of theological reflection anchored in local experiences. See Gutiérrez, *Theology of Liberation*, xxxi. Gutiérrez contends that when faith is severed from social practice, it cannot effectively champion the marginalized.

shoulders.⁷ By dialoguing with feminist theologians, gawani theology may further highlight how gender inequalities sometimes hamper full communal sharing, urging new forms of empowerment for women's roles in Malawian society. This integrated approach envisions a broader network-oriented theology, weaving together local cultural insights, shared pastoral responsibilities, and the theoretical scaffolding of liberation, feminist, or other progressive theologies.

2.4. ECOLOGICAL AND CULTURAL DIMENSIONS

Furthermore, gawani theology addresses global environmental crises and cultural homogenization, looking toward the ancient Chewa wisdom that regards land, water, and wildlife as part of a God-given inheritance to be shared, not exploited. Some theologians in Malawi propose rereading biblical mandates—like the call to "tend and keep" the garden in Gen 2:15—considering gawani precepts. If farmland is held communally or distribution of produce is collectively arranged, that communal approach could curb exploitative agricultural practices. Tutu himself underscores that an "ubuntu-based ethic" includes conscientious stewardship of the environment since communal flourishing inherently depends on stable ecological conditions.⁸

Moreover, globalization can overshadow local customs under Western-driven consumer culture. By revitalizing gawani-based social norms, gawani theology offers a counternarrative emphasizing communal sufficiency over insatiable consumption. This fosters cultural self-confidence and defends indigenous knowledge systems from being dismissed as archaic. According to van Breugel, certain Chewa rituals, though easily misunderstood as superstitions, hold valuable knowledge about communal cohesion and natural resource management.⁹ By integrating these

---

7. Feminist theologians note that in many African contexts, the practical burden of sharing daily resources falls disproportionately on women. Chichewa speaker Phiri highlights how these roles, though empowering in certain respects, can also mask underlying gender inequities. Phiri, *Women, Presbyterianism and Patriarchy*, 32. A gawani approach that spotlights women's labor is therefore an avenue for bridging feminist concerns and communal theologies.

8. Tutu contends that "the ethic of ubuntu necessarily encompasses stewardship," since communal well-being is inseparable from ecological stability. Tutu, *No Future*, 35. This extends gawani's communal notion of shared humanity to nonhuman creation, reframing environmental activism as an expression of theological solidarity.

9. Van Breugel points out that some Chewa rituals, while interpreted by outsiders

rituals into broader theological discourse, gawani theology repositions local tradition as an indispensable partner in theological reflection.

2.5. TOWARD A GLOBAL NETWORK-ORIENTED THEOLOGY

In sum, gawani theology highlights how an ethic of sharing in Malawian contexts merges seamlessly with biblical imperatives. It insists that local cultural frameworks are not peripheral but central to incarnational Christian practice. While gawani arises from a specific cultural-linguistic milieu, its impetus for collective responsibility and shared well-being finds broad resonance. Contemporary African theologians thus envision gawani theology as a fresh instance of what some might call "network-oriented theology," bridging distinct theological lineages—liberation, feminist, minjung, ecological—to coconstruct an inclusive, people-centered Christian witness. The synergy with other theological movements aligns with the Christian affirmation that redemption necessarily embraces whole societies, not just discrete individuals, and that loving one's neighbor is concretized most vividly when communities stand shoulder to shoulder, bearing each other's burdens.

By promoting gawani, believers no longer regard Christian discipleship as a private moral path; rather, they see it as inherently communal, shaped by the day-to-day realities of giving and receiving. The wide applicability of such a theological stance emerges in local parishes, extended family units, and grassroots networks, all of which, it is argued, become microcosms of an alternative social order. In advancing from a purely conceptual horizon to a practically lived framework, gawani theology provides impetus for tangible acts: from neighborhood food banks to coops for essential commodities, from inclusive child-care services to collective efforts in addressing structural injustices. Indeed, as some Malawian scholars articulate, gawani theology has the capacity to speak with an African accent, echoing the diverse experiences of communities historically overshadowed by global narratives. When placed in a constructive dialogue with other currents of contextual theology across continents, it potentiates a Christian tradition ever more vibrant and integral.

---

as mere folklore, in fact encode essential knowledge of land management and conflict resolution, generationally transmitted as a communal ethic. See van Breugel, *Chewa Traditional Religion*, 41. Through gawani theology, such rituals are reexamined as theological resources that promote collective harmony.

2.6. CONCLUSION: GAWANI THEOLOGY AS A PATH OF COLLECTIVE FAITH AND TRANSFORMATIVE SHARING

Gawani theology, as explored in this chapter, provides a structured view of how communal practices in Malawian culture can merge with biblical teachings to create a form of Christianity centered on mutual responsibility. It draws its name from the Chichewa verb "to share," reflecting the principle of distributing resources, time, and supportive care within relationships that extend beyond one's immediate household. What results is a model of faith that sees belonging, stewardship, and collective well-being as interwoven commitments, challenging any framework that reduces spirituality to private or individualistic behavior.

The starting place for gawani is the daily practice of ubale, or belonging, a concept that binds communities together not only in times of abundance but equally when hardships arise. Whether driven by political distress or economic scarcity, the tradition underscores how Malawian groups have coped by exchanging labor, pooling meager goods, and nurturing emotional resilience. Gawani thereby codifies ordinary survival methods as theological convictions, transforming what might appear as small gestures into core expressions of an integrated faith that respects cultural tradition and biblical imperatives.

As a theological perspective, gawani connects local Malawian experiences with New Testament calls to communal solidarity, stewardship, and hospitality. Beyond citing scriptural passages in an abstract manner, it insists that Christian authenticity emerges when resources are shared in tangible ways. Acts 2:44, with its image of believers holding everything in common, aligns with everyday communal practices that unify neighbors under a shared moral vision. This stands in contrast to frameworks where generosity remains a personal choice; gawani challenges the church to adopt structural methods—like communal land use or cooperative ventures—that express a collective ethic.

Such commitments demand ongoing creativity in contexts of rapid urbanization, youth migration, and the pressure of global consumer culture. Certain Malawian scholars have proposed forming base communities that draw on gawani norms to meet the shifting realities of city life, weaving in the best of local traditions with new forms of activism. Whether addressing ecological damage or advocating for fair wages, these endeavors show that gawani is not locked in the past. Instead, it represents an adaptable heritage that speaks into present-day challenges, urging believers to coordinate their spiritual convictions with pragmatic strategies.

Gawani also finds resonance in various streams of contextual theology. It shares with liberation thought the view that care for the poor is an essential biblical thread, and it welcomes dialogue with feminist theology by recognizing how women's everyday labor drives communal wellbeing. This inclusive stance also intersects with ecological theology, as it highlights the moral need to preserve land, water, and biodiversity for the flourishing of the entire community. In every case, gawani foregrounds how local wisdom, tested in history, can work in concert with broader movements seeking justice and participation.

Moreover, gawani contributes to broader discussions on the clash between local cultural identities and widespread commercial norms. By reclaiming communal sharing as a potent social model, it offers a counternarrative to market-driven individualism. While consumer culture promotes unrestrained acquisition, gawani's ethic of sufficiency and neighborly compassion invests local traditions with renewed importance. Viewed from an African perspective, practices such as clan-based support or rereading biblical stewardship from a communal vantage underscore that the best defense against external cultural pressures often arises from rooted values.

At the same time, gawani's emphasis on local symbols and rituals, such as *nyau* dance, demonstrates a commitment to incarnational expressions of theology. Worship cannot remain an abstract set of liturgical elements; it must incorporate community routines, dances, or gatherings that link present believers to their ancestors, each other, and God. Far from trivializing such heritage, gawani invites them into the center of church life, illustrating how cultural continuity can deepen a collective sense of faith and responsibility.

By presenting gawani theology as a network-oriented approach, Malawian theologians underscore the potential for forging global partnerships that honor diverse traditions. This constructive orientation transcends borders as it dialogues with movements in Latin America, Korea, or other regions where local experiences, structural analysis, and spiritual conviction combine. Gawani thus enriches the global theological landscape with a distinctly African accent, reminding outsiders that, in Malawi, community survival is a spiritual matter calling forth shared devotion, resource management, and social advocacy.

In practical church life, gawani fosters a shift from one-off acts of charity to ongoing modes of collaboration. Congregations might prioritize cooperative agriculture projects, joint childcare systems, or rotating microloans. Such changes reorganize Christian practice around everyday partnerships rather than hierarchical charitable gestures, empowering all members to shape the common welfare. This daily interplay, combining moral obligation and cultural memory, shapes a social order where each neighbor's well-being becomes everyone's task.

Ultimately, gawani theology testifies that an approach grounded in local customs and everyday relationships can speak strongly to contemporary dilemmas. As younger generations face uncertain futures, as ecosystems are threatened, and as social inequities persist, gawani's ethic of shared belonging calls believers to stand together, bridging differences of status or background. This chapter's focus on gawani concludes with the assertion that communal life—rooted in cultural understanding and guided by biblical mandates—can revive hope, maintain dignity, and nurture a spirit of cooperation, marking a faithful path toward collective flourishing.

3.

Viewing the World Through a Worm's Eye

Critical Perspective and Practical Wisdom in Gawani Theology

A worm's eye outlook focuses on communities that typically remain unnoticed in mainstream accounts, reframing how theological and social perspectives are understood. Instead of beginning with dominant structures or influential voices, this approach highlights experiences of those living on the edges of society. This shift promises not only to refine interpretive practices but also to strengthen ethical reflection, since it compels scholars, faith leaders, and communities to remain accountable to the everyday struggles of marginalized populations.

Such an orientation underscores the gap between prevailing narratives—often celebrating influential institutions or heroic figures—and the realities of workers, the economically vulnerable, or minor religious groups. By highlighting lives commonly overlooked, the worm's eye stance unpacks alternative forms of collaboration, resilience, and moral insight. These grassroots stories, rather than serving as peripheral examples, frequently become the key to rethinking long held assumptions about power and communal relationships.

This perspective resonates with gawani theology, which grounds its convictions in the lived experiences of individuals facing systemic hardship. Whereas some theological models might stress abstract doctrines, gawani emphasizes how convictions take shape when faith communities interact with those in precarious conditions. Through resource sharing, communal care, and advocacy, gawani theology practices an engagement that aligns with the worm's eye lens: vital knowledge arises when those grappling with daily burdens speak for themselves, shaping both church initiatives and theological reflection.

Gadamer's hermeneutical focus on dialogue and practical wisdom adds another dimension. He contends that understanding is not produced in isolation but through open encounters with traditions and contexts. A worm's eye orientation welcomes narratives of those historically dismissed by institutional authority, thereby energizing dialogue with voices that mainstream interpretations have often neglected. This process enlarges interpretive horizons by incorporating fresh experiences into discussions about faith, social policy, and historical development.

A commitment to the worm's eye vantage also proposes that knowledge is tied to ethical choices. Engaging with individuals on the margins means adopting practical forms of cooperation and self-reflection, ensuring interpretive acts are intertwined with social responsibility. Organizations, whether churches or civic groups, cannot remain neutral bystanders; they must reexamine their attitudes and institutional frameworks in light of testimonies offered by communities confronting systemic injustice. Such encounters often unsettle conventional power arrangements, thereby prompting fresh discernment in how leadership and mutual accountability are defined.

Through this methodology, categories such as mission, service, and leadership are broadened to include reciprocity and cocreation of knowledge. Instead of approaching marginalized communities primarily as recipients of aid, a worm's eye angle reveals their essential role as contributors to collective wisdom. By treating these communities as partners, not mere objects of outreach, interpreters and church leaders can craft collaborative strategies aimed at genuine transformation. This approach aligns with gawani's idea that theological truths come alive when they engage actual human challenges, be they oppression, economic crisis, or lack of representation.

In this chapter, the goal is to explore how a worm's eye perspective enriches theological and historical scholarship, especially when it converges with gawani theology's emphasis on shared agency and daily-level faith practices. Focus will be placed on examining how grassroots experiences reshape accepted narratives, how Gadamerian dialogue connects to marginalized voices, and how ethical action arises from this collaborative vantage. The core assertion is that both scholarship and ministry deepen when communities no longer view those at the periphery as peripheral, recognizing instead that wisdom, compassion, and the seeds of renewed social structures often emerge from below.

3.1. PHRONESIS, DIALOGUE, AND ETHICAL COMMITMENT

The worm's eye vantage aligns with Hans-Georg Gadamer's hermeneutical emphasis on "phronesis"—the form of practical wisdom that manifests through lived engagement—and dialogue as key components of genuine comprehension.[1] Gadamer insists that knowledge is not simply gleaned from detached observation but unfolds within active encounters with tradition, context, and the other. When interpreters include underprivileged groups among their primary interlocutors, these encounters can be drastically reconfigured. No longer confined to academic speculation or abstract discourse, interpretation becomes an ethical practice, one aimed at understanding how structural inequities concretely affect communities. By integrating these marginalized stories into broader dialogues, the worm's eye perspective ensures that interpretive acts assume a dimension of moral accountability and potential societal impact.

In *Truth and Method*, Gadamer maintains that tradition, rather than functioning as a static inheritance, can be revitalized through collaborative encounters with new or challenging perspectives.[2] The worm's eye approach capitalizes on this dynamic by foregrounding how vulnerable communities critique and adapt inherited norms, whether religious, political, or cultural. Such reappropriations highlight the fact that tradition grows most vigorously when it interfaces with concrete, and often disquieting, human experiences. In the realm of gawani theology, this interplay becomes critical: religious commitments, initially framed in doctrinal statements or liturgical practices, acquire renewed life when reinterpreted considering systemic oppression, poverty, or social exclusion. Put differently, theological reflection gains ethical vigor to the extent that

---

1. Gadamer, *Truth and Method*, 312. Gadamer highlights phronesis as integral to ethical discernment in hermeneutical encounters.

2. Gadamer, *Truth and Method*, 369. Engaging new perspectives reinvigorates tradition, preventing it from becoming static or dogmatic.

it engages the worm's eye vantage as a legitimate, indeed necessary, conversation partner.

3.2. REDEFINING HISTORIOGRAPHY AND POWER FROM BELOW

One of the central convictions of a worm's eye stance is that official histories—composed of legislative achievements, documented elite quarrels, or monumental acts of conquest—fail to capture the intricate networks of mutual support, quiet resilience, and everyday endurance among those at the bottom rungs of society. By spotlighting laborers, small-scale farmers, or itinerant workers, we uncover microhistories that collectively reveal alternative modes of community formation.[3] These smaller narratives do not merely add texture to dominant accounts; they confront those accounts by exposing how systemic inequalities were maintained, contested, or sometimes bypassed in the daily lives of marginalized populations.

Gadamer's notion of "erfahrung"—experience as transformative—elucidates the stakes of this historiographical shift.[4] When historians and theologians immerse themselves in testimonies of disenfranchised groups, they may discover that these experiences disrupt well-established interpretive categories, revealing hidden power imbalances or moral dilemmas that standard frameworks overlook. Such disruptions can serve as catalysts for rethinking conventional wisdom. In effect, the worm's eye posture refuses to treat impoverished or otherwise marginalized communities as a mere footnote to mainstream narratives; instead, it asserts that these communities function as critical agents, shaping historical events and forging new paradigms of cooperation even under conditions of exploitation.

3.3. TRADITION AND INNOVATION: THE WORM'S EYE AS A SOURCE OF RENEWAL

Although a worm's eye viewpoint can appear to undermine or negate tradition, it also often revitalizes tradition by subjecting it to moral scrutiny informed by concrete suffering and hope. Gadamer's fusion of

---

3. Hill, *World Turned Upside Down*, 1634. Hill documents microhistories of mutual support and underground resistance.

4. Gadamer, *Truth and Method*, 319. Erfahrung underscores the transformative dimension of direct encounters with adversity or unexpected experiences.

horizons—the concept whereby inherited interpretive horizons merge with the perspectives of the present—attains sharpened relevance when the present vantage emanates from communities historically viewed as powerless.[5] In precisely this way, a congregation in a marginalized setting may reinterpret religious doctrines or scriptural passages through the lens of daily struggle, uncovering dimensions of faith that remain concealed under more complacent or privileged interpretive regimes.

Christopher Hill's investigation of radical groups during the English Revolution underscores that tradition does not unravel when confronted by previously sidelined voices.[6] On the contrary, the doctrinal and political revelations that sprang from poorer segments of society often revitalized debates about governance, individual conscience, and the legitimate scope of religious authority. Hence, rather than overthrowing tradition outright, marginalized voices appropriated and reframed it, thereby unveiling its latent transformative potential. The worm's eye vantage thus illustrates how alternative viewpoints can breathe life into seemingly fixed systems of thought by compelling them to respond to emergent social and theological concerns.

3.4. TWOFOLD LIBERATION: OPPRESSED AND OPPRESSOR

An especially noteworthy feature of the worm's eye method is the belief that systemic injustice constrains not just the oppressed but also the oppressor. Although at first glance paradoxical, this conviction mirrors Schleiermacher's notion that inclusive and dialogical religious engagement can release all participants from the confines of alienation.[7] Within such an engagement, the strong and the weak, or the privileged and the disenfranchised, encounter each other in a collaborative exchange that erodes entrenched dynamics of dominance and subordination. The worm's eye posture thereby transcends a purely polemical stance by envisioning the possibility that even those wielding power might discover a renewed moral horizon by surrendering their monopoly on control.

---

5. Gadamer, *Truth and Method*, 414. Gadamer's notion of "fusion of horizons" encapsulates how tradition evolves when confronted by distinct vantage points.

6. Hill, *World Turned Upside Down*, 1640. Radical voices expanded doctrinal and political discourse during the English Revolution.

7. Schleiermacher, *On Religion*, 9. Schleiermacher posits that inclusivity can liberate both marginal and dominant participants.

Paulo Freire's critical pedagogy further affirms the necessity of embracing the perspectives of the oppressed to dismantle deeply rooted inequities.[8] While Freire's educational context differs from that of theological or historical hermeneutics, the principle of mutual cocreation of knowledge resonates strongly with the worm's eye ethic: interpretive insights do not merely trickle down from experts or elites, but arise from the cooperative labor of those typically excluded from academic or doctrinal authority. Failing to embrace such reciprocity, interpretive communities risk upholding an implicit hierarchy that privileges privileged viewpoints—thereby reinforcing the exact injustices they may profess to oppose.

3.5. GAWANI THEOLOGY: BRIDGING PRAXIS AND MARGINALIZED EXPERIENCE

Gawani theology situates itself at the intersection of faith praxis and the immediate realities of those facing structural hardship, insisting that theological reflection must integrate the lived struggles of marginalized communities in tangible, day-to-day encounters. Far from being a mere theoretical stance or an abstract doctrinal position, it advances the idea that genuine spiritual commitments materialize when believers collaborate with the dispossessed in acts of mutual support, grassroots advocacy, and the formation of shared resilience networks. In this sense, gawani theology prioritizes ground-up partnerships that reshape traditional power imbalances, inviting community members themselves to shape and refine theological discourse. By aligning itself with Hans-Georg Gadamer's articulation of phronesis—the notion that ethical discernment is inseparable from concrete contexts—gawani theology underscores the responsibility of local faith communities to respond compassionately and effectively to the struggles around them.[9]

This orientation departs from models that treat those on society's periphery merely as recipients of charity or objects of distant moral concern. Rather, gawani theology urges believers to acknowledge vulnerable populations—whether they be the displaced, the hungry, or the politically

---

8. Freire, *Pedagogy of the Oppressed*, 2018, 53. Freire's approach to cocreated knowledge resonates with the worm's eye emphasis on reciprocity.

9. Gadamer, *Truth and Method*, 71. Gadamer underscores that phronesis—moral discernment linked to concrete situations—demands ethical engagement, mirroring gawani theology's emphasis on communal agency.

disenfranchised—as coauthors of religious reflection, with unique insights into shared survival strategies. In such a theological framework, reciprocal caring practices are not optional extras but lie at the heart of faith itself. When ministers, lay leaders, and everyday believers immerse themselves in the realities of social and economic marginalization, they discover new dimensions of spiritual wisdom rooted in resilience, interdependence, and solidarity. Gawani theology thus demonstrates how communal agency—in the form of resource pooling, empowerment initiatives, and collaborative decision-making—can serve as a catalyst for what might otherwise be relegated to impersonal, top-down charity.

Moreover, this approach shapes how scripture is read, how worship is organized, and how doctrinal positions are formulated. Interpreting biblical texts within contexts of hardship compels a direct confrontation with the stark realities of exploitation, illness, and displacement.[10] Rather than settling for abstracted readings that emphasize universal truths alone, gawani-minded communities reflect upon how biblical passages speak to the necessity of neighborly care, mutual responsibility, and concrete justice. Indeed, narratives like the exodus—where God is portrayed as hearing the cries of an oppressed people—take on renewed urgency in contexts of contemporary sociopolitical crisis. In gawani theology, such biblical motifs become the impetus for robust ethical engagement, challenging adherents to facilitate institutional reforms and public activism aimed at dismantling oppressive structures.

By foregrounding a worm's eye vantage, gawani theology also highlights the moral imperative to see the world through the lens of those who suffer. According to this principle, genuine spiritual insight emerges when believers not only witness but also participate in addressing the fundamental needs of marginalized groups. This conviction resonates with scriptural depictions of God's alignment with the powerless—symbolically descending from a lofty realm to experience human distress and initiate liberating change.[11] In so doing, gawani theology refuses to confine matters of faith to abstract speculation or disembodied devotion; it insists on the urgency of an intimate, daily-level encounter with the afflictions that shape many believers' lives. Hunger, forced displacement, wage injustice, and other socioeconomic pressures are not peripheral

---

10. Kang, *Theology of Gawani*, 6–7. Kang expounds on the idea that God hears the plight of the oppressed, linking a worm's eye view with divine empathy.

11. Kang, *Theology of Gawani*, 7.

concerns; rather, they constitute the sphere within which theological commitments are tested for authenticity.

Such an approach prompts a reevaluation of mission itself, displacing paternalistic or hierarchical models of charity in favor of reciprocal empowerment. Gawani practitioners do not offer help as a unilateral gesture; instead, they walk alongside those in distress, enabling collaborative problem-solving and mutual enrichment. From this perspective, theological reflection arises not in secluded academic halls but in the context of urgent, practical dilemmas: procuring food for a neighbor's household, securing safe housing for a displaced family, or advocating for inclusive local governance. In short, gawani theology converts what might otherwise remain pious intentions into dynamic avenues for social transformation, propelled by the spiritual depth that emerges when faith communities immerse themselves in the everyday realities of those on the margins.

When a worm's eye hermeneutic converges with these commitments, traditional theological categories—dogmas, liturgical forms, or ecclesial structures—must adapt to the pressing need for justice-based interventions. Such adaptation entails recognizing that theologically sound insights are inseparable from—and shaped by—the wisdom of individuals whose voices have historically been excluded. This dialogical stance, which draws upon the collaborative synergy between intellectual tradition and marginalized perspectives, invokes what Gustavo Gutiérrez describes as the imperative to interpret scripture and tradition in solidarity with "the afflicted and the hungry," understood not as metaphor but as lived, material realities.[12] Gawani theology deepens that imperative by emphasizing daily acts of resource sharing, locally governed cooperatives, and bottom-up forms of leadership that embody this ethos of accompaniment.

Ultimately, gawani theology showcases how a faith-based commitment to localized struggle can reconfigure communal norms. In this model, theological reflection is no longer the purview of an elite subgroup, nor is it restricted to abstract doctrinal pronouncements. Instead, it thrives as a communal enterprise entwined with the challenges and hopes of those at the socioeconomic periphery. Indeed, the worm's eye angle widens the interpretive horizon by insisting that authentic Christian

---

12. Gutiérrez, *Theology of Liberation*, xxxi. Gutiérrez argues that theology must emerge from and return to the historical and social realities of the oppressed, thereby fueling communal transformation.

praxis—expressed through persistent solidarity, reciprocal learning, and structural advocacy—forms an integral dimension of theological inquiry. By unveiling how moral agency takes shape in contexts of adversity, gawani theology stands as a living testament that robust spirituality arises precisely where faith communities heed the wisdom, resilience, and leadership of those whose struggles most urgently call for a transformative response. In so doing, it reinforces the proposition that shared agency, coauthored by marginalized individuals, can lay the groundwork not only for philanthropic interventions but also for deep-seated institutional reforms that challenge entrenched injustices.

3.6. HIDDEN POWER STRUCTURES AND THE CAPACITY FOR GRASSROOTS REINTERPRETATION

A worm's eye hermeneutic frequently uncovers the ways in which legal mandates or religious edicts might be repurposed—or even subverted—by marginalized communities confronting punitive conditions. In seventeenth-century England, as Hill documents, impoverished people or radical sects reinterpreted official rules through the lens of practical survival, communal fairness, and spiritual conviction.[13] From an institutional vantage, these grassroots reinterpretations may seem disruptive or heretical. Yet from a worm's eye perspective, they often represent necessary adaptations that make official decrees more consonant with local realities.

Gadamer's concept that interpretive frameworks evolve when confronted with unexpected realities is directly applicable here.[14] For instance, when an ostensibly universal religious prohibition or a government directive collides with immediate, life-threatening circumstances in a poor community, it may be reconfigured to address urgent survival needs. Such reconfiguration reveals that interpretive authority does not reside exclusively in official pronouncements or learned commentaries; instead, it emerges dynamically whenever communities' fashion new meanings to navigate hardships. The worm's eye stance, therefore, does more than highlight neglected voices—it illuminates how these voices recalibrate the very structures presumed to control them.

13. Hill, *World Turned Upside Down*, 1637. Grassroots interpretations frequently diverged from official decrees.

14. Gadamer, *Truth and Method*, 52. Previously unanticipated contexts necessitate recalibrating interpretive frameworks.

Dispelling the Myth of Neutral, Objective Hermeneutics

Another substantial contribution of the worm's eye approach is its rejection of the claim that interpreters can stand in a purely objective or detached position. By underscoring that every interpretive act is historically situated, the stance reveals how disclaimers of neutrality can mask power interests.[15] Gadamer likewise notes that all understanding emerges from within particular horizons, thus nullifying the notion that one might occupy a vantage free from bias or tradition.[16] An interpreter who neglects to identify their own cultural, economic, or ideological entanglements risks perpetuating injustice through well-intentioned but fundamentally imbalanced discourses.

Within theological discussions, this acknowledgement of subjectivity resonates closely with the impetus behind gawani theology. Top-down missionary models or "charitable" outreach can become paternalistic if they fail to perceive the latent power asymmetries at play. By contrast, a worm's eye lens fosters a form of humility that situates interpreters—whether they are pastors, theologians, or scholars—on an equal footing with communities in precarious conditions. It is precisely through the reciprocity of this dialogical exchange that ethically grounded transformations can unfold, echoing Gadamer's insistence on dialogue as the core locus of understanding.

3.7. REIMAGINING TRADITION AND COMMUNITY THROUGH COLLABORATIVE DIALOGUE

Far from advocating a simple reversal of hierarchical structures, the worm's eye posture calls for an inclusive dialogical space in which multiple perspectives converge to reassess cultural inheritance and normative claims. By exposing lesser-known stories of defiance, cooperation, and resilience in the face of oppression, it expands the interpretive arena to accommodate a broad spectrum of experiences, including those previously deemed insignificant.[17] This expanded arena injects creative energy

---

15. Herder, *Philosophical Writings*. 114. Herder stresses that claims of objectivity often obscure hidden biases.

16. Gadamer, *Truth and Method*, 116. Understanding is always shaped by one's own preconceptions and historical embeddedness.

17. Huizinga, *Homo Ludens*, 90. Creative engagement can spark reformist or transformative energies.

into interpretive processes, fostering moral responsibility for redressing social disparities through collective reflection and deliberate action.

Gadamer's emphasis on the transformative power of aesthetic or participatory engagement underscores how immersion in lived experience can reveal facets of meaning obstructed by mere intellectual distance.[18] Analogously, the worm's eye standpoint insists that direct encounter with marginalized realities compels interpreters to reevaluate accepted truths. Just as aesthetic participation dislodges superficial readings of art, so too does the worm's eye vantage unravel superficial assumptions about society. In line with gawani theology, this recognition moves beyond abstract moralism, urging interpreters to seek concrete pathways for social revitalization—be it through collaborative agricultural projects, fair distribution of resources, or grassroots advocacy.

3.8. BROADENING THE FUSION OF HORIZONS TO ENCOMPASS LIBERATION

At the heart of Gadamer's conceptualization is the claim that understanding emerges from the reciprocal interplay, or the "fusion," of the interpreter's horizon and that of the text or phenomenon under scrutiny.[19] The worm's eye perspective intensifies this principle by arguing that those who inhabit the social margins occupy a horizon fundamentally shaped by daily struggles for acknowledgment, resources, and survival. When these marginalized horizons confront established interpretive traditions, the ensuing dialogue can be both unsettling and revelatory, propelling communities toward deeper moral insight. Such an encounter not only challenges the comfortable presuppositions of privileged interpreters but also paves the way for a more inclusive and justice-oriented communal framework.

Viewed through the lens of liberation theology, including gawani theology, the worm's eye approach bolsters the argument that subaltern voices form a crucial corrective to interpretive distortions that gloss over structural oppression. Bernard Lonergan's concept of self-appropriation clarifies how identifying and dismantling internalized biases can dramatically expand the range of communal possibility.[20] When interpretive

---

18. Gadamer, *Truth and Method*, xxviii. Active participation reveals layers of meaning concealed by purely theoretical approaches.

19. Gadamer, *Truth and Method*, 525. Horizon-fusion denotes the encounter of distinct interpretive horizons, often yielding novel insights.

20. Lonergan, *Method in Theology*, 31. Self-appropriation helps identify biases and

communities commit to hearing the experiences of those who endure exploitation, they begin to transform theological reflection from an intellectual pursuit into an ethical mandate that fosters shared discernment, practical service, and communal solidarity.

3.9. CONCLUSION: BUILDING A SHARED HORIZON THROUGH THE WORM'S EYE VANTAGE

One theme woven throughout this chapter is the idea that a worm's eye vantage reframes social, historical, and theological reflection by concentrating on people whose lived experiences are often missed in conventional accounts. This view offers more than an academic exercise in inclusivity; it calls for a change in how groups understand and address real challenges such as wage injustice, land disputes, or political suppression. By making these overlooked perspectives a starting point, communities gain a way to reassess existing power relations and generate moral strategies that align with actual human conditions.

A second theme involves how this vantage echoes Gadamer's emphasis on dialogue, where knowledge arises not through detached study but through patient engagement with tradition and context. In a worm's eye posture, this dialogue includes direct relationships with those on the socioeconomic edges, ensuring that interpretive processes remain accountable to material constraints. Rather than limiting theology or historical study to abstract theory, this approach anchors reflection in shared interaction, leading to communal learning and fresh ethical awareness.

A third thread concerns how grassroots stories of resistance, ingenuity, and solidarity form alternative histories that challenge official records. Whether exploring events in seventeenth-century England or modern-day contexts, the worm's eye lens shows that so-called ordinary individuals often reshape communities in unrecognized ways. Highlighting these smaller narratives does not merely add extra detail to elite accounts; it demands a reevaluation of how power is maintained and how social progress can unfold from below.

Another dimension underlines how a worm's eye vantage can make tradition more responsive to moral questions raised by social exclusion. Rather than discarding past teachings or customs, individuals on the margins adapt and reinterpret them to address contemporary issues. This

---

enlarge communal possibility.

capacity for renewal suggests that tradition itself can evolve, provided it is open to fresh inputs from those directly facing daily adversity. The result is a tradition more aligned with human dignity and communal well-being, echoing the thrust of gawani theology's emphasis on day-to-day solidarity.

One more aspect is the shared liberation that emerges when the needs of those at the bottom rungs become a collective concern. A worm's eye framework recognizes that systemic injustice confines both those on top, who benefit from its structures, and those on the receiving end. Naming this reality sets the stage for collaborative solutions where the privileged also break free from the illusions of power. In theological terms, such liberation implies a broader sense of mutual accountability, suggesting that real transformation requires the involvement of all parties in a community, not solely the disenfranchised.

A related theme is Paulo Freire's principle that knowledge does not move exclusively from the expert to the learner. Instead, the worm's eye orientation proposes that everyone in a community—whether academically trained or not—has a vital role in shaping theological interpretation or historical understanding. This collaborative ethos challenges the notion of top-down charity, urging faith communities to see vulnerable neighbors as cocreators of meaning and practice. In gawani circles, resource sharing and empowerment are more than moral ideals; they are the daily outworking of a partnership that values each person's viewpoint.

Another observation concerns gawani theology's approach to praxis, which blends theological reflection with tangible acts of care among those experiencing structural hardship. This perspective moves beyond statements of compassion to real collaboration with the displaced, impoverished, or politically silenced. The worm's eye vantage intensifies that effort by exposing how daily struggles serve as the ground where faith communities either confirm or discredit their stated values. In short, an ethos of walking alongside the marginalized is not an add-on, but essential to shaping a credible theology.

An additional issue addressed here is how biblical interpretation shifts when the marginal becomes active readers. Passages once considered abstract or purely spiritual reveal themes of injustice and solidarity with renewed clarity. Gawani theology underscores this effect: exodus narratives highlighting God's concern for the oppressed, or teachings on neighbor love, take on immediate relevance for communities confronting displacement or want. This reorientation of Scripture not only influences mission strategies but also redefines worship, prayer, and the shape of congregational life.

Next, the worm's eye vantage raises critical questions about interpretive neutrality. By accepting that all understanding is historically situated, interpreters are prompted to examine their own biases and cultural entanglements. In theological contexts, this often means discarding the illusion that a privileged observer can pronounce doctrinal truths free from social commitments. Instead, communities discover that the legitimacy of their readings depends on transparent engagement with the real conditions of those who have suffered from hierarchical or biased interpretations.

There is also a collective sense of tradition and community reformation. Marginalized perspectives are not bent on erasing heritage or confession; rather, they revitalize them by insisting that doctrines or canons prove their worth in practice. In the worm's eye approach, older teachings about unity, grace, or holiness find renewed application in settings of oppression, pointing to how faith and solidarity belong together. Themes like covenant or neighborly care become urgent tasks, not historical curiosities.

Another paragraph highlights the aesthetic dimension Gadamer describes. Immersion in marginalized contexts—akin to immersing oneself in an artwork—can unsettle previous assumptions, opening a path for new approaches. In parallel, an encounter with local traditions, farming practices, or self-made cooperatives can yield forms of moral reflection that remain invisible to more distant observers. In effect, this aesthetic-like participation fosters a theology that values experience and lived knowledge as much as scholarly expertise.

Continuing, the worm's eye vantage supports the idea that faith-based reflection and social action intertwine. For many historically dominant traditions, theology sat in the realm of theory, while social activism was considered optional. By contrast, a perspective shaped by gawani theology and subaltern experiences reveals that the impetus for activism emerges directly from biblical imperatives and communal reflection. Social and ecological initiatives, therefore, reflect an integrated view of discipleship that ties worship to public responsibility.

A further focus deals with how power structures are challenged when communities prioritize the well-being of those at society's edges. This recentering compels a rethinking of governance within churches, nonprofits, and local councils, unveiling new roles for community members who have previously been silenced. Thus, the worm's eye vantage does not merely critique established hierarchies; it outlines alternative leadership patterns grounded in collaboration, reciprocity, and humility, aligning with gawani's emphasis on shared agency.

One more theme relates to how gawani theology merges local expertise with religious tradition. Both are taken seriously: the knowledge emerging from specific neighborhoods or occupations intersects with biblical teachings to forge approaches that address real challenges such as hunger or unfair labor. This synergy stands apart from theoretical ideals untested in daily life; instead, it underscores how faith communities can remain relevant by paying heed to immediate circumstances.

Finally, this chapter reaffirms that a worm's eye vantage broadens theological horizons by making room for the input of those excluded from mainstream narratives. In gawani terms, this move exemplifies how the gospel fosters active care for neighbors, turning typical missionary or philanthropic models into partnerships. As congregations place subaltern voices at the heart of collective decision-making and theological discourse, they enact an inclusive ethic that nurtures hope and fosters sustainable change. The practice of everyday solidarity thus becomes the living sign of a faith that refuses to leave the marginalized as bystanders, inviting them to coauthor a shared future shaped by compassion and justice.

4.

Gawani in Creation and Salvation

An Interdependent Relationship Linking God, Humanity, and Nature

Gawani theology presents an interconnected approach in which creation and salvation function as complementary aspects of God's covenant with humanity. Rather than isolating environmental stewardship from divine redemption, it affirms that care for the earth and care for fellow human beings belong together. The Genesis narrative about being made in God's image offers a perspective of stewardship rather than unchecked dominion, challenging any view that grants unbounded authority over nature. At the same time, the Exodus account of liberation suggests a calling for believers to oppose systems of exploitation, underscoring that neglecting either the ecological or social dimension undermines the shared mission to foster communal flourishing.

Within this framework, Genesis portrays an intricate relationship between humanity and the rest of creation, with humans placed in a carefully ordered world intended for growth and reciprocity. The earth is not a passive resource but a part of the covenant community, receiving diligent care so that it can continue to sustain life. This arrangement contrasts with reading dominion as mere license to extract; it instead signifies moral responsibility to preserve the integrity of ecological systems. Rather than encouraging exploitation, Genesis points to a bond of service, calling humans to reflect the Creator's compassion through protective stewardship.

Exodus then depicts how God's liberating action extends beyond spiritual matters to confront oppressive structures that degrade human life. When the Israelites cry out in bondage, God intervenes to restore communal well-being, revealing that divine action includes standing with those who suffer and reorienting social patterns that permit injustice. From a gawani viewpoint, this same principle applies to the modern world: caring for creation and pursuing social equity converge, because both are part of God's intention to nurture life and relationships. Economies built on exploitation threaten not only human welfare but also the balance of creation, echoing pharaoh's hoarding that curtailed freedom for many.

Gawani theology strengthens these biblical motifs by integrating the call to serve with a focus on cooperative relationships. Genesis describes shared stewardship that respects each partner's place in creation, while Exodus highlights the necessity of forging laws and practices that protect the vulnerable. Gawani interpreters see these accounts as frames for a covenant ethic promoting both environmental responsibility and communal justice. Solidarity with those who lack power becomes inseparable from recognizing creation's inherent value, pointing believers toward practical choices that reflect the covenant's inclusive nature.

Natural theology offers another layer of reflection, contending that human reason and observation of the natural world can reinforce biblical themes. Gawani advocates this dialogue, suggesting that science, cultural wisdom, and ecological studies can illuminate how interconnectedness operates in tangible ways. Such an outlook respects Gadamer's hermeneutical method, where tradition and context shape understanding. By carefully listening to local histories, environmental data, and the biblical witness, gawani practitioners affirm a unified interpretation that honors both revelation and reality.

In conversation with liberation theology—particularly Gutiérrez's focus on "the afflicted and the hungry"—gawani broadens the horizon to include the earth as a participant in human welfare. If the vulnerable are left without resources or dignity, the entire relational network suffers. By the same token, when environmental devastation occurs, communities on the margins typically endure the worst impacts. Uniting these concerns, gawani and Gutiérrez both assert that Scripture's call includes addressing material inequities and systemic pressures that destabilize families and ecosystems alike.

The chapter thus proposes that creation care and the pursuit of social justice are not competing agendas but integral parts of one covenant mission. By interpreting Genesis and Exodus as a cohesive message, gawani theology identifies shared stewardship and compassion for the oppressed as essential obligations. Properly understood, this commitment extends beyond spiritual devotion or occasional charity, urging believers to align their entire communal and ecological footprint with God's design for harmony. Through this blend of biblical reflection, natural theology, and local contexts, the chapter aims to present a renewed vision of redemption that embraces both humanity's bond with the Creator and the shared household of creation.

4.1. GENESIS AND THE GAWANI ETHOS: IMAGE-BEARING FOR COMMUNAL STEWARDSHIP

The biblical foundation for gawani theology originates in the book of Genesis, which presents humanity as created "in our image" (Gen 1:26). This well-cited passage does more than acknowledge the dignity of human life; it provides a primary calling for humankind to manifest the Creator's compassion and inventiveness. In the gawani framework, bearing God's image is never an endorsement for unrestrained dominion but rather a call for ethical cooperation, reframing human beings as cocaretakers tasked with fostering the well-being of the wider creation.[1] This perspective challenges readings that interpret "dominion" solely as the right to exploit, underscoring that power must be understood as a form of accountability, bound to the flourishing of ecological systems rather than their subjugation.

Many longstanding doctrines posit that, because humans bear the *imago Dei*, they possess a singular status of authority over other living beings. Gawani theology shifts this viewpoint by placing the emphasis on reciprocity: Genesis situates humanity on the sixth day—after the unfolding of cosmic and earthly habitats—to highlight that humankind emerges within a sophisticated, interwoven environment, one that

---

1. Kang, *Theology of Gawani*, 5. Kang highlights that human beings are "speech-creatures par excellence," suggesting that God's unique address to humanity implies a vocation of creative agency and communal dialogue.

imposes responsibility rather than absolute control. Humans indeed display capacities for creativity, moral judgment, and reflection, but these traits are meant to empower, not to suppress, the broader community of life. According to Walter Brueggemann, the "mandate of power" in Gen 1:28 coincides with an equally significant "mandate of responsibility," urging interpreters to consider that dominion cannot be viewed in isolation from the ongoing patterns of divine artistry.[2]

However, appreciating this mandate in comprehensive terms demands a reexamination of the scriptural text. Gawani theology stresses that humanity's mandate includes safeguarding the ecological order, building communities of justice, and recognizing that all creation shares in the sanctity of life. Such a commitment redefines conventional models of authority, encouraging believers to renounce paradigms that reduce the earth to a resource bank subject to limitless extraction. The creation narrative thus conveys an intricate message: even though humans hold a unique role, this role is oriented toward stewardship, ethical collaboration, and continuous reverence for the Creator's handiwork.

When turning to the second creation account (Gen 2), the biblical narrative highlights that God formed humans from "the dust of the ground" (Gen 2:7). This imagery underscores two essential truths. First, people remain deeply tied to the ecological surroundings, requiring sustenance from the earth's bounty to persist. Second, humanity partakes of God's spiritual essence, indicating that identity is neither purely physical nor entirely spiritual but a harmonious combination of both. Gawani theology interprets this as a statement that humans are called to honor their physical interdependence alongside their spiritual bond, grounding them in a context where the divine breath coexists with earthly finitude. The result is an ethos that values respect for creation, emphasizes the Creator's generosity, and views existence as a continuous invitation to commune with God's life-giving spirit.[3]

Such theological reflection has far-reaching implications for how individuals and faith communities might reevaluate their own roles. Rather than celebrating human autonomy as an excuse for unaccountable power, gawani thinkers consider moral agency to be an outgrowth of divine companionship, whereby humans work in tandem with God

---

2. Brueggemann, *Genesis*, 31. Brueggemann maintains that dominion in Gen 1:28 is inevitably linked to responsibility, challenging uses of this text to endorse unfettered dominance and reminding readers of the interdependent character of creation.

3. Kang, *Theology of Gawani*, 6.

to maintain the interconnected tapestry of existence. This understanding informs ethical choices in fields such as environmental conservation, social welfare, agricultural policy, and even economic structures. Gawani theology thus proposes an integrative vision in which spiritual devotion intersects with social responsibility, pointing to a holistic concept of creation care.

Gawani theology pays particular attention to the way Gen 2 describes the creation of man and woman. Instead of instituting a hierarchical chain of command, Gen 2:23 articulates mutual belonging: "bone of my bones, flesh of my flesh." Gawani interpreters highlight this reciprocal dynamic as an example of what might be called the gawani dynamic, wherein man and woman serve as helpers for one another. This term does not convey subordination but rather interdependence, suggesting that both parties carry unique, complementary responsibilities, unified by divine intention. Within gawani reading, the phrase "bone of my bones" exemplifies a lived reality of partnership, indicating that each partner's well-being is entwined with the other's.

Moreover, the first human pair in Gen 2 shares a common vocation: tending the garden that symbolizes the fullness of creation—encompassing land, animals, vegetation, and potential for cultivation. In a gawani perspective, this vocation extends beyond immediate domestic tasks, pressing upon all spheres of communal and societal life to adopt a framework of cooperative development. By recognizing that humanity's existence is part of an established natural cycle, believers are reminded that any distortion in these ecological or social webs is at odds with God's creative objective. Consequently, tasks like addressing climate issues, ensuring equitable resource distribution, and promoting sustainable living become integral expressions of faithfulness to the mandate described in Genesis.

Gawani theology acknowledges that, historically, several Christian communities have used Genesis to validate patriarchal or exploitative practices, often reducing the rich narrative to a single principle of dominion. Yet if dominion is assessed only as an excuse for unlimited control, such interpretations run counter to the wider biblical portrayal of God as deeply involved with and benevolent toward creation. Gawani interpreters argue that these texts were never intended to endorse mechanical or coercive understandings of authority.[4] Instead, creation is presented

---

4. Brueggemann, *Genesis*, xlii.

as something that operates in harmony with the Creator's will, thriving when humans function as responsible caretakers.

This reading also addresses the importance of cosmic order in Gen 1–2, highlighting that divine speech shapes creation into a place designed for thriving relationships. Creation day by day emerges from the creative word of God, which is answered not through coercion but through a cooperation that resonates throughout the cosmos.[5] When dominion is understood as reflecting the Creator's compassion, it ultimately signifies an imperative to preserve, enliven, and sustain what God has entrusted to human stewardship.

By incorporating the gawani perspective, faith communities are invited to explore a more comprehensive viewpoint on authority. This approach questions any tendency to separate the spiritual or theological realm from the material or social realm. The text suggests instead that divine-human relationships are manifest in ecological respect and social equity. If God cares about how creation functions, then every dimension of human life—economic policy, social justice, environmental stewardship, family relations—can be reimagined through the lens of gawani principles.

Adopting a gawani lens implies that religious practice is not confined to abstract reflection; it insists on ethical action informed by biblical values. Faith communities inspired by gawani theology might undertake initiatives such as establishing sustainable agricultural methods, advocating for environmental conservation, and championing fair labor practices, all as an embodiment of the Genesis mandate to care for the community of life. The pursuit of social justice, too, resonates with this theology, as each person is made in the Creator's image, deserving dignity and consideration within societal structures.

Moreover, the covenant language in Gen 2, whereby man and woman unite in shared responsibility, amplifies this call to unity. The partnership extends beyond family structures to community dynamics: collective decision-making, mutual reliance, and a commitment to serving the marginalized. By framing human relationships in terms of connectedness, gawani theology contends that concerns for ecology and communal well-being are not merely optional philanthropic gestures but indispensable expressions of what it means to be in relationship with God.

---

5. Brueggemann, *Genesis*, xi.

This perspective also invites a critical reassessment of passages in the later biblical tradition that appear to subordinate women or condone exploitative power structures. Gawani scholars point out that such interpretations often reflect contextual readings shaped by later social and political pressures, rather than the formative witness of Genesis. Through a careful study of the text's emphasis on cooperation, equality, and the idea of both man and woman sharing in divine creativity, gawani theology encourages communities to reject narrow or hierarchical readings that disconnect the creation mandates from the Creator's inclusive character.[6]

In sum, gawani theology offers a broad reading of Genesis that foregrounds humanity's vocation to exemplify the Creator's compassion and inventiveness. By locating dominion within the framework of stewardship and affirming that humans are simultaneously earthly creatures and recipients of divine breath, gawani theologians recover the biblical call to tend and cultivate, rather than exhaust and conquer. This perspective has extensive social and ecological implications, calling believers to challenge exploitative attitudes and commit themselves to a cooperative ethos of creation care.

Ultimately, gawani theology underscores that God's creation narrative in Genesis revolves around community—encompassing human relationships, the human-divine bond, and humanity's cooperation with the broader web of life. The image-bearing mandate thus functions as an impetus for shaping ethical, socially engaged, and ecologically sensitive communities that recognize their bond with both the Creator and the creation. When interpreted through this lens, Genesis promotes a balanced yet dynamic view of human authority, framed by a responsibility to nurture the ongoing vitality of life. In doing so, it invites faith communities to craft lifestyles, ministries, and communal policies that harmonize with the overarching biblical message: humanity's call to participate in God's work of sustaining and restoring the shared household of creation.

4.2. EXODUS: GAWANI SOLIDARITY WITH THE SUFFERING AND COMMUNAL LIBERATION

The exodus narrative holds a vital place within gawani theology, illustrating in detail how God not only observes but also decisively intervenes

---

6. Kang, *Theology of Gawani*, 6.

in oppressive sociopolitical systems to reestablish communal wholeness.[7] This biblical account centers on the Creator's intentional alignment with marginalized people in bondage, as seen in the declaration, "I have surely seen the affliction of my people. . . . I know their sorrows" (Exod 3:7). The text depicts God as deeply aware of human suffering and as a liberating agent who dismantles exploitative power structures rather than merely condemning them from a distance. For proponents of gawani theology, this portrayal underscores a defining principle: divinity is not remote or indifferent but fully engaged with those subjected to injustice.[8] By descending to share in human trials, God indicates a commitment to overturning systems that endanger both human dignity and the larger creation. This central motif inspires the conviction that religious communities, in every era, must confront subjugation head-on, responding to the needs of the vulnerable through moral, social, and structural transformation.

From a gawani viewpoint, the subjugation described in Exodus emerges out of pharaoh's monopolization of economic and political resources—an arrangement that systematically reduces people to a subordinate status.[9] Pharaoh's approach, which included gaining control over land and sustaining an ever-expanding surplus of grain, exemplifies how economic manipulation transforms free individuals into an expendable labor force forced to survive by serving the empire. This unfolding drama underscores that exploitation is not simply a historical footnote but a persistent threat whenever resources are hoarded by an elite minority, leaving ordinary people deprived of autonomy and coerced into gratitude for even minimal subsistence. In the Exodus context, peasants eventually declare, "You have saved our lives. . . . We will be slaves to pharaoh," revealing how oppressive regimes can condition the oppressed to normalize subjugation. Gawani theologians highlight this phenomenon as a clarion call for modern readers to examine how contemporary forms of

---

7. This introductory statement highlights the overarching claim of gawani theology that Exodus is not only about historical liberation but also provides a timeless framework for understanding divine participation in human struggles. See Kang, *Theology of Gawani*, 6–7.

8. The idea that God actively descends to share in human trials underscores the gawani principle of solidarity with those who are marginalized or oppressed, rejecting any view of the divine as aloof from worldly suffering.

9. See Brueggemann, *Deliver Us*, 6. Brueggemann underlines how pharaoh's control over land, labor, and economic transactions systematically disempowered the Hebrew slaves.

power—be they corporate, governmental, or ideological—frequently seek to maintain control through economic dependency or fear of scarcity.[10]

Yet, Exodus also signals that liberation is more than a political rearrangement; it establishes a covenant-centered community in which the newly freed Israelites engage in laws and practices designed to preserve shared welfare.[11] Walter Brueggemann interprets this reconstitution of society as a paradigmatic event, applying to diverse contexts such as neoliberal capitalist regimes or exilic conditions that perpetuate "anxiety, injustice, and exploitation." By situating laws like the Decalogue within the narrative of freedom from Egypt, Exodus implies that genuine emancipation endures when social norms and legal frameworks prioritize communal responsibility over oppression. In gawani theology, these covenantal dimensions are not abstract regulations but practical blueprints for a social order rooted in neighborly concern, equitable stewardship of resources, and reverence for the sustaining rhythms of creation. Consequently, Exodus functions as a scriptural invitation to reconstruct societies around values that challenge systemic greed, exploitation, or disregard for ecological integrity.

A key element of this account lies in Yahweh's personal encounter with those in bondage. The text states that God "heard their cry ... and knew their sufferings" (Exod 3:7–8), revealing a direct involvement that defies conceptions of a distant, removed divinity.[12] Terence Fretheim notes that God's immediate address in Exodus "sets all that follows into motion," showing a deity willing to be vulnerable to humanity's cries and intimately engaged in the physical and emotional weight of enslavement. According to Fretheim's interpretation, for God to "know" suffering is for God to experience it deeply, choosing to adopt an "eye of compassion" rather than maintain an untroubled celestial vantage.[13]

---

10. Gawani theologians often connect these insights to modern economic and political systems that can trap communities in cycles of dependence, mirroring pharaoh's consolidation of resources.

11. The shift to a covenant-centered order, especially at Mount Sinai, is crucial for understanding how Exodus frames liberation as an ongoing, communal practice rather than a one-time event.

12. The dual emphasis on God's action—both "hearing" and "knowing"—demonstrates a personal investment in human distress, thereby distinguishing Yahweh from distant deities of the ancient Near East.

13. Fretheim, *Exodus*, 59–60. Fretheim asserts that God's knowledge of suffering is neither abstract nor merely intellectual, but a deep empathic resonance that propels God to intervene directly.

Gawani theology emphasizes this divine solidarity as evidence that authentic worship and social ethics must converge. If God does not shy away from oppressive conditions, neither should faith communities. Instead, they are mandated to recognize modern parallels to pharaoh-like forces, working actively to liberate laborers ensnared by exploitative industries, regions harmed by environmental hazards, and populations disenfranchised by systematic injustice.

This liberative framework unfolds through a twofold movement: first, God defeats the empire's structures, and second, God shapes the freed people into a covenant-bearing community.[14] The plagues and the parting of the sea represent divine acts that disrupt the empire's stranglehold, revealing how creation itself—through phenomena like hail, frogs, and the parted waters—may be mobilized to expose the fragility of an oppressive regime. As gawani theologians interpret it, the natural world is not a passive backdrop but an active witness to God's commitment to defend life's inherent worth. The storyline thus intersects with the concerns of Genesis: the same Creator who establishes a balanced, harmonious cosmos actively intervenes when that harmony is undermined. From a gawani lens, this continuum between Genesis and Exodus underscores that ecological well-being and social justice are inseparable. When humans exploit land or deprive others of freedom, they violate the integrated fabric of life God has shaped.[15]

Moreover, Exodus demonstrates that emancipation is incomplete without a transformative social ethic. After crossing the sea, Israel encounters Yahweh at Mount Sinai, receiving decrees oriented toward communal well-being, such as caring for foreigners, instituting Sabbath practices, and honoring the fundamental dignity of every community member.[16] In gawani reading, these ordinances make explicit the responsibilities that freed individuals carry for maintaining an equitable social framework. Rather than reproducing hierarchical or extractive patterns, covenantal norms encourage them to recall their prior status as slaves

---

14. This twofold movement is central to gawani theology's reading of the plagues and the Red Sea crossing, illustrating the pattern of dismantling oppressive power before constructing a liberated community.

15. Genesis and Exodus share a narrative thread that integrates creation's welfare with social justice, suggesting that environmental degradation and human enslavement violate the same divine ethic.

16. Brueggemann, *Deliver Us*, xv, notes how the Decalogue forms part of a broader legal corpus that seeks to foster an alternative social vision, one inimical to pharaoh's exploitative model.

in Egypt, using that collective memory to prevent new forms of oppression from emerging among themselves. Consequently, Exodus does not terminate in the exodus event alone; it progresses toward the forging of a community shaped by mutual accountability, reflective of God's gawani character that embraces the marginalized.

This message resonates in modern domains, where economic disparities, exploitative labor conditions, and political repression persist.[17] Gawani theology teaches that Exodus provides a theological archetype for all generations, urging them to identify and challenge pharaoh-like conditions that sabotage human flourishing and degrade creation's integrity. Taking cues from Yahweh's response—compassionate, direct, and unyielding toward injustice—faith communities might commit to legislative advocacy, environmental stewardship, and grassroots mobilization for vulnerable groups. Such engagement is not optional but foundational, given that the biblical paradigm of covenant demands that once-liberated people safeguard the freedom of others. In effect, Exodus insists that liberation is cyclical: as a community experiences freedom, it bears a moral obligation to uphold similar freedoms for its neighbors, including the land and its resources.

Additionally, gawani theology perceives in Exodus a new creation echo, paralleling the relational aspirations of Genesis.[18] Kang argues that the exodus event functions as a restoration of God's design for human existence, overcoming the dehumanizing systems that thwart the life-giving vocation initially entrusted to humanity. This perspective reinforces the notion that each act of communal liberation, whether in the ancient Middle East or the contemporary world, reflects God's overarching plan to recover wholeness amid fractured realities. In practical terms, this restoration of wholeness can manifest in campaigns for living wages, corporate responsibility, environmental protection, or policies that reconcile deep societal divides—each avenue affording believers the opportunity to enact the covenant values championed in the desert journey of Exodus.

Furthermore, the exodus narrative invites reflection on divine partiality for the least of these. Yahweh's choice to identify with abused

---

17. Gawani theology applies Exodus principles to contexts of modern injustice, recognizing how structural factors continue to disenfranchise individuals and communities worldwide.

18. Kang, *Theology of Gawani*, 6–7. Kang argues that the exodus event parallels the creation mandate of Genesis by restoring humanity to its intended role as stewards and coparticipants in God's flourishing design.

laborers rather than powerful elites subverts ordinary expectations of monarchy or sovereignty.[19] Gawani theologians highlight that God's mercy is not paternalistic; rather, it is an empathy so extensive that it challenges hierarchical structures from within, empowering the oppressed to become agents in their own liberation. This divine inclination warns contemporary faith communities against aligning themselves exclusively with privileged interests. Instead, they are beckoned to engage in gawani solidarity, which Kang describes as God's participatory involvement with human hardship.[20] Such solidarity creates new possibilities for forging alliances that transcend social stratification, focusing on the shared objective of dismantling the chains of servitude in whichever forms they appear.

Finally, Exodus underscores that liberation is not solely about removing people from bondage; it is about guiding them into a relational framework where cosmic shalom can take root.[21] Following the crossing of the sea, the people receive commandments that incorporate rhythms of rest—Sabbath and Sabbatical Years—demonstrating that creation itself requires cycles of renewal. Gawani theology integrates this observation into a wider ecological ethic, insisting that emancipation from pharaoh's tyranny must include freedom for the earth from ceaseless exploitation. The laws and rituals in Exodus support an ethos that regards land, labor, and human relationships as interconnected. Thus, contemporary believers are compelled to address environmental crises and global inequalities not as extraneous political issues but as essential aspects of living out the legacy of Exodus.

In conclusion, Exodus, through a gawani lens, depicts divine solidarity that extends from empathetic observation of Israel's suffering to an active reordering of societal structures grounded in covenantal norms. Pharaoh's empire, rooted in monopolization of resources and severe oppression, stands as an enduring image of any sociopolitical system that turns fellow human beings into tools for profit or coerces them through

---

19. Fretheim, *Exodus*, 60, explains how Yahweh's preferential alignment with slave laborers subverts ancient assumptions about divine allegiance, which was often presumed to favor royal or elite classes.

20. Kang, *Theology of Gawani*, 7. The term "gawani solidarity" describes a model of divine-human relationship wherein God shares intimately in human affliction to effect transformative change.

21. These relational frameworks—Sabbath, Sabbatical Years, and hospitality codes—anchor Israel's ethical posture, ensuring that liberation translates into sustained communal well-being and ecological care.

the threat of scarcity.²² God's intervention disrupts these patterns, forging a new communal identity committed to fairness, hospitality, and the conscientious use of creation's bounty. By linking the cosmic vision of Genesis with the communal liberation of Exodus, gawani theology affirms that the Creator's dedication to life's flourishing spans both ecological and social spheres. Modern faith communities, therefore, inherit the Exodus challenge: to recognize present-day forms of oppression, cultivate empathy, and collaborate to dismantle repressive structures. In doing so, they embody the gawani solidarity made visible when Yahweh confronted pharaoh, liberated the enslaved, and called a people into a covenant that resonates with justice, mercy, and enduring care for creation.

4.3. A HERMENEUTICAL APPROACH TO LIBERATION: ENGAGING GUTIÉRREZ'S PERSPECTIVE ON THE AFFLICTED AND THE HUNGRY

A hermeneutical lens that incorporates the lived realities and voices of faith communities is indispensable for connecting theological discourse to the complex sociopolitical challenges of the modern world. Such an approach underscores the significance of diverse cultural and historical contexts, illustrating how faith can shape social structures in practical, transformative ways. Gutiérrez proposes that the experiences of those who are poor and oppressed should occupy a central place in any serious theological project, urging that abstract or metaphysical reflection alone will not suffice to dismantle systemic injustice.²³ His emphasis on sociopolitical engagement demonstrates why liberation theology—far from being a purely theoretical system—calls for genuine, tangible changes within communities contending with pervasive inequality.

Within this paradigm, the ideas of "the afflicted" and "the hungry" go beyond metaphorical constructs; they highlights actual human beings trapped in oppressive circumstances.²⁴ In Luke's Gospel, these figures

---

22. Pharaoh's empire serves as a paradigm of structural oppression that extends beyond the ancient context, prompting modern faith communities to confront similar "empires" wherever they appear.

23. Gutiérrez, *Theology of Liberation*, xxxi. Gutiérrez contends that theology must engage thoroughly with political, social, and historical dimensions rather than retreating to purely abstract speculation.

24. Gutiérrez, *Theology of Liberation*, 254. Gutiérrez insists that "the afflicted and the hungry" signify real socioeconomic oppression, challenging the church to enact

epitomize the social, economic, and political disenfranchisement characteristic of many in Jesus's milieu, demanding that the church extend its witness beyond purely individual spirituality. As Gutiérrez claims, to shrink "the afflicted and the hungry" to spiritual allegories alone obscures the urgent sociohistorical dimensions presented by the biblical text, hampering the church's capacity to respond effectively. His critique echoes the notion that the initial three Beatitudes in Luke form an interconnected message, beckoning both individual and communal responses aimed at eradicating poverty in all its forms—political, economic, and cultural.[25]

In addition, Gutiérrez raises critical questions about how non-Western religious and cultural traditions can contribute to the broader goals of liberation theology. Employing the example of Aloysius Pieris, Gutiérrez engages "Asia's longstanding contemplative tradition," contending that the "deeply contemplative side" cultivated over centuries is far more than a refuge from the pains of daily life.[26] Rather, this form of meditation can serve as a reservoir of spiritual energy fueling real societal transformation. Gutiérrez cautions, however, that if religion or meditation becomes merely a coping mechanism to evade "the troubles and sufferings of daily life," it risks sustaining or masking structural injustice.[27] His perspective underscores the possibility that, when aligned with the cause of the poor, meditative practices may spark a deeper sense of accountability and conscientious action within the community.

Gutiérrez's reflections extend into an ecclesial mandate for solidarity with the marginalized. He asserts that Luke's Beatitudes articulate Jesus's profound concern for the economically disadvantaged, illuminating the concrete socioeconomic backdrop of first-century Palestine.[28] The impetus, he argues, lies not in mere charity but in reconstructing exploitative systems—laws, policies, and cultural norms—that perpetuate

interventions in the face of tangible hardship.

25. Gutiérrez, *Theology of Liberation*, 254. Emphasizing the Beatitudes as a cohesive message, Gutiérrez appeals for a communal approach to eradicating systemic poverty and injustice.

26. Gutiérrez, *Theology of Liberation*, xxxii. Referencing Aloysius Pieris's work, Gutiérrez suggests that contemplation need not contradict activism but can undergird the pursuit of structural changes.

27. Gutiérrez, *Theology of Liberation*, xxxii. Gutiérrez warns that if contemplative practice merely serves as an escape from real-world suffering, it risks reinforcing the status quo and deflecting attention from needed reforms.

28. Gutiérrez, *Theology of Liberation*, 254. In Gutiérrez's reading, Luke's Beatitudes are deeply embedded in the material conditions of first-century communities, urging the church to move beyond general charity toward systemic restructuring.

cycles of deprivation. Historical evidence in Latin America affirms this stance, as base communities have actively challenged structural barriers to empowerment, ensuring that the church's response to poverty transcends simplistic or paternalistic models. Alongside these experiences, further analyses propose that Luke's first three Beatitudes be interpreted collectively, emphasizing the shared responsibilities that arise for the community of disciples.[29] In so doing, the biblical narrative extends from affirming individuals in hardship to commissioning the wider faith community to subvert the very mechanisms that engender dispossession.

French exegete Alexandre Dupont provides a complementary reading by highlighting the prophetic tenor running throughout Luke's Gospel.[30] Dupont's study reinforces Gutiérrez's argument that the biblical text is not a static repository of moral principles but rather a living call for societal renewal and liberation. This is particularly salient where the text exposes "the afflicted and the hungry" as a genuine social category in need of concrete remedies, thus summoning readers to rethink their complicity within systems of structural inequality. Gutiérrez embraces this interpretation, insisting that scholars and communities move beyond narrow moralism to embrace a more robust, justice-oriented application of Scripture.

On a global scale, Gutiérrez's engagement with Asian and African voices manifests the adaptive potential of liberation theology to diverse cultural settings. His concept of a preferential option for the poor may have originated amid specific Latin American conditions, yet the problem of poverty and oppression remains a pressing concern worldwide. By prioritizing context, Gutiérrez's hermeneutical approach allows for the integration of varied spiritualities—like that of Pieris—into the broader dialogue on liberation. In this sense, local histories and practices do not detract from the theological core but rather energize it with new perspectives and possibilities for action. Consequently, this integrative method transforms theology into a dialogue inclusive of intersecting realities, thereby equipping communities to advocate policies that protect human dignity, challenge exploitative labor practices, and ensure equitable resource distribution.

---

29. Gutiérrez, *Theology of Liberation*, 254. This interpretation asserts that Luke's first three Beatitudes should be understood collectively, underscoring shared responsibilities within the disciple community.

30. Dupont, *Les Béatitudes*, 49–51, 139. Here, Dupont clarifies the prophetic impulse driving Luke's Gospel, contending that "the afflicted and the hungry" represent a call to concrete social and political renewal.

In closing, Gutiérrez's viewpoint underscores the necessity of placing the concrete experiences of impoverished and marginalized groups at the heart of biblical interpretation. He proposes that the church must view "the afflicted and the hungry" as actual subjects living under systemic burdens rather than symbolic figures used merely to illustrate abstract doctrines. Alongside recognizing Luke's "prophetic dimension," Gutiérrez also demonstrates how liberation theology entails tangible political and social implications, guiding communities to refashion institutional structures with the explicit goal of nurturing justice and collective flourishing. By acknowledging local cultures and traditions, faith communities can expand theological reflection beyond insular boundaries, pursuing forms of solidarity that surpass superficial charity. Hence, hermeneutical and liberationist currents converge to remind us that theology remains incomplete if it fails to respond to oppression with unified, transformative action.

In conclusion, the preceding discussion demonstrates how gawani theology and Gutiérrez's outlook converge on themes of creation care, communal ethics, and active liberation. The interweaving of Genesis and Exodus conveys not merely doctrinal statements but a cohesive paradigm in which ecological well-being, social justice, and spiritual devotion are united under a covenant that calls for collective responsibility. Both perspectives direct believers toward an awareness that theological reflection must avoid detachment from daily realities, choosing instead to confront the practical needs of societies in transition. Through this focus, they uphold the significance of covenantal fidelity, showing how scriptural texts can be catalysts for tangible reformation in modern contexts.[31]

A notable contribution of this framework emerges in the idea that dominion, far from excusing exploitative control, signifies a requirement to cultivate and nurture all forms of life. Gawani theology highlights the Genesis mandate to steward creation while underscoring that genuine authority always carries obligations to protect and sustain.[32] Simultaneously, Gutiérrez underscores that faith-based reflection loses its vitality if it remains isolated from the daily struggle of impoverished and marginalized individuals. Consequently, both stances converge on the principle that any authentic reading of Scripture must incorporate the experiences

---

31. Kang, *Theology of Gawani*, 7.
32. Brueggemann, *Genesis*, 31.

of those bearing the heaviest social and economic burdens, thus energizing collective pursuits of structural change.

Furthermore, these approaches underscore that liberation is never merely a personal or spiritual matter. While gawani interpreters turn to the biblical accounts of creation and exodus to reveal the close bond between ecological harmony and social welfare, Gutiérrez accentuates Luke's Beatitudes as an invitation to address inequities in law, policy, and cultural attitudes.[33] Such a shared vision clarifies that religion cannot be restricted to ceremonial practices or dogmatic pronouncements; instead, it seeks to catalyze real-world improvements in how resources are distributed, how governance is conducted, and how communities are structured. By situating "the afflicted and the hungry" at the center, theological discourse is pressed to examine where and how injustice persists, prompting believers to challenge any status quo that normalizes the oppression of people or devastation of nature.

A consistent theme involves a covenant-based orientation toward society, whereby believers are reminded to recall past instances of enslavement, exploitation, or environmental disruption and resist reproducing similar dynamics. Gawani interpreters see the second creation account as an affirmation of human connectedness to both God and the earth, urging believers to form partnerships that sustain all creatures within an interdependent web of existence.[34] Likewise, Gutiérrez's advocacy for solidarity with the vulnerable illuminates a covenantal calling: to stand actively with those dispossessed of resources and rights, fostering a climate of protection and fairness that echoes biblical injunctions against oppression.[35] By synthesizing these notions, faith communities learn to see policy reform, environmental stewardship, and social activism as indispensable expressions of religious identity.

An additional dimension arises in the prioritization of empathy as an essential characteristic of the divine-human relationship. Where gawani theology underscores God's empathetic descent in Exodus, Gutiérrez points to Luke's Gospel to illustrate how the biblical narrative consistently sides with the powerless.[36] Such depictions carry implications for modern believers, who are called to recognize that worship divorced from practical compassion becomes inadequate. Religious institutions,

---

33. Gutiérrez, *Theology of Liberation*, xxxi.
34. Kang, *Theology of Gawani*, 5.
35. Gutiérrez, *Theology of Liberation*, 254.
36. Fretheim, *Exodus*, 59–60.

therefore, have a duty to advocate policies that defend the vulnerable, remedy systemic wrongdoing, and champion equitable opportunities for all. Hence, empathy, articulated as a divine attribute, becomes a guiding norm for faith-driven social engagement.

Alongside these emphases, both gawani theology and Gutiérrez's liberation approach call for inclusive dialogue with local cultural and religious insights. By acknowledging non-Western contemplative traditions—as illustrated through Aloysius Pieris—Gutiérrez shows how spiritual disciplines can support social action, provided they do not devolve into escapism.[37] Gawani theology, similarly, integrates ecological perspectives from diverse communities, affirming that sustainable agriculture, communal land management, and indigenous wisdom can deepen collective moral frameworks. This acknowledgment fosters an adaptable theology, one that avoids a monolithic model and instead encourages reciprocal learning between tradition and context.

Moreover, the insistence on structural transformation reflects the ongoing nature of covenant obligations. Gawani advocates a continuous rethinking of human governance, resource allocation, and economic structures to ensure that the environment remains hospitable for coming generations.[38] Gutiérrez's analysis of institutionalized poverty in Latin America shows a parallel conviction that believers must go beyond temporary assistance, promoting lasting modifications in legal, political, and social systems. Both perspectives advise that new forms of injustice inevitably arise over time, so communities must renew their commitments and remain vigilant in defending dignity against encroaching forces of exclusion.

Beyond immediate contexts, these theologies point to an ever-present need for reexamining authority. Gawani interpreters challenge hierarchical applications of biblical language, noting that "dominion" can serve as a tool for caring rather than subjugating. Gutiérrez, for his part, critiques interpretations that uphold patriarchal or class-based privilege at the expense of the marginalized, contending that divine concern for the oppressed should reconfigure ecclesial priorities.[39] This realignment envisions leadership that fosters collaboration and mutual respect, undermining any assumption that top-down power structures reflect scriptural mandates.

37. Gutiérrez, *Theology of Liberation*, xxxii.
38. Kang, *Theology of Gawani*, 6.
39. Gutiérrez, *Theology of Liberation*, 254.

Equally essential is the call for a worshipful life that transcends inward devotion. In gawani theology, this involves celebrating the Creator's artistry through communal actions—such as reforestation projects, protection of watersheds, and fair labor campaigns—that demonstrate a practical acknowledgment of creation's value. Gutiérrez's stance similarly rejects any notion of purely inward spirituality, emphasizing that liturgy and ritual gain relevance when they address present injustices and mobilize believers to respond effectively. By connecting praise with policy, reflection with reformation, and ritual with radical neighborliness, both perspectives articulate a faith that unites the spiritual with the socioeconomic.

Finally, these approaches converge on an enduring optimism about the capacity for meaningful change. Gawani theologians cite the biblical themes of creation and exodus as historical testimonies to God's unwavering resolve in sustaining life and restoring broken communities.[40] Gutiérrez, likewise, asserts that no matter how embedded unjust systems become, believers can find in Scripture a rationale for challenging oppressive dominion. This shared confidence nurtures a constructive posture, inviting believers to actively participate in shaping laws, social norms, and global partnerships that elevate the worth of people and preserve the environment. Rather than resigning themselves to cycles of domination, communities that embrace these teachings can commit to renewal in each generation, embodying the covenant blessings of freedom, compassion, and continuous care for the shared household of creation.

4.4. CONCLUSION: INTEGRATING CREATION AND LIBERATION IN GAWANI THEOLOGY

One key theme drawn from this chapter is that gawani theology proposes a unified view of creation and redemption, insisting that both must be understood as facets of a single covenantal plan. Creation is not reduced to a backdrop for human activity but is vital to the fabric of communal existence. By interpreting Genesis as a commission for stewardship rather than domination, gawani underscores humanity's role as responsible caregivers within God's ecological community. This framework contrasts sharply with any reading that interprets authority only as control,

---

40. Kang, *Theology of Gawani*, 6–7.

highlighting instead that service, accountability, and shared growth characterize humanity's unique status in creation.

A second theme relates to Exodus, which shows how God acts decisively when oppressive forces degrade human worth and disrupt social order. Gawani interprets divine liberation in Exodus as a deliberate engagement with unjust structures—an affirmation that God identifies with the burdened, empowering them to resist dehumanizing conditions. This realization further indicates that religion must not retreat from systematic inequities; rather, it should stand with those seeking equitable transformation. In linking liberation and covenant, the Exodus narrative shows that freed communities are called to form new patterns of shared life, forging social norms that protect human dignity and the well-being of nature.

A third focus is the role of empathy, demonstrated by God's compassion toward enslaved Israel. Gawani readings emphasize that genuine faith communities mirror this empathy by acknowledging the challenges faced by vulnerable groups. Whether addressing forced labor or environmental exploitation, the call is to reject complacency and to work toward societal frameworks that reflect covenant values. Such a perspective ties spiritual devotion to the willingness to confront practical issues, affirming that the biblical message demands more than personal piety or ceremonial acts.

An additional observation involves creation's active participation in liberation. The exodus plagues show how the natural world becomes a catalyst exposing the fragility of oppressive powers. Gawani suggests that the same Creator who shapes the cosmos can mobilize creation to reveal and undermine exploitative regimes. This image resonates with modern ecological movements, encouraging faith communities to see environmental stewardship not simply as an option but as an extension of God's liberating work. Care for the earth emerges as integral to the covenant, uniting the well-being of people with the flourishing of all creation.

A further perspective arises in gawani's emphasis on structural change. Both Genesis and Exodus are not confined to moral ideals; they outline how social and economic life might be reoriented around respect for life. Dominion, reimagined as caretaking, sets a precedent for reevaluating power relations in settings such as agriculture, public policy, and corporate practices. The exodus story, in particular, shows that new laws and rituals guide the community toward fairness. Gawani thus urges modern believers to confront present-day "pharaohs," whether they appear as systemic poverty, corporate greed, or exploitative labor conditions.

A related idea deals with worship that embraces social responsibility. Gawani argues that devotion to God is incomplete if it overlooks real injustices harming neighbors and the environment. Reflecting on divine compassion in Exodus leads to an understanding of liturgical life as connected with everyday acts of solidarity. This stands as a counter to a privatized faith, calling congregations to ensure that worship services inspire tangible steps to protect human dignity and ecological balance. In this way, religious ceremonies become occasions for renewing a collective commitment to equity and sustainability.

Another dimension emerges when exploring how Gutiérrez places the afflicted and the hungry at the center of theological reflection. He asserts that theology is diminished if it neglects the voices of those living under unjust constraints. Gawani theology aligns with this approach by encouraging communities to hear marginalized experiences as direct appeals for structural justice. The Genesis commission, interpreted through this lens, becomes a mandate to safeguard not just the land but all who depend on it, ensuring that resources are shared, and oppression is challenged.

There is also an important continuity between the compassion of the Creator in Genesis and the liberation in Exodus. Gawani sees these accounts as unified by God's intention to uphold life at every level. When creation is threatened—whether by environmental degradation or socioeconomic imbalance—gawani-based interpretations view that threat as contrary to the Creator's purpose. Consequently, faith communities find impetus to address injustices that might otherwise go unchallenged, whether in small-scale local contexts or in large-scale global networks.

An additional aspect concerns the covenant-based ethos that emerges from these biblical narratives. Gawani highlights how covenant demands collective accountability. The creation stories offer a cosmic context for this covenant, while Exodus details concrete ways of building a society that resists domination. Fostering such covenantal ethics in contemporary settings means moving beyond isolated personal morality and adopting community-driven solutions. Schools, workplaces, and civic structures all become arenas where covenant ideals guide practical decisions toward equity and sustainability.

A further notion arises in examining the complementarity of men and women as indicated in Genesis. Gawani underscores that "bone of my bones" signals mutual partnership rather than hierarchical subordination. In turn, this leads faith communities to reimagine relationships in ways that elevate respect and collaboration among all members. The same ethic extends to broader social structures: just as man and woman are presented as cocaretakers of creation, so are believers called to form inclusive teams that promote ecological stewardship, fair labor practices, and just governance.

An important reflection involves how these narratives challenge readers to reevaluate the conventional understanding of power. Traditional interpretations sometimes use biblical texts to defend exploitative dominion. In contrast, gawani frames authority as a means to uphold life's integrity, whether human or nonhuman. This approach prompts believers to question any practice that treats creation merely as a resource for personal gain. It also invites leaders to adopt a servant-leadership style that fosters collective well-being rather than personal advantage.

Further observation relates to the transformative character of gawani-based activism. By integrating creation care, social equity, and worshipful devotion, Gawani theology positions believers to engage the world holistically. Congregations might sponsor sustainable agriculture, offer legal advocacy for underpaid workers, or lobby for environmental protections—all seen as manifestations of the covenant. Since Exodus shows God using a range of methods to free the enslaved, gawani interprets modern activism as a faithful participation in that same liberating enterprise.

Another dimension concerns worship that celebrates creation's abundance while recognizing human limits. Genesis portrays a Creator who forms an environment capable of sustaining life, yet also sets boundaries to foster balance. Gawani advocates an ethic of restraint, encouraging responsible consumption and balanced economic practices. Rather than romanticizing nature or overlooking resources, the approach urges respect for creation's capacity while challenging believers to adopt lifestyles that minimize harm.

A final theme centers on hope. Whether through the Exodus liberation or Genesis stewardship, these biblical portrayals exhibit God's unwavering dedication to preserving and renewing life. Gawani theology interprets that dedication as an ongoing call for communities to challenge injustice while trusting that their efforts align with a divine plan for wholeness. Such confidence fuels persistent activism, motivating believers to persist even when faced with daunting problems like pollution, income inequality, or institutional discrimination. Because both creation and redemption emerge from divine compassion, faith communities are assured that transformative change, however gradual, remains possible.

All these discussions converge with creation and salvation as an intertwined movement of responsibility and renewal. Far from relegating religion to abstract doctrine, gawani theology brings biblical narratives into direct conversation with today's social and ecological dilemmas. Recognizing God as a companion in human struggles, believers find reason to resist domination, tend the land responsibly, and foster partnerships that defend human and environmental integrity. This chapter thus closes on a perspective of integrated covenant life, in which the same God who shapes the cosmos is the God who liberates the oppressed, calling every faith community to join in sustaining and restoring the shared household of existence.

5.

A Contemporary Reconsideration of the Kingdom of God Through Liberation Theology and the New Political Theology

In contemporary Christian discourse, the kingdom of God has gained renewed prominence as theologians increasingly highlight its capacity to spur sociopolitical transformation and communal flourishing. Traditional eschatological readings tend to emphasize the kingdom as a future event—one that will finally establish divine justice and bring human history to its consummation. More recent approaches, however, underscore the kingdom's implications for present ethical engagement, insisting that God's reign entails active solidarity with the marginalized here and now.

Crucial to this reframing are two major currents of modern theology—liberation theology and the new political theology—which examine the kingdom through the lens of structural injustice, political power, and the lived experiences of oppressed communities. At the same time, gawani theology—rooted in Joseph Kang's articulation of wholeness, self-giving, and the restoration of life—broadens the conversation, addressing how the kingdom of God can be reimagined for African contexts, particularly in Malawi. Gawani theology integrates Africa's rich communal ethos with a biblical emphasis on service (διακονία), thereby infusing classical doctrines of salvation with a communal, justice-oriented focus.

This essay navigates these intersecting perspectives on the kingdom of God. First, it revisits key New Testament texts—especially in the Synoptic Gospels, the Johannine tradition, and the book of Revelation—to clarify how Jesus's proclamation of divine reign challenges prevalent socioreligious structures. Next, it connects these scriptural insights with Gustavo Gutiérrez's emphasis on liberation from systemic poverty and Johann Baptist Metz's insistence on public responsibility within Christian faith. Finally, it situates gawani theology at the heart of contemporary debates by illustrating how Kang's vision of "restoration of wholeness of life" not only resonates with African communal values but also provides a practical blueprint for combating corruption, poverty, and inequality. In so doing, the kingdom of God emerges not as a distant, purely spiritual ideal, but as an embodied ethic—a call for believers to live out their faith through concrete acts of hospitality, resource sharing, and advocacy for the vulnerable.

5.1. KINGDOM OF GOD AND THE MALAWIAN CONTEXT

In recent decades, theologians in Malawi and the broader African context have increasingly reimagined classical Christian doctrines, seeking to address pressing social challenges such as systemic injustice, poverty, gender-based inequities, and long-standing colonial legacies.[1] Among these doctrines, the kingdom of God occupies a critical place, not merely as an eschatological horizon but as an ethico-spiritual paradigm that promises liberation in tangible ways. Joseph Kang's conception of gawani theology—or the "restoration of wholeness of life"[2]—resonates with African communal values and underscores the call to reconfigure social, economic, and political structures in light of God's sovereign rule.

Gawani theology, with its emphasis on service, self-giving, and restoration, converges with Malawian theological priorities, where the idea

---

1. For an overview of Malawian contexts and theologies, see Nasambu-Mulongo, "Bosadi," where the author explains how sociopolitical histories shape hermeneutical frameworks.

2. Kang, *Theology of Gawani*, 7–9. Kang clarifies that gawani involves both "giving" and "restoring," thus making Christ's ministry a model for communal transformation.

of ubuntu or relational personhood often guides local Christian ethics.[3] This essay examines how the New Testament portrayals of the kingdom of God—especially in the Synoptic Gospels, the Gospel of John, and the book of Revelation—can be reimagined within a Malawian context striving for holistic liberation. By integrating insights from Kang, Gustavo Gutiérrez, Johann Baptist Metz, and Derrida's deconstructionist perspectives, we will explore how this kingdom vision prompts a hermeneutics of transformation, challenging both local religious paradigms and sociopolitical structures.

5.2. THE SYNOPTIC GOSPELS: GAWANI THEOLOGY AND COMMUNITY FLOURISHING

The Synoptic Gospels—Matthew, Mark, and Luke—offer multiple vantage points on God's reign. Mark's opening proclamation, "The time is fulfilled, and the kingdom of God is at hand," underscores the immediacy of divine intervention within earthly realities.[4] Joseph Kang observes that both Mark and Luke employ the phrase ἡ βασιλεία τοῦ θεοῦ forty-six times, whereas Matthew, reflecting Jewish reverential sensitivities, frequently uses ἡ βασιλεία τῶν οὐρανῶν.[5] Within a Malawian theological framework, where oral traditions and respect for sacred realities are keenly felt, the substitution of "heaven" for "God" invites fruitful reflection: it signals the reverential approach to the divine name while simultaneously affirming the earthly and communal dimensions of the kingdom.

Malawi, often called the "Warm Heart of Africa," faces persistent socioeconomic challenges, including poverty, healthcare crises, and a colonial legacy that shaped its political structures.[6] Within this setting,

---

3. Kang, *Theology of Gawani*, 17; cf. Mbiti, *African Religions*, 106, for background on the communal ethos in African moral philosophy.

4. Mark 1:15 (NRSV). See also Kang, *Theology of Gawani*, 7, who emphasizes the immediate tone of Jesus's inaugural proclamation.

5. Kang, *Theology of Gawani*, 7, 9. Kang remarks that Matthew's phrase ἡ βασιλεία τῶν οὐρανῶν respects Jewish piety while preserving the same theological reality as "kingdom of God."

6. Cf. Moyo, "Naming Practices," 10, 12–13. In this study, Moyo argues that colonial naming customs exerted a powerful influence on Malawi's sociopolitical identity, revealing how external impositions altered local power structures and shaped subsequent governance patterns. These insights illustrate that Malawi's colonial history remains a critical factor in interpreting modern social conditions and reformulating strategies for equitable development.

the kingdom proclamation can be reimagined as a public call to justice and restorative communal relations. The gawani notion of "restoration of wholeness" dovetails with local theological aspirations to see the reign of God tangibly address the aspirations of ordinary Malawians—access to education, equitable distribution of resources, and communal solidarity.

Matthew's Gospel, especially in the Sermon on the Mount (Matt 5–7), stresses the kingdom's ethical implications, insisting on righteousness, mercy, and poverty of spirit as core virtues.[7] In a Malawian context, these teachings gain urgency amid socioeconomic disparities. Gawani theology echoes this ethical dimension by highlighting self-giving (gawani) and communal care.[8] This perspective aligns with African communal values that emphasize collective well-being over Western individualism. Consequently, the Matthean Beatitudes (Matt 5:3–12) and the Lord's Prayer (Matt 6:9–13) not only call disciples to personal piety but also challenge local churches to address systemic injustices—be they in local governance, international aid policies, or gender dynamics within the family structure.

Luke's emphasis on inclusivity further cements the kingdom's liberative thrust. By foregrounding Jesus's ministry among the poor, the sick, and those marginalized by purity codes (Luke 4:18; 7:22), Luke's Gospel resonates with gawani theology's call to build communities of healing.[9] Applied to a Malawian context, this invites both ecclesial and para-church ministries to champion hospitality, healthcare initiatives, and economic empowerment as vital expressions of God's kingdom.

5.3. JOHN'S GOSPEL: "ETERNAL LIFE" AND THE COMMUNAL DIMENSION OF GAWANI

In contrast to the Synoptic tradition, the Gospel of John only intermittently invokes "kingdom of God," preferring the term "eternal life" (ἡ ζωή αἰώνιος) to describe Christ's mission.[10] John 3:16 crystallizes this motif, shifting the focus from a geocentric notion of kingdom to relational

---

7. Kang, *Theology of Gawani*, 17. The Sermon on the Mount exemplifies Jesus's radical ethic that shapes kingdom-centered living.

8. Kang, *Theology of Gawani*, 9. Gawani theology insists on the principle of service (διακονία) as integral to the kingdom's manifestation.

9. Metz, *Faith in History*, 15. Metz's vision of liberation intersects with Luke's portrayal of radical inclusion.

10. Gutiérrez, *Theology of Liberation*, 98–104. Gutiérrez acknowledges the shift in John's terminology yet sees continuity in the liberative thrust.

communion with God. Joseph Kang suggests this shift parallels the early Christian community's "interiorization" of divine sovereignty, emphasizing personal transformation that bears communal fruit.[11]

Malawian theological perspectives often align with John's stress on abiding (μένειν) in Christ (John 15:4–5). A communal ethos that valorizes mutual belonging and collective resilience finds an apt biblical correlate in the Johannine call to remain in Jesus as branches on the vine, drawing nourishment for a life of love and fruitfulness.[12] In the Malawian church, where liturgical life and social support systems often blend, the idea of abiding underscores a shared identity: individual faith is nurtured within the broader ecclesial fellowship, which in turn extends outwards to the wider community through acts of hospitality, care for vulnerable populations, and initiatives for local development.[13]

This abiding theme, when cross-referenced with gawani theology, suggests that the relational essence of eternal life has structural implications for how believers organize their economy, approach land stewardship, and foster interreligious dialogue in a pluralistic society.[14] Consequently, John's Gospel in Malawi may not be read as an otherworldly or purely mystical text but as an invitation to solidarity-building, peacemaking, and social transformation, all undertaken as expressions of abiding in divine love.

5.4. REVELATION: APOCALYPTIC HOPE AND AFRICAN ESCHATOLOGICAL IMAGINATION

The book of Revelation broadens New Testament eschatology by envisioning "a new heaven and a new earth," a cosmic renewal that finalizes God's redemptive work.[15] In a Malawian and wider African context, marked by histories of colonial exploitation and struggles for postcolonial identity,

---

11. Kang, *Theology of Gawani*, 9–10. Kang argues that the early church in John's community reinterpreted the kingdom motif to highlight interior transformation and mutual belonging.

12. Kang, *Theology of Gawani*, 9. Kang notes that abiding (μένειν) in Christ fosters communal identity in both spiritual and practical dimensions.

13. On the interplay of worship and social action in Malawi, see Kayange and Charles Verharen, *Ethics in Malawi*, 89–92, 159–60, 163.

14. Derrida, *Of Grammatology*, xxxvi–lv. Derrida's approach to deconstructing boundaries can inform how Malawian Christians navigate socioreligious pluralism.

15. Rev 21:1 (NRSV). Cf. Kang, *Theology of Gawani*, 7, on the eschatological language shared among NT apocalyptic texts.

Revelation's promise of divine justice resonates powerfully. Johann Baptist Metz affirms that Christian apocalyptic hope is never an evasion of the present world; rather, it is an ethical impetus that galvanizes believers to stand against oppression and embody the values of the future kingdom in current realities.[16]

In conversation with Johann Baptist Metz's emphasis on political engagement, liberation theologian Gustavo Gutiérrez argues that authentic eschatology propels believers to confront social injustices, actively dismantling entrenched structures that foster poverty and dehumanization.[17] Gutiérrez's theological framework, while rooted in Latin American realities, has found resonance among Malawian thinkers who perceive in the book of Revelation's portrayal of a new creation a powerful mandate to reimagine social order in light of the final restoration.[18] These Malawian theologians, influenced by historical and cultural contexts marked by political suppression and shifting Christian missions, look to eschatological hope as more than a purely spiritual escape; rather, they see it as an urgent call to transform oppressive economic and cultural systems in anticipation of God's promised renewal.

Gawani theology, emerging in contemporary Malawian discourse, emphasizes restorative wholeness as vital to apocalyptic expectation, advancing the idea that the coming harmony of a new heaven and new earth underscores God's intention to bring about liberation that integrates spiritual renewal with practical reforms.[19] This holistic perspective

---

16. Metz, *Faith in History*, 55, 109–10. Metz contends that eschatological hope energizes political and ethical commitments.

17. Gustavo Gutiérrez sets forth the premise that eschatological beliefs must drive concrete social action. Here, he contends that theological reflection, if merely speculative, cannot address the real-life forms of suffering that communities endure. His argument underscores the necessity of dismantling social and political structures that perpetuate human indignities, rather than confining hope to a realm of abstract promises. Gutiérrez, *Theology of Liberation*, xxxi.

18. Malawian theologians draw on Gutiérrez's liberationist insights in their own contexts, interpreting the book of Revelation's vision through a lens shaped by Malawi's political and cultural history. See Ross and Mulwafu, *Politics, Christianity and Society*, 11, 32, 35, 37. Ross and Mulwafu outline how enduring political structures, even after the Banda era, continue to affect ecclesial and civic engagement.

19. Gawani theology's stress on "restorative wholeness" aligns with Gutiérrez's claim that faith cannot be divorced from praxis. Theologians in Malawi interpret apocalyptic texts as exhortations to promote justice in socioeconomic domains, echoing Gutiérrez's position that the church carries a responsibility to effectuate meaningful change. On the interplay of meditative traditions and social activism, see Gutiérrez, *Theology of Liberation*, xxxii. Gutiérrez points to the importance of contextualizing theological ideas

includes active advocacy for equitable resource distribution, communal empowerment, and structural accountability—all dimensions understood to be integral to the eschatological vision. In such an approach, apocalyptic hope intersects with real-world concerns, galvanizing faith communities to pursue social policies that champion the dignity of the marginalized.

Moreover, by framing the unity of new heaven and new earth as a divine disclosure of holistic liberation, gawani theologians contend that faith communities should not reduce eschatology to detached spiritual speculation. Instead, they propose that genuinely embracing this vision necessitates economic equity and robust communal well-being, both of which demand an alliance between theological conviction and sociopolitical action. This alliance, grounded in the local historical tapestry of Malawi, acknowledges that achieving communal restoration often requires persistent advocacy, including the reform of entrenched power structures and unwavering support for healthcare, education, and human rights. In this regard, gawani theology stands as both a critique of passive religiosity and a constructive call for an engaged, justice-oriented practice of faith.

By drawing on Revelation's vivid imagery—where sorrow, pain, and death are eradicated (Rev 21:4)—Malawian congregations can cultivate a theology of resilience that fortifies communal efforts against corruption, economic stagnation, and social fragmentation. Moreover, this eschatological outlook fosters ecumenical collaboration, as different Christian traditions in Malawi unite around the conviction that God's final victory is both a future certainty and a present source of hope, inspiring cooperative strategies for developmental projects, healthcare initiatives, and educational programs.

5.5. JOINT PROCLAMATION OF THE KINGDOM: JOHN THE BAPTIST AND JESUS IN THE MALAWIAN MILIEU

The narratives depicting John the Baptist and Jesus—both heralds of divine reign—retain relevance in contexts of poverty and social upheaval. John the Baptist's "baptism of repentance" established a moral baseline, urging readiness for an imminent transformation of historical conditions.[20] In Malawi, where changes in political leadership and civic

---

within particular historical struggles.

20. Mark 1:2–3. On John the Baptist's transitional role, see Gutiérrez, *Theology of*

structures often evoke hope for a new era, John's call remains a potent metaphor for authentic spiritual and societal renewal: it is not enough to await God's kingdom passively; one must reconfigure one's life in anticipation of divine justice and community uplift.[21]

Jesus expands John's message by demonstrating the kingdom through healing miracles, exorcisms, and consistent outreach to societal outcasts.[22] Joseph Kang comments that Jesus's table fellowship with marginalized individuals exemplifies a "reordering of power," shattering pollution boundaries and instigating relationships of dignity and equality.[23] In a Malawian context, where hierarchical social structures can perpetuate elitism or patriarchy, Jesus's radical inclusivity challenges churches to reflect on how worship spaces, leadership roles, and communal resources might be redistributed in the spirit of gawani theology.

These healing narratives, in turn, speak to the healthcare crises Malawi continues to face, including but not limited to the ongoing struggle against HIV/AIDS.[24] Jesus's embodied compassion invites Christian communities to see medical interventions, counseling, and anti-stigma campaigns not merely as charitable activities but as kingdom imperatives that model Christ's inclusive fellowship and liberating presence.

5.6. MIRACLES AND PARABLES: HERMENEUTICS OF LIBERATION FOR MALAWI

Miracles such as the feeding of the five thousand (Mark 6:30–44; John 6:1–14) have been interpreted by modern scholars not just as supernatural displays but as symbolic enactments of divine generosity.[25] Gutiérrez frames these miracles within the biblical movement from death to life and from injustice to justice.[26] In a Malawian context, where daily bread

---

Liberation, 98.

21. Kang, *Theology of Gawani*, 9. The impetus for repentance emerges as a corporate as well as individual mandate, shaping how communities prepare for divine intervention.

22. Luke 4:18; Cf. Mark 1:15 (NRSV).

23. Kang, *Theology of Gawani*, 9–10. Zacchaeus's transformation in Luke 19:1–10 exemplifies Jesus's challenge to established social orders.

24. On healthcare challenges, see Willms et al., "Malawi Faith Communities," 23–32.

25. Gutiérrez, *Theology of Liberation*, 103. Miracles are seen as part of God's broader historical movement from injustice to redemption.

26. Gutiérrez, *Theology of Liberation*, 113. Gutiérrez argues that each sign in the

A CONTEMPORARY RECONSIDERATION OF THE KINGDOM 65

is never guaranteed for many households, the feeding miracle stands as both inspiration for mutual support and critique of unequal resource distribution. Joseph Kang's language of gawani— "giving of oneself" and "restoration of wholeness"—intensifies the economic implications: local churches are called to adopt sustainable agriculture programs, cooperatives, and microfinance initiatives as manifestations of kingdom values.[27]

Jesus's parables often challenge deep-seated social norms by showing how genuine compassion transcends conventional barriers of culture, status, or tradition.[28] Among these, the good Samaritan parable (Luke 10:25–37) stands out as a compelling instance in contexts marked by ethnic heterogeneity or strong factional identities, because it highlights the principle that loving one's neighbor must exceed all national, tribal, and even denominational boundaries.[29] In Malawi, where regional affiliations and tribal identities can still influence resource distribution and political coalitions, the Samaritan's act of mercy radically confronts the logic of favoritism, calling believers to a broader solidarity that dismantles exclusive allegiances.[30] Viewed through the lens of Jacques Derrida's 'deconstruction,' this parable positions an alienated outsider as the paradigm of neighborly love, thus undermining the categories by which certain communities might be labeled less deserving of empathy, social services, or public advocacy.[31] By centering the story on a figure typically disdained

---

Gospels embodies the inbreaking kingdom.

27. Kang, *Theology of Gawani*, 5–6. Gawani underscores God's provision as communal sharing.

28. Gutiérrez, *Theology of Liberation*, xxxi. In this influential work—first published in Spanish in 1971—Gustavo Gutiérrez argues that theological reflection must remain closely connected to sociopolitical and historical circumstances, lest it devolve into purely abstract speculation. His emphasis on concrete solidarity with those on the margins finds resonance in how Jesus's parables consistently reorient cultural assumptions toward inclusivity.

29. Cf. Ross and Mulwafu, *Politics, Christianity and Society*, 45–58. The contributors in this volume document how tribal and regional identities in Malawi have historically affected both resource allocation and political alliances, demonstrating why the good Samaritan story remains relevant in critiquing favoritism.

30. The parable's illustration of love that transcends communal boundaries cuts against the grain of ethnocentric loyalties, particularly in societies where local affiliations still wield considerable influence. In the Malawian setting, this message disrupts partisan loyalty, urging faith communities to reexamine how social benefits and communal resources are distributed.

31. Derrida, *Of Grammatology*, 37. Derrida's deconstruction invites readers to question the frameworks that support hierarchical or exclusionary distinctions. By offering a reviled foreigner as the exemplar of neighborly concern, Jesus effectively disassembles

within the prevailing cultural framework, Jesus unravels the binaries that reinforce prejudice, inviting Malawian churches and civic institutions to reimagine relationships across sociopolitical lines. In turn, believers are prompted to practice a form of hospitality that extends beyond mere personal benevolence, embracing systemic changes to ensure that all groups—irrespective of regional or cultural backgrounds are welcomed into tangible expressions of support and concern. This perspective not only challenges individuals to transcend their ingrained biases but also mobilizes local congregations to promote equity at the institutional level, aiming to embody a communal ethic that values human dignity above narrow partisanship.

Similarly, Zacchaeus's encounter with Jesus (Luke 19:1–10) highlights how personal redemption spills over into structural transformation: the wealthy tax collector's restitution to the poor becomes a paradigmatic moment of gawani, signifying how economic repentance revitalizes communal relationships.[32] Thus, parables function as narrative roadmaps, revealing that the kingdom of God entails radical reorientation of personal finances, social alliances, and even cultural norms of belonging.

Across the New Testament witness, the kingdom of God emerges not as a static concept but as a dynamic, life-giving reality that intersects profoundly with human struggles for justice, communion, and holistic well-being. The Synoptic Gospels stress the immediacy of God's reign through Jesus's proclamations and deeds, whereas John reframes the same reality as "eternal life," calling believers to abide in Christ's love. Revelation broadens the horizon, envisioning a cosmic renewal wherein God's sovereignty reaches its ultimate expression. Taken together, these strands converge in gawani theology's affirmation that God's kingdom manifests whenever communities practice service, redistribute resources, and tear down barriers of impurity and exclusion.

In Malawi's sociopolitical climate—marked by a history of colonial influence, ongoing developmental challenges, and vibrant Christian witness—reimagining the kingdom of God in terms of liberation means engaging systematically with issues such as economic injustice, political corruption, and healthcare inequities. Gawani theology foregrounds

---

societal presumptions that categorize certain groups as less deserving, a process analogous to Derrida's notion of unraveling normative binaries.

32. Kang, *Theology of Gawani*, 9. Zacchaeus's economic repentance represents both personal and structural realignment under the kingdom.

the restorative and communal dimensions of this kingdom, challenging churches and individual believers to embody what they proclaim.

Ultimately, the kingdom of God in Malawian hermeneutics stands as both promise and task it announces a future of eschatological shalom while simultaneously demanding the transformation of present social orders. By drawing upon the theological resources of Kang, Metz, Gutiérrez, and Derrida—alongside the local wisdom and communal ethos characteristic of Malawi—Christian communities can reinterpret and apply the biblical vision of God's sovereign rule in ways that liberate and empower. Far from remaining a distant doctrinal point, the kingdom thus becomes an ever-present invitation to reimagine societal structures, reinvigorate spiritual life, and foster holistic flourishing in the Warm Heart of Africa.

5.7. CONCLUSION: THE KINGDOM OF GOD AND MALAWI'S PATH TO WHOLENESS

One theme emerging from this chapter is that the kingdom of God involves more than a future event or a private belief system; it requires communities to consider economic, social, and political relationships in tangible ways. By looking at how Jesus proclaimed God's reign in the Synoptic Gospels, and by drawing connections to Malawian contexts, the discussion shows that local churches benefit when they see the kingdom as an ongoing invitation to challenge oppressive norms and renew communal practices.

A second theme highlights how the kingdom vision resonates with African concepts of communal solidarity. The chapter describes how gawani theology weaves together Kang's emphasis on service, African understandings of relational identity, and biblical priorities of compassion. In Malawi, where social bonds are often shaped by extended family ties and communal ethics, kingdom language encourages believers to share resources, collaborate in development efforts, and stand alongside those marginalized by economic inequalities.

A further topic examines how John's Gospel reframes the kingdom idea through motifs such as eternal life. This approach underscores a relational dynamic that calls believers to abide in divine love. When applied to Malawi, abiding signals that spiritual growth happens in the midst of real-life challenges, whether related to healthcare shortages or educational disparities. The abiding theme, therefore, points local churches to consider how worship, communal prayer, and everyday action can merge to form a consistent ethic of care.

Another element involves the apocalyptic perspective found in Revelation, which envisions a renewed creation where suffering is abolished. Such a portrayal resonates with Malawian thinkers who, faced with the legacy of colonial structures, interpret the new heaven and new earth as a call to transform current systems. Instead of viewing eschatology as an otherworldly escape, local communities can embrace it as a motivating factor for social change, ensuring that faith does not ignore issues like corruption or environmental damage.

The chapter also references the joint messages of John the Baptist and Jesus, both announcing God's imminent reign in first-century Palestine. For Malawi, the Baptist's baptism of repentance echoes the continuous need for moral reorientation in the public arena. Meanwhile, Jesus's deeds of healing and deliverance provide an example of how tangible acts of mercy embody the kingdom. When churches in Malawi translate these deeds into healthcare outreach, educational programs, or dialogue about governance, they affirm that discipleship includes social responsibility.

From a historical perspective, theological voices such as Gustavo Gutiérrez and Johann Baptist Metz insist that the kingdom can never be a passive or purely spiritual concept. The chapter applies these perspectives to Malawi's reality, where structural poverty and political imbalances challenge believers to become agents of liberation. Faith, in this sense, is not cut off from public life; rather, it seeks to reform policies and practices that keep entire communities in hardship.

The discussion also addresses the role of Derrida's deconstruction, particularly how certain parables undermine dominant categories of worthiness or status. This approach fits well in Malawi, a context where entrenched social hierarchies sometimes harm vulnerable groups. By reading biblical narratives through a lens that unveils hidden forms of exclusion, churches can shape ministries that reach beyond tribal, regional, or class divisions.

Miracles, parables, and table fellowship stories provide a shared script for believers who seek to apply kingdom values in concrete ways. The chapter points out how the feeding of the five thousand can be interpreted as both an act of compassion and a symbol of communal sharing. In a nation where daily food security remains a concern for many, such narratives challenge Christians to organize cooperatives, microfinance initiatives, and other programs that promote an equitable distribution of resources.

Another feature of the chapter is its focus on restitution and economic repentance, illustrated by the example of Zacchaeus. This motif has strong relevance in places where corruption and unfair practices persist. By taking seriously the idea that personal conversion includes remedying injustices, Malawian churches can present the gospel as something that breaks cycles of exploitation. This approach not only changes individual hearts but also restructures communal life.

The text pays close attention to the pastoral dimension of kingdom teaching. Ministers and lay leaders are encouraged to help congregations see how worship and social engagement are unified. Through preaching about Zacchaeus, the good Samaritan, or other biblical figures, they can spark reflection on whether the local church fosters dignity for outsiders, invests in vulnerable groups, and supports those lacking a voice.

Malawi's own concept of ubuntu, or communal personhood, can interface constructively with Christian ideas of neighborly love and kingdom service. Both traditions highlight that an individual's well-being is bound up with the welfare of the entire group. By aligning these ideas with biblical portrayals of Jesus's inclusive fellowship, churches can cultivate a climate where mutual help is seen as a sacred responsibility, not merely a voluntary option.

One of the practical outcomes the chapter emphasizes is the formation of alliances between congregations, civil society, and even governmental bodies. By addressing poverty, environmental challenges, and public health crises together, believers model a kingdom vision that crosses institutional boundaries. They refuse to settle for minor acts of charity, instead adopting systemic approaches that lead to long-lasting improvements.

The chapter also identifies how New Testament eschatology can strengthen hope, even in the face of daunting obstacles. Revelation's prophetic vision reinforces that the ultimate future belongs to God, offering courage to Malawian faith communities when they confront injustice or ecological threats. Such hope is neither naïve nor escapist; rather, it invites determined efforts to align present structures with God's future intentions.

Gawani theology takes on a prominent role here, framing service and restoration as markers of the kingdom's presence. Rather than separating spiritual renewal from political transformation, gawani underscores the unity of both dimensions. In Malawi, this might translate into projects that directly reduce economic hardship, such as agricultural training or community-led businesses, rooted in shared Christian convictions about stewardship and compassion.

The discussion reiterates that worship itself can be a sphere of transformation. When the church assembles, it rehearses patterns of inclusion and justice, modeling kingdom relationships that stand in contrast to prevailing social norms. Malawi's ecclesial gatherings, therefore, may become laboratories where the practical outworking of unity, generosity, and reconciliation is consistently tested and refined.

A further topic highlights the potential for interreligious collaboration when it comes to championing kingdom-like values in a broader society. While gawani theology is explicitly Christian, its emphasis on hospitality and wholeness can resonate with other spiritual or cultural traditions that also seek community uplift. Partnerships with secular NGOs or local leadership structures can extend the reach of ministries, demonstrating that faith is relevant to common concerns.

The future orientation of the kingdom does not negate the importance of addressing present inequality. The text suggests that eschatological promises mobilize believers to challenge world powers, whether expressed in exploitative labor conditions or limited healthcare access. By applying a biblical vantage, Malawian churches see the Holy Spirit's power as a resource for ethical courage, enabling them to persist in advocacy and structural reform.

In the final analysis, the chapter argues that the kingdom of God calls Malawian Christians to embrace both spiritual practices and social action, shaping a reality where no one is forgotten. Such an emphasis fits well in contexts where daily survival can overshadow long-term planning. The kingdom perspective elevates the communal imagination, encouraging believers to think beyond immediate crises toward a shared destiny of restored life.

The concluding approach reminds readers that neither liberation theology nor gawani theology claims to solve every problem overnight. Instead, they create an ongoing process of faithful engagement with the real conditions of ordinary people. In Malawi, where political shifts are frequent and global economic pressures remain high, the kingdom motif offers an enduring challenge: will churches settle for a privatized spirituality, or will they stand as catalysts for equitable change?

Bringing the entire discussion together, the chapter portrays the kingdom of God as a reality that invites every believer in Malawi—and elsewhere—to reevaluate priorities. By emphasizing hospitality, justice, and humble service, the biblical texts show how worship of God connects to practical deeds. Integrating the local communal ethos with theological reflection, gawani theology proposes that living under God's rule means forging relationships and institutions that reflect shared human dignity.

In this perspective, Malawi's specific challenges become opportunities for believers to manifest God's reign in ways that are culturally grounded and ethically bold. Whether through feeding programs, legal advocacy, or grassroots collaboration, the kingdom gains expression whenever communities align their resources and passions toward the flourishing of all. Such a commitment resonates with John's eternal life, Matthew's Sermon on the Mount, Luke's concern for the marginalized, and Revelation's hope of a redeemed creation.

The final takeaway is that the kingdom is not merely a topic for theological speculation; it is a summons to reimagine how life can be structured for the common good. Because Malawian society holds firm ties to communal identity and faith-based networks, churches have a strong platform to promote change grounded in biblical values. When gawani theology and liberationist perspectives converge, the kingdom emerges as a comprehensive framework for social renewal, championing both personal conversion and institutional fairness. Such an approach ensures that the Warm Heart of Africa continues to seek wholeness under the liberating reign of the God who calls all believers to a living hope.

6.

Gawani Christology

The Son of Human Being and the Restoration of Humanity in the Gospels and Acts

The unpublished work of Joseph Kang, tentatively entitled *Opening Gawani Theology: Seeking Interconnection and Wholeness—Focusing on the Gospels and Acts*, offers a sweeping reevaluation of New Testament Christology by centering on Jesus's distinctive self-referential title: "the Son of Human Being."[1] Although various labels—such as "Messiah," "Lord," or "Son of God"—appear in the Gospel narratives, Kang highlights that Son of Human Being uniquely reflects Jesus's own choice in naming His role and ministry.[2] By paying close attention to how this term is used across the Synoptic Gospels and the book of Acts, Kang suggests that the Son of Human Being concept is not peripheral but, in fact, undergirds an expansive theological vision. This vision—what Kang terms a gawani theology—encompasses God's in-breaking kingdom, sociopolitical liberation, eschatological hope, and, above all, the restoration of human dignity.[3]

---

1. Kang, *Theology of Gawani*, 10–14.

2. Kang, *Theology of Gawani*, 4, 16: Kang underscores that the Son of Human Being stands apart from other titles that are typically conferred on Jesus by either crowds or the early Christian communities.

3. Kang, *Theology of Gawani*, 3–4: Kang defines gawani as a guiding ethic of interconnectedness, insisting that the biblical witness portrays Jesus's ministry as a decisive manifestation of divine solidarity.

This article provides an expanded discussion of Kang's gawani Christology, integrating detailed biblical exegesis with insights from liberation theology and covenant theology. The guiding premise here is that any comprehensive interpretation of Jesus's ministry must confront the reality of social exclusion and economic exploitation.[4] Kang maintains that Jesus strategically employed the title Son of Human Being to illuminate immediate acts of solidarity and to project a vision of comprehensive cosmic renewal. Far from functioning as a merely symbolic or esoteric phrase, "Son of Human Being" underscores a call to rehumanize those living under oppressive circumstances—an imperative that centers communal flourishing on empathetic action and the promotion of human dignity. Building on this premise, gawani theology invites faith communities to expand discipleship beyond personal piety, challenging them to foster an ethic of radical empathy that seeks to transform exploitative structures.

In Kang's framework, the Son of Human Being theme simultaneously critiques systems of domination and foreshadows an eschatological horizon in which all of creation experiences justice and restoration.[5] This interpretation resonates with Gustavo Gutiérrez's view that a genuinely liberative theology refuses to separate spiritual concerns from sociopolitical realities, since severing these dimensions impoverishes both domains.[6] By affirming that religion ceases to be truly redemptive when confined to private devotion or leveraged merely for political expediency, Gutiérrez underscores the necessity of confronting institutionalized injustice, particularly when it masquerades as order.[7] Kang's reinterpretation of Son of Human Being, as shaped by gawani theology, aligns with this conviction by positing that authentic Christian praxis must address systemic exploitation, whether enacted through governmental policies,

---

4. Gutiérrez, *Theology of Liberation*, xl. Gutiérrez insists that marginalizing either the political or the religious domain reduces the potency of both, thereby urging a holistic approach that unites social justice with spiritual commitments.

5. Kang presents Jesus's ministry as fulfilling present sociocultural interventions while also unveiling a sweeping eschatological vision, a perspective that frames Son of Human Being language as pivotal in the Gospels.

6. Gutiérrez, *Theology of Liberation*, xl, 64. He argues that compartmentalizing the spiritual and the political impoverishes any authentic pursuit of liberation, prompting a reexamination of how theology interacts with societal structures.

7. Gutiérrez, *Theology of Liberation*, 64. Gutiérrez condemns institutionalized violence that legitimizes oppression in the name of sustaining order, highlighting the moral imperative to resist such distortions of stability.

economic practices, or cultural assumptions. Such an approach emphasizes that disciples of Jesus are called to participate in reciprocal relationships of caring, thereby converting theological convictions into tangible, justice-oriented initiatives.

Moreover, by intertwining immediate solidarity with an expectation of eventual cosmic renewal, gawani theology highlights a faith that is both prophetic and pragmatic. In other words, the struggle against entrenched inequities does not merely echo a distant eschatological promise; it constitutes a profound embodiment of that promise in the present.[8] In Kang's view, the gawani commitment is evidenced when believers intentionally share one another's burdens and resources, recognizing that personal well-being and communal welfare are inseparable. Such an ethic of shared responsibility dovetails with the broader liberationist principle that meaningful transformation—social, cultural, or economic—must involve a direct reordering of power. By locating Jesus's self-reference within this liberating paradigm, gawani theology suggests that the church's calling extends beyond abstract pronouncements into concrete engagement with the marginalized. Hence, Kang offers a Christological interpretation that simultaneously upholds spiritual depth and confronts oppressive realities, urging faith communities to embody the very solidarity and compassion exemplified by the Son of Human Being.

In what follows, we will explore how Kang's approach reconfigures standard scholarly debates on the Son of Human Being, investigate his perspective on the Gospels' testimony regarding Jesus's compassion for the marginalized, and illustrate how Acts continues Jesus's Son of Human Being mission in the earliest Christian community. We will then consider how these insights connect to covenant motifs and to modern theological discourse. By merging biblical scholarship, historical analysis, and systematic reflection, this article aims to reveal the robust theological potential of Son of Human Being language, as Kang envisions it, for confronting contemporary forms of injustice and alienation.

---

8. Gutiérrez, *Theology of Liberation*, 216. When gradual reforms prove insufficient, Gutiérrez urges a radical challenge to systemic injustice, which parallels Kang's notion of a gawani-driven solidarity that fosters enduring social change.

6.1. THE CENTRALITY OF SON OF HUMAN BEING IN GAWANI THEOLOGY

Unique Self-Reference in the Synoptic Gospels

Kang argues that Son of Human Being stands out among the array of Christological titles because Jesus himself repeatedly employs it to articulate his identity and mission.[9] The Gospels occasionally record the crowds or disciples addressing Jesus with other designations—such as "Rabbi" or "Son of David"—but Son of Human Being emerges as a distinctly self-ascribed term. In the Synoptic narratives (Matthew, Mark, Luke), Jesus utilizes this phrase in three broad categories: earthly ministry, suffering and resurrection, and eschatological judgment.[10] Kang maintains that all three categories are indispensable for understanding Jesus's role as a liberative figure who both engages in present transformative acts and anticipates the final unveiling of God's righteous rule.

Contrary to the historical-critical viewpoint that Jesus referred only to an earthly Son of Human Being while later church expansions shaped the eschatological or suffering dimensions, Kang posits that the Gospels preserve authentic clues to Jesus's own intentions. Kang thus concludes that the early church did not fabricate the Son of Human Being sayings in their entirety but rather preserved them to reflect Jesus's conscious self-depiction.[11] The triple emphasis on earthly compassion, sacrificial suffering, and ultimate judgment underscores the integrative scope of Jesus's identity as Son of Human Being.

---

9. Kang, *Theology of Gawani*, 8–12. While other appellations (Messiah, Son of David) are used by various speakers, the Son of Human Being appears consistently as Jesus's self-chosen form of address in the Synoptic tradition.

10. Kang, *Theology of Gawani*, 7–8. The consensus among many scholars is that the Gospels present three main sets of the Son of Human Being sayings—earthly ministry, passion/resurrection, and future judgment—though debates remain regarding their original contexts.

11. Kang, *Theology of Gawani*, 11. Kang suggests that the diverse references to the Son of Human Being reflect a cohesive Christological aim that derives from Jesus's authentic ministry, rather than merely from post-Easter editorial developments. He states, "It is crucial, as far as those 'Son of Human Being' sayings are concerned, to understand why the early Christian communities identified Jesus of Nazareth with the Son of Human Being and depicted it as Jesus' own self-description. This self-designation of Jesus as the 'Son of Human Being' cannot be separated from the Gospel witness of his teaching and action for the sake of the dawning rule of God, in terms of human restoration over against all kinds of dehumanizing evil forces. In this respect, Ps 8 and Ezekiel could be taken into christological consideration along with Dan 7."

Gawani and the Restoration of Human Dignity

Gawani adds a further layer to the Son of Human Being discourse by focusing on human dehumanization.[12] At its core, gawani points to a collective ethic in which practical care is extended to those existing on the margins of society—economically disenfranchised, culturally devalued, or politically oppressed. Drawing from the Gospels, Kang highlights that Jesus's recourse to Son of Human Being language regularly appears in contexts where structural injustices are called into question. Thus, the Son of Human Being emerges not only as an eschatological figure but also as the one who challenges and reverses social hierarchies in the here and now. Through healing, table fellowship with outcasts, and explicit condemnation of exploitative systems, Jesus exemplifies the gawani ethic, inviting his followers to do likewise.

Zacchaeus, a tax collector deemed both ritually impure and morally suspect, was presumed to belong to society's margins—shunned by devout circles and systematically distanced from communal life.[13] Yet, when Jesus publicly insists on lodging at Zacchaeus's house (Luke 19), he effectively extends a gawani invitation—an invitation to share life in a way that transcends conventional boundaries and hierarchies. Zacchaeus, responding with eager hospitality, welcomes Jesus and his disciples into his home. To the onlookers, Jesus's act appears scandalous—"He has gone in to be the guest of a sinner (ἁμαρτωλῷ)!" (v. 7)—but it is precisely this radical association that dismantles the prevailing purity barriers. By consciously choosing to engage with Zacchaeus rather than condemn him, Jesus disarms the pollution ideology that had wedged sinners apart from both community and God. In so doing, he ushers in the possibility of authentic relational renewal and transformative healing. Notably, Luke's wording in verse 6b—using the term δεῖ ("must")—underscores the irrevocable nature of Jesus's decision to abide with Zacchaeus, emphasizing that their encounter constitutes neither a matter of convenience nor a mere courtesy, but rather a definitive enactment of gawani's rehumanizing ethic.[14]

---

12. Kang, *Theology of Gawani*, 11. Kang's concept of dehumanization involves restoring individuals and groups who have been dehumanized by socioeconomic hierarchies and prejudices.

13. Kang, *Theology of Gawani*, 9.

14. The Greek verb δεῖ in Luke 19:6 conveys an imperative necessity, highlighting that Jesus's choice to stay with Zacchaeus is not optional but rather an essential component of his mission to restore dignity to those excluded by social and religious norms.

6.2. THE MULTIPLE DIMENSIONS OF THE SON OF HUMAN BEING

Earthly Ministry: Solidarity and Compassion

Jesus's earthly ministry of solidarity remains one of the most prominent Son of Human Being motifs, manifested in his direct engagement with individuals on society's margins. The Gospels depict him traveling throughout Galilean towns, proclaiming the kingdom of God, tending to the sick, and befriending those considered outcasts. Kang describes this present aspect of the Son of Human Being as an immediate embodiment of gawani, wherein Jesus tangibly participates in human weakness and establishes relationships with marginalized people.[15] Such an outlook asserts that Jesus's mission was not merely oriented toward a distant eschatological future; rather, he actively confronted daily hardships and extended concrete compassion to disenfranchised communities.

In contrast to Jewish eschatological traditions that might have cast the Son of Human Being solely as a future apocalyptic figure, the Gospel accounts highlight a ministry deeply immersed in real-world suffering. This portrayal resonates with Gustavo Gutiérrez's argument that theology must remain anchored in actual sociopolitical realities rather than devolving into abstract speculation.[16] By alleviating immediate injustices and forging bonds of solidarity with individuals at the fringes, Jesus demonstrates how the Son of Human Being paradigm transcends theoretical constructs and embraces pragmatic love. Consequently, his example challenges faith communities to engage in similar practices of solidarity, upholding human dignity and cultivating transformation in both personal encounters and broader social structures.

Moreover, Kang presents Jesus's earthly compassion as an intentional and defining feature of his ministry, rather than a peripheral flourish. By emphasizing that "the criterion for judgment is not a confession of faith in Christ; neither are grace, justification, or forgiveness of sins,"

---

15. Kang emphasizes that Jesus's "present" engagement with human suffering characterizes the Son of Human Being as actively reorienting oppressive contexts here and now, rather than waiting for a purely apocalyptic fulfillment. Kang, *Theology of Gawani*, 11.

16. Gutiérrez underscores that authentic Christian practice should intertwine spiritual reflection with tangible action against systemic inequality, contending that an overly abstract faith undercuts any effective pursuit of liberation. See Gutiérrez, *Theology of Liberation*, xxxi.

Kang underscores a holistic vision wherein genuine discipleship hinges on whether one practices gawani—actively sharing love and caring for individuals in need.[17] This approach reframes salvation as inseparably bound to communal well-being, refusing to isolate redemption within a merely spiritual or future-oriented domain. Instead, Kang proposes that "doing the will of the Father" entails concrete acts of empathy and mercy directed especially toward those who have been victimized or marginalized by structural injustice.[18] In so doing, the Son of Human Being identifies personally with those society deems least, thereby modeling a form of solidarity that dismantles exclusionary barriers and restores dignity to the oppressed. Far from treating forgiveness of sins as a private spiritual transaction, Kang's perspective situates it in the realm of tangible relationships, where restored fellowship and equitable social arrangements stand as central manifestations of divine grace. By highlighting the communal dimensions of Jesus's compassion, this reading of the Son of Human Being challenges faith communities to integrate spiritual devotion with social responsibility, forging a redemptive ethic that empowers the powerless, heals fractured bonds, and anticipates the full realization of God's compassionate reign.

Suffering and Resurrection: The Redemptive Power of Self-Giving

Alongside earthly compassion, the Son of Human Being sayings repeatedly highlight Jesus's forthcoming suffering, death, and resurrection. Kang contends that this is not a separate theological layer but part of a single narrative through which Jesus reveals himself as the agent of human renewal.[19] He notes that this "suffering Son of Human Being" subverts both the Roman imperial logic of domination and the religious aspiration for a purely triumphant messiah. By choosing the path of

---

17. Kang stresses that this understanding of salvation unites interior transformation with outward justice, insisting that love and mercy must guide every interaction—especially with those whom social and religious structures have consistently devalued. Kang, *Theology of Gawani*, 12.

18 Kang, *Theology of Gawani*, 12.

19. Kang, *Theology of Gawani*, 14–15. The "suffering, death, and resurrection of the Son of Human Being" motif underscores that Jesus's journey to the cross emerges from a deliberate mission to confront oppressive powers.

suffering and crucifixion, Jesus demonstrates that true authority arises from self-giving love.

Here, Kang aligns with theologians such as Jon Sobrino, who maintain that the crucified Christ embodies a uniquely "liberating power" directly opposed to the logic of domination and violence.[20] In expanding upon this perspective through a gawani lens, Kang depicts the Son of Human Being as more than a distant eschatological figure: he decisively enters into the suffering of the marginalized and fully assumes their burdens—a process culminating in the cross. What emerges, then, is not merely a display of passive sacrifice but rather an active confrontation with oppressive regimes, wherein divine love undermines structures built on force and coercion. Sobrino's view of the crucified God dovetails with Kang's emphasis on self-emptying solidarity, illuminating how the Son of Human Being's path entails radical vulnerability as the wellspring of transformation.

Doubling the resonance of this paradigm, the resurrection stands as God's definitive testimony that a self-sacrificial form of engagement is not futile but rather endowed with a capacity to unsettle long-entrenched structures of injustice. As Jürgen Moltmann argues, the crucifixion must be apprehended alongside the resurrection, generating an "eschatological paschal faith" that weaves Jesus's historical suffering directly into divine identity.[21] In so doing, the victory over death underscores that compassion-driven social frameworks are not merely utopian ideals reserved for a remote future; instead, they are practicable avenues for enacting justice in the present.[22] Once the empty tomb is held in tension with the cross, believers are confronted with a theological vision that refuses to isolate redemption within personal piety or spiritual abstraction.[23] Rather, Jesus's

---

20. Sobrino articulates that true redemptive power arises from identifying wholeheartedly with those who suffer, rather than relying on coercive strategies. Sobrino, *Christology*, 15.

21. Moltmann maintains that the cross, when paired with the resurrection, intertwines Jesus's suffering with God's own identity rather than relegating it to a purely apocalyptic horizon. See Moltmann, *Crucified God*, 52.

22. Moltmann further posits that this "eschatological paschal faith" defies any notion that transformation must await the end of time, contending that the crucifixion-resurrection event disrupts established power structures in the immediate social sphere See Moltmann, *Crucified God*, 57.

23. Once the resurrection is read in concert with Golgotha, redemption can no longer be privatized or extracted from historical realities, a point Moltmann reiterates in his discussion of how the suffering of Jesus implicates God's very nature. Moltmann, *Crucified God*, 58–59.

crucifixion and resurrection converge into a forceful critique of oppressive power structures, revealing that genuine liberation arises from an unreserved solidarity with those deemed powerless.

From Kang's vantage point, this revelation redefines what constitutes success and challenge, urging faith communities to gauge their authenticity by how fully they adopt a cross-resurrection dynamic in their communal practices. Liberated from narrow concerns of purely individualistic devotion, the Son of Human Being's path compels disciples to confront systemic wrongs with the same unwavering resolve demonstrated by Christ's passion and vindication. By centering sacrificial love as the linchpin of Christian witness, Kang insists that believers not only criticize but also decisively counter hierarchical frameworks reliant on coercion. Consequently, the resurrection validates an alternative paradigm marked by mutual care and radical inclusivity, resonating with Gustavo Gutiérrez's contention that any authentic hope must be anchored in concrete sociohistorical engagement.[24] In this light, Kang's approach illuminates how the cross and resurrection offer not simply a personal consolation but a transformative impetus to construct communities grounded in gawani's principle of rehumanizing communion—an ethic that dismantles exclusionary boundaries and fosters genuine shared flourishing in the here and now.

Eschatological Judgment: Ethical Accountability and Final Renewal

A prominent facet of the Son of Human Being motif emerges in the context of eschatological judgment, particularly as articulated in Matthew's Gospel. Within Matt 25:31–46, the Son of Human Being is portrayed as the ultimate judge who separates the nations based on concrete acts of love toward the needy—feeding those who are hungry, welcoming the stranger, clothing individuals lacking basic necessities, and visiting the imprisoned.[25] This scene highlights a form of divine justice rooted in tangible mercy, rather than mere doctrinal affirmation, thereby underscoring

---

24. Gutiérrez emphasizes that liberating praxis entails more than theoretical constructs, insisting on a theologically grounded involvement in real sociopolitical contexts. Gutiérrez, *Theology of Liberation*, xxxi.

25. Matt 25:31–46 portrays the Son of Human Being convening all nations, testing their commitment to practical compassion instead of theological correctness alone. See Trilling, *Das Wahre Israel*, 14.

the Son of Human Being's concern for the socioeconomic realities of human life. According to Kang, the Son of Human Being's identification with the least indicates that the authenticity of one's faith is tested by the willingness to serve and embrace marginalized individuals.[26] Instead of relegating the moral dimension to a peripheral status, the text suggests that love of neighbor, exhibited in practical compassion, determines who genuinely partakes in God's consummated reign. This reading resonates with the core principle of gawani theology, which emphasizes that outward deeds of solidarity with vulnerable groups function not as optional virtues but as indispensable markers of true discipleship.

Matt 25 further underscores the sweeping scope of this eschatological moment by noting that "all the nations" are assembled before the Son of Human Being (Matt 25:32). Scholarly interpretations vary on whether this phrase extends beyond Israel to include every people group, thus reinforcing the universality of the final evaluation.[27] Trilling, for instance, argues that the phrase connotes a comprehensive horizon for divine judgment, while Waetjen demonstrates how Matthew employs ethnic language to point toward an inclusive vision of God's people.[28] Kang builds on this perspective to maintain that the Son of Human Being's global authority is expressed through merciful justice, insisting that acts of empathy rather than tribal or religious identity constitute the decisive standard.[29] This dynamic, wherein personal piety must translate into active care, embodies the gawani insistence that theological commitments be measured by how thoroughly they overturn exclusionary structures and champion the well-being of the marginalized.

Kang's viewpoint dovetails with Gustavo Gutiérrez's broader argument that salvation encompasses more than private or spiritual consolation; it must also entail the liberation of those trapped in oppressive social conditions.[30] From a Gutiérrezian perspective, any theology that

---

26. Kang observes that "the least" references all who are marginalized or devalued, adding that the Son of Human Being's empathy becomes the benchmark for discerning authentic kingdom participation. See Kang, *Theology of Gawani*, 11–12.

27. The phrase "all the nations" has been interpreted in various ways—some propose it extends to every ethnic group, thereby underscoring the universal scope of final judgment.

28. Trilling, *Das Wahre Israel*, 14. See also Waetjen, *Matthew's Theology*, 258–59, for additional discussion on ethnic dimensions in Matthew's narrative.

29. Kang, *Theology of Gawani*, 11–12.

30. Gutiérrez highlights that salvation loses coherence if it fails to address social and economic disparities that incarcerate the poor. For his discussion on sociopolitical

professes concern for eternal destinies yet ignores systemic inequities risks devolving into an abstract discourse detached from the anguish of the poor. By contrast, Kang's gawani framework—echoing Matt 25—advocates an embodied faith in which one's response to the afflicted directly reveals the integrity of one's devotion. Within this construction, neither individual smugness nor institutional complacency has room to coexist with genuine righteousness. If the Son of Human Being judges the nations primarily based on their treatment of the least, then the central question for faith communities becomes "Are they willing to engage in concrete, sacrificial action for those deemed insignificant by prevailing power structures?"

Such an eschatological scenario reframes the ultimate judgment as deeply relational and communal: the Son of Human Being stands in solidarity with the voiceless, the disenfranchised, and the forgotten. Through this lens, Kang contends that the parable's injunction against apathy elevates gawani practice to a theological imperative—one that implicates both private moral commitments and social practices. Embodying gawani compassion thus becomes essential for living out the Son of Human Being's comprehensive mission, culminating in a final assessment where love of neighbor defines the boundary of God's realm. In effect, the Matthean vision challenges Christians to recognize that an authentic approach to God cannot be severed from tangible acts of mercy, signifying that genuine discipleship is displayed not by formulaic statements of faith but through an ongoing effort to dismantle injustice and to restore dignity to those whom society discards. This holistic outlook insists that an eschatological hope rooted in the Son of Human Being's teaching must encompass liberative initiatives in the present, advancing the belief that divine judgment is integrally connected with ethical accountability and the renewal of both persons and communities.

6.3. GAWANI THEOLOGY AND THE BOOK OF ACTS

Continuation of Jesus's Ministry in the Early Church

Kang's analysis persuasively argues that the gawani ethic, originally modeled by Jesus during his earthly ministry, not only survives but is further developed in the formation of the early church as depicted in the Acts of

---

structures, ecclesial concerns, and the intersection of grace with historical contexts, see Gutiérrez, *Theology of Liberation*, 90, 148, and 245.

the Apostles. In Acts 4:32–37, we encounter a vivid portrait of communal life in which believers share their possessions so that "there was not a needy person among them." This radical practice of economic and social sharing is not an incidental feature but a deliberate enactment of the inclusive fellowship that Jesus himself modeled during his ministry. Kang contends that such practices, deeply embedded in the gawani framework, echo the table fellowship of Jesus and signal an ongoing commitment to rehumanizing relationships that defy prevailing power structures.[31] Moreover, this community model serves as a transformative counterpoint to traditional hierarchical and individualistic forms of social organization, offering instead a living testimony to the restorative vision of God's kingdom.

Kang further elucidates that the impetus behind this communal life is found in the Spirit's empowering presence, as described in Acts 1:8 and vividly realized at Pentecost. When the Holy Spirit descends upon the disciples, it not only unites them across linguistic and cultural barriers but also commissions them to continue Jesus's mission of witnessing—thus extending the gawani ministry into every sphere of human interaction.[32] The Pentecost event, therefore, is not merely a supernatural occurrence; it is the dynamic catalyst that transforms a scattered group of followers into a cohesive community marked by a radical reordering of social relations. This reordering is characterized by an ethos of mutual care, where the early Christians exemplify a living together that defies conventional expectations of exclusivity. Such a paradigm shift compels later generations of believers to see communal solidarity not as optional charity but as a core element of authentic discipleship.

The Martyrdom of Stephen: Identifying with the Son of Human Being

Further illustrating this continuity, Kang draws attention to the martyrdom of Stephen in Acts 7:54–60 a moment that encapsulates the full

---

31. Kang contends that the model of communal sharing described in Acts 4:32–37 is a deliberate enactment of the gawani principle, which calls for a reordering of social relations through mutual care and economic redistribution. Kang, *Theology of Gawani*, 17.

32. Kang highlights that the Pentecost event, as narrated in Acts 1:8, dissolves long-standing cultural and linguistic barriers, thereby uniting believers in a single mission that embodies the gawani ethic of rehumanization. Kang, *Theology of Gawani*, 18.

cost of bearing witness to the gawani ethic. As Stephen, on the brink of execution, beholds "the heavens opened" and the Son of Human Being standing at the right hand of God, his vision powerfully affirms that the divine mission of dehumanization persists even in the face of mortal opposition.[33] Kang interprets Stephen's fearless acceptance of suffering as a definitive manifestation of the gawani commitment: a willingness to share in the burdens of the marginalized and to stand as a counterforce to oppressive social and religious systems. This episode, in which Stephen's vision and subsequent martyrdom serve as a symbolic vindication of sacrificial love, underscores the idea that the legacy of Jesus's ministry is not confined to his earthly life but continues robustly in the lives of his followers. By merging Christ's exaltation with an uncompromising call to sacrificial service, the early church is thus depicted as a community that both inherits and actively perpetuates the transformative power of the cross and resurrection.[34]

Kang's interpretation, therefore, challenges modern faith communities to reevaluate their own practices. In his view, the authentic embodiment of the gawani ethic requires that churches not only embrace a communal mode of living but also actively confront and dismantle all forms of systemic injustice. Such a commitment involves a dual focus: maintaining an inward, spiritually rich community life and simultaneously engaging in outward, justice-oriented actions that transform societal structures. By anchoring the mission of the church in both the shared experience of the Holy Spirit and the uncompromising call to social equality, Kang's analysis affirms that the early church's model of rehumanizing communion remains a vital and provocative paradigm for contemporary Christian practice.

---

33. In Acts 7:54–60, Stephen's vision of the Son of Human Being at God's right hand is presented as an affirmation of the cost and reward of sacrificial witness, illustrating how the early church internalized the transformative power of the cross. Witherington, *Acts of the Apostles*, 253–254, identifies ten clear parallels between Stephen's trial and Jesus' passion, portraying Stephen's martyr-witness as exemplary solidarity with the oppressed; this reading illuminates the mutual burden-sharing (gawani) emphasized in the present chapter. See also Kang, *Theology of Gawani*, 18.

34. Kang posits that Stephen's martyrdom is not merely a tragic end but a powerful testimony that the legacy of Jesus's ministry endures in the faithful, challenging both individuals and institutions to embrace a holistic, justice-oriented discipleship. Kang, *Theology of Gawani*, 18. Witherington, *Acts of the Apostles*, 283–284, interprets Acts 7:55–56 ("the Son of Man standing") as both a vindication of sacrificial love and a commission for the church to reproduce the cross-and-resurrection pattern in communal service, a vision that coheres with the gawani commitment outlined here

6.4. GAWANI THEOLOGY IN THE BROADER BIBLICAL CONTEXT

Covenant, Promise, and the Son of Human Being

Son of Human Being language in the Gospels can be understood within a broader covenant tradition that links the Old and New Testaments in a single narrative of divine-human relationship. When one reads the calling of Abraham (Gen 12) and the liberation of the Israelites in Exodus (Exod 3), it becomes evident that God's commitment to rescue and bless people is not limited to any one group.[35] Kang maintains that this overarching covenant theme is heightened in the ministry of the Son of Human Being, who identifies with those under oppression and calls them into restored life. By viewing the Son of Human Being as part of this unfolding covenant history, one recognizes that Jesus's engagement with marginalized individuals is not an isolated phenomenon but the continuation—and amplification—of a narrative already established in the Hebrew Scriptures.

Such an understanding conveys that the Son of Human Being enacts a new exodus dynamic, delivering individuals from burdens that mirror Israel's ancient enslavement.[36] In other words, just as Yahweh took the side of the enslaved in the Old Testament, Jesus stands in solidarity with those hampered by unjust social structures in the Gospels. Kang's discussion shows how this commitment to liberation aligns with a covenant perspective in which God takes the initiative to form relationships grounded in restoration. Even as the Old Testament covenants highlight the theme of deliverance from bondage, the New Testament Gospels reinforce it by depicting the Son of Human Being's ongoing engagement with individuals who have been silenced or scorned by societal norms.

Furthermore, this covenant emphasis reaches far beyond a single group. God's interaction with Abraham, as seen in Gen 12:3, anticipates that "all families of the earth" will be embraced within God's covenant

---

35. See Gen 12:3, Exod 3:7–8, and Kang, *Theology of Gawani*, 4–5.

36. The analogy between the exodus event and Jesus's movement toward the marginalized demonstrates how covenant deliverance in the Old Testament foreshadows Jesus's liberative mission. See Kang, *Theology of Gawani*, 15. Here Kang appeals to the idea that material wealth, if accumulated through systemic injustice, fails to yield genuine human flourishing. He relates this to a broader biblical narrative where God intends covenant fidelity to bring personal and societal benefits, not oppression. Cf. Frankl, *Man's Search for Meaning*.

plan. Although the book of Acts portrays the expansion of the early Christian community—from Judea through Samaria to the ends of the earth, thereby including Gentiles—Professor Kang does not explicitly recount this expansion in his discussion. Instead, he suggests an inclusive framework embedded within the broader covenant tradition, leaving the detailed narrative of expansion to be inferred from the wider biblical context.[37] This progression demonstrates that God's intention has consistently extended beyond the boundaries of any single nation or ethnicity, highlighting the covenant's all-encompassing scope.

Within this framework, the Son of Human Being does not supersede or negate older expressions of God's resolve to rescue. Instead, the ministry of Jesus forms a continuation of the Old Testament idea that God is both transcendent and intimately connected with human needs. In Kang's account, the Son of Human Being deepens the old covenant notion of God's empathy by stepping directly into the experiences of individuals suffering under various forms of oppression. This includes those afflicted by spiritual alienation, physical ailments, economic hardship, or the cumulative injuries caused by a hierarchical social system that disfavors the vulnerable.

In this way, biblical covenants highlight both divine fidelity and human responsibility. Kang argues that the Son of Human Being's solidarity with human affliction demonstrates the costliness of covenant love, as Jesus not only preaches deliverance but enters fully into the conditions that necessitate it. Believers who acknowledge this covenant reality are thus called to embrace conduct that supports God's intention for social and communal renewal. Kang's reference to Acts portrays how the early Christian community grappled with expanding the covenant mission beyond Israel, grappling with cultural barriers and prejudices while remaining committed to the Son of Human Being's inclusive mission.

This covenant perspective also implies that confession of Jesus as the Son of Human Being is not a discrete doctrinal assertion detached from lived practice. Rather, it is part of a comprehensive story in which God covenants with people for their restoration and well-being. Kang emphasizes that the covenant extends to economic justice, interpersonal relationships, and ethical action that prioritizes those harmed by societal structures. The Son of Human Being model in the Gospels, therefore, illuminates the covenant's purpose: to restore individuals, families, and

---

37. Kang, *Theology of Gawani*, 15.

A CONTEMPORARY RECONSIDERATION OF THE KINGDOM

nations into a state of holistic welfare, erasing boundaries that keep certain populations in perpetual subjugation.

Such a reading resists any narrowing of covenant concepts to abstract theology. It instead places the covenant in actual human contexts where real suffering occurs and where God's deliverance can be made tangible. As Kang sees it, the old covenant's portrayal of a liberating God is brought into sharper focus in the person and work of Jesus, who fulfills the divine promise to stand against entrenched power systems on behalf of the exploited. This approach also invites readers to participate in a covenant community that continues Jesus's priorities, thereby creating tangible expressions of God's enduring initiative to redeem and to reconcile.

Sin, Estrangement, and Forgiveness

Within this covenant outlook, the Son of Human Being addresses the interconnected reality of sin, communal estrangement, and forgiveness in a holistic way. According to Kang, an emblematic illustration of this occurs in Mark 2:5–12, where Jesus forgives a paralyzed man's sins while also performing a physical healing.[38] Such an event exhibits that Jesus's declaration of forgiveness is more than a private release from guilt; it is also a catalyst for the restoration of communal well-being.

Kang's position asserts that sin damages relationships by fostering cultural, social, and economic barriers that alienate individuals from one another and from God. This perspective elevates sin beyond the personal sphere, highlighting how societal norms can perpetuate forms of exclusion and hierarchy. For example, Kang interprets the Markan motif of a reordering of power to mean that Jesus's acts of healing and forgiveness disrupt longstanding systems of domination, symbolized by new cloth and new wine in Mark 2:21–22.[39] Hence, divine forgiveness extends to dismantling frameworks that cause dehumanization, advocating a renewed order in which people experience reconciliation.

A suitable instance is the story of Zacchaeus in Luke 19:1–10. Kang observes that Zacchaeus is described as a wealthy tax collector who has

---

38. In Mark 2:5–12, Jesus's healing of the paralytic is linked to the declaration of forgiveness, reflecting the interconnected reality of spiritual and social restoration. Kang describes this as part of a "reordering of power." See Kang, *Theology of Gawani*, 8; cf. Waetjen, *Reordering of Power*.

39. Kang, *Theology of Gawani*, 8.

likely contributed to social exploitation.[40] When Jesus notices Zacchaeus in the sycamore tree and calls him by name, Jesus effectively engages in a personal and communal gesture of reconciliation. By inviting himself to Zacchaeus's house, Jesus undoes the stigma that would otherwise distance Zacchaeus from the broader society. This event underscores a significant feature of gawani theology: relational restoration that leads to constructive action. Zacchaeus responds by giving half of his possessions to those in need and promising to restore fourfold what he has taken from others.

Kang references Martin Buber's *I and Thou* to show how addressing someone by name removes the barrier between them, generating a context for genuine encounter.[41] Such an encounter reveals a covenantal dimension of forgiveness, wherein Jesus integrates individuals once deemed pariahs back into the community. Zacchaeus's transformation is not confined to moral rectitude in a personal sense; it also involves rectifying previous injustices, thus exhibiting the covenant principle that social reconciliation is intertwined with spiritual renewal.

This pattern of holistic forgiveness challenges any conceptualization of piety that lacks an impact on society. Kang contends that Jesus's mission as the Son of Human Being involves a collective scope, enabling entire communities to reimagine their priorities. When sin is framed as a structural force in addition to a personal failing, believers are called to address injustice, stand with those harmed by societal bias, and practice forms of compassion that mirror Jesus's own mode of engagement.[42]

Also relevant is the depiction of Jesus's way as one marked by continual movement toward Jerusalem in the Synoptic Gospels. Kang interprets this journey as Jesus's enactment of a new communal order that inverts established hierarchies (Mark 9:35). Through repeated predictions of his suffering, Jesus illustrates the cost of realigning social relationships, since those invested in the power structure often find this reordering threatening. Despite this risk, the Son of Human Being persists in upholding those who have been silenced by the dominant system.

Kang's examination aligns forgiveness with the tangible dismantling of oppression, as seen in Jesus's willingness to share meals with ostracized

---

40. The Zacchaeus narrative (Luke 19:1–10) displays forgiveness that culminates in communal reconciliation. Kang explains that Jesus's decision to stay at Zacchaeus's home undoes social stigmas and enables the tax collector to commit to just practices. See Kang, *Theology of Gawani*, 9; cf. Buber, *I and Thou*.

41. Kang, *Theology of Gawani*, 9.

42. Kang, *Theology of Gawani*, 9.

individuals and to counter cultural taboos. This reorientation illustrates that the Son of Human Being's authority to forgive transcends legal or ritual boundaries; it is an authority that heals and reconciles on multiple levels. In Mark 2:10, Jesus explicitly declares that he has the authority to forgive sins on earth. By coupling this authority with acts of inclusion and physical healing, he reveals that such forgiveness affects everyday life rather than functioning solely as a theological abstraction.

Forgiveness as Social Restoration

Kang devotes particular attention to the communal dimensions of forgiveness, asserting that real restoration requires changes in relationships, economic practices, and moral perceptions.[43] In Luke 19:10, Jesus's pronouncement that "redemption happened" at Zacchaeus's house underlines how personal transformation leads to community benefit. By calling Zacchaeus "lost" and then welcoming him, Jesus reframes the notion of who belongs in the covenant community. This reframing is not limited to religious rites; it shows God's aim to rebuild a community grounded in hospitality and reciprocity.

When Zacchaeus proclaims that he will offer restitution to those he defrauded, his actions echo covenant themes by restoring equity. Kang clarifies that this dimension of forgiveness links the spiritual and the societal: salvation in the Gospels includes ethical responsibility toward one's neighbors. Rather than presenting forgiveness as a discrete event that leaves existing structures untouched, the Son of Human Being fosters a new kind of relationship (gawani) in which mutual care and responsibility are foundational.

Following the same rationale, Kang addresses the larger biblical narrative in which personal piety is always related to communal wellbeing. The Old Testament often highlights that worship divorced from justice is incomplete (e.g., Isaiah 58). Kang argues that Jesus's ministry, as the Son of Human Being, emphasizes this same principle by urging followers to support just relationships and to attend to marginalized voices. Zacchaeus's choice to distribute his assets stands as an instance of that principle, illustrating an actual shift in economic behavior triggered by an encounter with Jesus.

---

43. Kang, *Theology of Gawani*, 9.

The Cross and the Cost of Transformation

Kang also discusses how resistance to Jesus's message arises from vested power interests.[44] The Synoptic Gospels show that Jesus's journey to Jerusalem is accompanied by escalating conflict with authorities who benefit from established patterns. Kang connects this conflict to covenant theology by noting that renewed relationships and social justice often clash with those invested in entrenched systems. The cost Jesus pays reflects the gravity of the transformation required to reshape entrenched perspectives, demonstrating that the new covenant is not merely symbolic but includes a tangible restructuring of human relationships.

In Mark 8:34, Jesus instructs, "If any wish to come after me, let them deny themselves and take up their cross and follow me." This directive implies that the cost of aligning oneself with the Son of Human Being's program is considerable. Kang interprets the cross as not only a personal burden but also a statement of solidarity with those who suffer unjustly.[45] By identifying with disenfranchised people, believers align themselves with a covenant that seeks the welfare of all, particularly those excluded from customary privileges.

Kang holds that the Son of Human Being's approach to forgiveness and healing cannot be divorced from this journey toward the cross, since the very structures that perpetuate sin will clash with an ethic of inclusive restoration. In this manner, the path to Jerusalem represents more than a geographical movement; it is a metaphorical journey toward the dismantling of hierarchical boundaries. The Son of Human Being's death, therefore, underscores the magnitude of the restoration he initiates, uniting personal and collective dimensions of redemption.

Conclusion

Kang's framework integrates covenant motifs from the Hebrew Scriptures with the portrayal of the Son of Human Being in the Gospels, highlighting a consistent emphasis on liberation, community renewal, and concrete acts of solidarity. The exodus story and the Abrahamic promise serve as foundational examples of God's plan to rescue, bless, and establish meaningful connections with humanity. Far from diverging from

---

44. Kang, *Theology of Gawani*, 9.
45. Kang, *Theology of Gawani*, 9.

this biblical tradition, Jesus's work intensifies it by demonstrating how deliverance is accomplished in real contexts of oppression. This continuity is shown in passages where Jesus forgives sins, welcomes the excluded, and reclaims social settings that have been marred by exploitation.

Seen in this way, the Son of Human Being's ministry is not only a climax of covenant history but also a signpost for ongoing faith communities that wish to follow his model. Kang's depiction of gawani theology invites believers to embrace forgiveness that reorients social structures and fosters renewed bonds between individuals and communities. Rather than reducing grace to a purely internal state, it insists on restitution, communal transformation, and shared well-being. The book of Acts reiterates this theme by describing how the early church overcame ethnic and cultural barriers, extending the reach of the Son of Human Being's inclusive call.

In sum, the Son of Human Being in Kang's presentation underscores how sin, estrangement, and forgiveness must be addressed within a network of relationships, grounded in an overarching covenant that spans both Testaments. This approach affirms that Jesus's acts of healing and reconciliation flow from a tradition of divine-human engagement. As such, the identity and mission of Jesus cannot be separated from the longstanding story of a God who hears the cries of the oppressed and responds with rescue. Kang's discussion thereby prompts readers to envision faith communities as agents of that same rescue: people who not only affirm the forgiveness available in Jesus but also embody its reality by removing systemic barriers and ensuring the welfare of all members of the covenant community.

6.5. IMPLICATIONS FOR CONTEMPORARY THEOLOGICAL PRACTICE

Liberation Theology and Socioeconomic Reform

Kang's interpretation of Son of Human Being language—in dialogue with gawani theology—aligns with the viewpoint that Christianity cannot be separated from the pursuit of social and economic justice.[46] He underscores

---

46. Kang sees this as central to Jesus's ministry of reordering power systems and uniting spiritual life with social responsibility. Kang, *Theology of Gawani*, 8. His focus on love and service is comparable to Paulo Freire's emphasis on praxis in *Pedagogy of the Oppressed*, though Kang advocates broadening the paradigm to include cosmic

that Jesus's life and ministry were not confined to an abstract moral realm but instead highlighted a decisive commitment to the disenfranchised, akin to Gustavo Gutiérrez's emphasis on engaging political, historical, and social contexts as integral to faith.[47] Gutiérrez claims that Christian communities must do more than offer temporary aid; they should become key agents working to dismantle the structures that perpetuate poverty and injustice, arguing that failing to address systemic inequality contradicts the central mandates of the gospel. Likewise, Kang stresses that the Son of Human Being's solidarity with marginalized groups exemplifies the Christian call to transformative action in the world.[48]

Yet Kang's scholarship does not merely restate established liberationist arguments; instead, he expands the scope of Christological reflection by focusing on the self-emptying love that defines the Son of Human Being's identity.[49] While various strands of liberation theology have underscored that faith demands social engagement, Kang highlights the connection between Jesus's redemptive role and his willingness to bridge cosmic and historical dimensions. Rather than viewing Jesus solely as a political figure, Kang portrays him as the embodiment of new humanity, someone who connects a grand eschatological vision with immediate acts of compassion.[50] His approach sheds light on how the crucifixion and resurrection establish a comprehensive framework for divine–human fellowship, confirming that the Son of Human Being's mission embraces both cosmic renewal and daily ethical responsibilities.

In practical terms, this perspective compels local congregations to question political mechanisms, labor injustices, and oppressive economic policies that undermine human dignity.[51] Inspired by Gutiérrez, Kang maintains that authentic discipleship is measured by actions aligning with the core message of Matt 25—providing food for the hungry, clothing for the naked, and advocacy for those who remain voiceless.

---

reconciliation.

47. Gutiérrez, *Theology of Liberation*, xxxi. Gutiérrez claims that real faith-based engagement requires intentional action to change structures that create or sustain poverty.

48. Kang, *Theology of Gawani*, 11. Kang contends that ignoring systematic injustice conflicts with Jesus's example in Matt 25.

49. Kang, *Theology of Gawani*, 14. Kang develops the notion of self-emptying love as the Son of Human Being's defining attribute.

50. Kang, *Theology of Gawani*, 10. He emphasizes that Jesus merges an eschatological promise with immediate social practice.

51. Kang, *Theology of Gawani*, 8. Kang links the kingdom of God to a radical reordering of existing economic and political conditions.

A CONTEMPORARY RECONSIDERATION OF THE KINGDOM 93

By concretely improving the lives of people at the margins, Christians mirror the self-giving spirit of Jesus, whose ministry did not separate personal piety from social accountability. In Kang's framework, spiritual disciplines and social justice efforts converge, encouraging believers to enact a communal ethic of genuine care, rather than engaging merely in superficial charity.

Confronting Present-Day Exclusions

In modern contexts, communities worldwide confront a variety of overlapping crises such as racism, misogyny, ecological devastation, and exploitation of labor.[52] Kang's interpretation of gawani theology underscores that a renewed focus on the Son of Human Being can guide churches toward addressing such injustices in both direct and structural ways. He views Jesus's boundary-crossing fellowship—seen in the Gospels when he associated with the marginalized—as a roadmap for present-day believers. When faith communities implement local outreach programs while simultaneously advocating policy changes, they continue the tradition of crossing social, economic, and political boundaries. Kang's perspective echoes Gutiérrez's claim that responding to hardship requires tackling the root causes of injustice, not merely applying temporary solutions.[53]

Kang further contends that faith communities should become spaces of comprehensive transformation, rather than sites offering only personal religious inspiration.[54] For instance, a congregation might provide shelter or meals to those who are homeless but also ask uncomfortable questions about property laws, wage gaps, and public health policies. Efforts to treat symptoms of inequality must be linked to structural advocacy, so that Christian ministry does not devolve into a series of disconnected volunteer projects. This holistic outlook resonates with the conviction—articulated in various liberationist writings—that political empowerment and spiritual renewal belong together, each reinforcing the other.

---

52. Kang, *Theology of Gawani*, 3. Kang argues that present-day evils must be confronted in a manner that mirrors Jesus's engagement with marginalized people in the Gospels.

53. Gutiérrez, *Theology of Liberation*, 254. He maintains that addressing poverty should include confronting its structural roots, not merely its outward manifestations.

54. Kang, *Theology of Gawani*, 12. Kang holds that Christian ministry must combine practical service with efforts aimed at lasting reform.

Additionally, Kang's theology extends beyond an oppressor–oppressed dichotomy, suggesting that gawani love, and solidarity can disarm hostility in more inclusive ways.[55] This approach encourages shared responsibility for dismantling hierarchies that produce constant polarizations. Rather than solidifying permanent divisions, gawani theology seeks to create partnerships where former adversaries can reshape social systems, revealing how self-emptying love is potent enough to reconstruct entire communities. In this way, contemporary churches, influenced by Kang's vision, should perceive activism for justice not as an optional pursuit but as a foundational dimension of their calling.

Ecclesial Renewal and Worship

Beyond the sphere of advocacy and reform, Kang's interpretation of the Son of Human Being has significant implications for worship practices and ecclesial life.[56] He notes that if the Son of Human Being represents divine self-limitation and active fellowship with vulnerable individuals, then Christian worship should embody humility, mutual service, and a willingness to relinquish social privilege. According to Kang, the church's liturgical gatherings must reflect the same spirit of self-giving demonstrated by Jesus, who washed his disciples' feet and broke bread for them.[57] This is not just a performance of ritual but a transformative act that signals new relationships among believers.

In sacramental celebrations, particularly the Lord's Supper, congregations do more than remember Jesus's body broken and his blood poured out. They are invited to practice genuine empathy by examining how collective worship might inspire transformative engagement on behalf of those who are disadvantaged. This perspective holds that the

---

55. Kang, *Theology of Gawani*, 4. Kang explains that gawani theology surpasses simple polarities and seeks solidarity that unites both oppressors and oppressed.

56. Kang, *Theology of Gawani*, 13. From the standpoint of true worship, Kang exposes the futility of liturgical arrangements that reinforce creaturely hierarchies. Confronted by the Lord who alone is exalted, the congregation is directed toward a doxological praxis of interdependence in which each member serves the other, and all together confess their common dependence upon the divine mercy.

57. Kang, *Theology of Gawani*, 14. With Johannine clarity, Kang discerns in the foot-washing (John 13:1–17) the normative form of ecclesial existence: the church is authorised to act precisely in the mode of her Lord's kenosis. In this humble service gawani becomes visible as the concrete shape of Christian witness and as the sign that the powers of domination have already been judged..

A CONTEMPORARY RECONSIDERATION OF THE KINGDOM   95

Eucharist should be regarded not only as a sacred memorial but also as an occasion to reaffirm the church's responsibility for concrete acts of service. When believers intentionally connect liturgical gestures—such as sharing bread and wine—with advocacy for those in need, the Lord's Supper becomes an enactment of solidarity rather than a purely symbolic ritual. Christian communities are thereby reminded that faith, to be authentic, must address systemic injustices rather than confining itself to inner spirituality or detached reflection.

Gutiérrez argues that a narrowly spiritualized approach to Scripture can lessen the church's ability to confront structural forms of evil, warning that any mode of worship which neglects socially transformative action cannot fully embody the message of the gospel.[58] This viewpoint suggests that believers fail to grasp the wider implications of the biblical narrative if they do not recognize how theological beliefs intersect with practical concerns in domains like economic inequality, political oppression, or cultural marginalization. Kang's perspective aligns with this claim, maintaining that reverence for Christ should be expressed by building honest relationships with those at the edges of society and by pursuing policies aimed at rectifying inequities.[59] When the Eucharist is celebrated in a way that unites communal devotion with everyday advocacy, the church preserves continuity between sacramental life and public witness, embodying a vision of faith that seeks both spiritual renewal and social responsibility.

To foster this sense of solidarity, worship should actively remove structures that maintain social, economic, or cultural privilege. By examining the ministry of Jesus—who frequently invited those on the periphery into table fellowship—Kang contends that congregations must ensure that the Lord's Supper and similar gatherings are genuinely accessible to all, without conditions.[60] In this view, the focus of worship

58. Gutiérrez, *Theology of Liberation*, 20. Gutiérrez contends that when congregations focus only on transcendental concerns, they risk bypassing the urgent ethical questions stemming from inequitable economic and political contexts. In his framework, biblical faith calls believers to take part in structural reform, thereby ensuring that worship remains connected to tangible acts of justice.

59. Kang, *Theology of Gawani*, 12. Kang summons the church to hear the decisive "Yes" and "No" of the living Lord: "Yes" to the liturgy that proclaims Christ's self-giving, "No" to every culture that shelters privilege. Where worship clings to ritual while refusing the neighbor's cry, it slips into what Barth calls "pious idolatry," forgetting that the One whom it names is also the Judge who dismantles all pretended securities.

60. Kang, *Theology of Gawani*, 12. Kang notes that Jesus's table fellowship consistently crossed social boundaries, indicating that communal practices should intentionally

is not restricted to a ceremony removed from everyday realities; rather, it deliberately urges believers to acknowledge and share resources with individuals or groups that might otherwise be ignored. Such an approach entails deliberate collaboration and ongoing self-examination so that the church does not inadvertently reaffirm social inequalities. Gawani theology, as outlined by Kang, thereby challenges faith communities to shape their gatherings around values of empathy, shared responsibility, and openhearted hospitality, reflecting a model of fellowship that Jesus demonstrated throughout his ministry.

Moreover, this vision implies that worship cannot be divorced from the real-life concerns of neighbors who face adversity daily. By situating mutual care at the very center of congregational life, gawani theology moves beyond traditional acts of piety and emphasizes communal accountability. Kang highlights that when congregations adopt practices such as collective discernment and transparent decision-making—especially in matters related to resource distribution—they embody a spirit of service that resonates with the selfless path Jesus walked.[61] This pattern is consistent with Gutiérrez's argument that focusing exclusively on spiritual components of faith risks neglecting the material and structural dimensions of oppression, thereby diminishing the church's potential to advance social well-being.[62] When believers translate devotion into tangible support for the defenseless, worship becomes a catalyst for holistic transformation instead of remaining an isolated event.

Finally, Kang stresses that worship rooted in God's self-giving character continually renews Christian communities in their commitment to the afflicted, ensuring that they do not view Sunday gatherings merely as havens from hardship.[2] He proposes that, rather than offering escape from the sorrow and tension of public life, the church gathering should equip participants with both the spiritual and practical resources needed to confront societal ills. In this manner, the church's vocation is not

---

oppose structures of exclusion.

61. Kang, *Theology of Gawani*, 13–14. Kang beholds the foot-washing as the revelatory moment in which glory and humility coincide. In stooping, the logos unveils true majesty; in serving, He exercises lordship. Thus the church, if it would live under this Word, is commanded to embody the same kenotic movement—"the community of the towel," called and sent to demolish the walls that divide and to build a fellowship whose ground is nothing other than the overflowing love of God in Christ.

62. Gutiérrez, *Theology of Liberation*, xxxi. He asserts that theologizing must address political, social, and historical environments. When churches lack structural awareness, their worship can inadvertently overlook pressing human realities.

A CONTEMPORARY RECONSIDERATION OF THE KINGDOM 97

limited to personal edification but includes proactively uplifting those lacking basic protections. By weaving reflection and concrete action into a unified whole, congregations embody the rehumanizing purpose of the Son of Human Being, forging shared unity in the pursuit of dignity for all. As Kang and Gutiérrez both maintain, the ultimate measure of the church's authenticity lies in its readiness to embrace marginalized persons, confront exploitative patterns, and direct all acts of worship toward a communal endeavor of God's reconciling work in the world.

6.6. FUTURE DIRECTIONS: ACADEMIC AND ECCLESIAL ENGAGEMENT

Scholarly Inquiry

Kang's extensive engagement with the Son of Human Being theme opens new possibilities for biblical scholars and theologians to reassess long-standing debates regarding apocalypticism, the historical Jesus, and the ecclesiastical developments visible in Acts. Although historical-critical methods have frequently focused on determining which sayings about the Son of Human Being might be the earliest, a gawani hermeneutic suggests that the heart of such discourse should focus on ethical transformation and communal restoration.[63] By centering human dignity and compassion for marginalized individuals, this perspective potentially shifts the criteria for determining authenticity away from purely textual or redactional considerations and toward the question of how effectively such texts advance an ethic of solidarity.

Furthermore, this approach motivates scholars to examine whether additional sources—beyond the Synoptic Gospels—can illuminate how early Christian communities recognized Jesus as the Son of Human Being. The possible role of Q or Johannine materials, for instance, may shed light on whether various Christ-following groups independently upheld this title, thus indicating a more widespread acceptance of its connotations.[64] Narrative-critical, social-scientific, and postcolonial methods

---

63. Kang, *Theology of Gawani*, 11–12. Kang refuses to let scholarship tarry among the ruins of mere source-analysis; he thrusts the reader to the frontier where the Son of Human Being breaks in as the living summons to solidarity. Here the text is measured not by antiquity alone but by its power to reconstitute human community in mercy and truth.

64. Kang, *Theology of Gawani*, 11. By linking Jesus to the apocalyptic figure of Daniel, Kang declares that the victorious "New Humanity" has already entered history

likewise stand to benefit from Kang's ideas. Such interpretive frameworks can uncover the sociopolitical resonances of Son of Human Being discourses and show how these narratives might validate the experiences of believers in communities facing oppression or systemic deprivation. If Jesus's life and ministry modeled an archetype of renewed humanity, as Kang suggests, then the Gospels offer a blueprint not merely for doctrinal reflection but for active engagement with the powers that diminish human worth.

Ecclesial and Pastoral Applications

On a congregational level, Kang's perspective summons churches to re-evaluate their commitments regarding mission statements, preaching, and theological education. Given that the Son of Human Being demonstrates unflagging concern for those who lack power or influence—whether due to economic, cultural, or political barriers—faith communities must consider how to address structural injustice in their daily contexts.[65] This directive may entail confronting oppressive realities such as institutional racism, patriarchal dominance, or exploitative labor systems. As Kang underscores, gawani theology calls local congregations to integrate worship, scriptural interpretation, and tangible activism so that the Christian message does not remain disconnected from social conditions.

In addition, theological training programs have much to gain by incorporating gawani theology. If future pastors, teachers, and lay leaders learn to read the New Testament with a mindset that interweaves compassion for marginalized populations and responsibility for addressing inequality, then theological reflection can become a catalyst for substantive change.[66] Instead of limiting exegetical practice to academic or devotional

---

under the sign of servanthood. The title is therefore no speculative label but a concrete pledge: God allies himself with those dehumanised, and the church may know this title only in the obedience that shares their burden.

65. Kang, *Theology of Gawani*, 17–19. Kang gathers the strands of Ps 8, Ezekiel, and the Gospels to show that exaltation and humiliation coincide in the same figure. The one who descends to the worm's-eye view is simultaneously invested with cosmic authority; thus greatness is rendered in self-emptying, and sovereignty appears precisely as lowly companionship with the oppressed.

66. Kang, *Theology of Gawani*, 17–19. From this vantage, the judgment scene of Matt 25 is no future abstraction but the unveiling of justice already operative wherever hungry bodies are fed and strangers embraced. The criterion is simple, devastating, and liberating: participation in gawani love. In that light every liturgy, every doctrine, every pious word stands or falls.

purposes, gawani theology prompts practitioners to see the biblical text as a driving force for moral accountability and communal well-being. This orientation aligns with what Gutiérrez argues concerning the necessity of linking spiritual convictions to the social realities of believers, warning that purely conceptual theology can weaken the pursuit of institutional reform.[67] From this angle, ecclesial vitality does not merely involve spiritual fervor but is validated through endeavors that restore human worth and extend concrete help to those who are often overlooked.

Conclusion

Joseph Kang's work, "Opening Gawani Theology: Seeking Interconnection and Wholeness—Focusing on the Gospels and Acts," offers a platform for reexamining how Son of Human Being traditions can inspire both scholarly conversations and the daily life of Christian communities.[68] By linking Jesus's self-reference as the Son of Human Being to divine covenant history, liberation from oppressive forces, and communal ethos, Kang highlights the unwavering compassion and radical openness embedded within the New Testament. This emphasis indicates that the Son of Human Being figure is not confined to eschatological or apocalyptic scenarios; rather, it resonates directly with current struggles against dehumanizing power structures.

In the Gospels, the Son of Human Being's ministry—marked by unrelenting hospitality, self-sacrifice, and attention to society's most vulnerable—continues within the Acts narrative as Holy Spirit-empowered communities model inclusive fellowship, equalizing resource sharing, and public testimony.[69] Stephen's vision of the Son of Human Being in the midst of martyrdom shows that following Jesus's path of suffering and restoration often demands costly devotion. Kang's gawani theology underscores that this cost, rather than signifying defeat, reveals the transformative essence of Christian identity.

Ultimately, viewing the Son of Human Being through the lens of gawani theology invites believers of every era to embrace acts of empathy,

---

67. Gutiérrez maintains that theology, when distanced from sociopolitical reality, becomes detached and cannot effectively challenge oppressive systems.

68. Kang, *Theology of Gawani*, 11–12. Kang underscores the potential for Christology to inform both academic study and grassroots Christian practice when rooted in an ethic of self-giving love.

69. Kang, *Theology of Gawani*, 17–19.

work for liberation, and nurture hope in God's future. Rather than dismissing Son of Human Being as an antiquated signifier, Kang clarifies that it stands at the center of Jesus's transformative proclamation—one that welcomes outsiders, critiques oppressive norms, and recasts authority through sacrificial service. In this way, Christology moves beyond doctrinal abstraction, becoming an active source for shaping ethical commitment and spiritual vigor. By combining serious biblical scholarship, liberation-oriented theological reflection, and current pastoral concerns, gawani theology awakens today's church and academy to the enduring mission of the Son of Human Being: healing fractured communities and restoring human dignity under God's reign.

6.7. CONCLUSION: THE PATH OF COMMUNAL TRANSFORMATION PRESENTED BY THE SON OF HUMAN BEING

A concluding reflection in this chapter is that the Son of Human Being theme underscores a vision of Jesus in relation to everyday concerns, especially those involving injustice and marginalization. By focusing on how Jesus interacts with economically oppressed or socially excluded individuals, the discussion shows that Christology is not merely about doctrine but also about transformative practice. This perspective suggests that believers should shape their communal life around the values of hospitality and the reordering of power.

A further aspect is the gawani emphasis, which calls faith communities to engage in more than sporadic giving. It portrays communal sharing as a regular way of living that breaks down barriers separating individuals of differing social standing. Through this lens, worship is not an isolated ritual but an invitation to reorganize wealth, resources, and time for the benefit of those who often remain unheard.

Another facet explored is how the Son of Human Being motif resonates with covenant patterns from the Hebrew Bible. The chapter connects Jesus's ministry to earlier examples of divine commitment, highlighting that biblical narratives consistently reveal God siding with those in bondage or relegated to the margins. When Jesus employs this title, it affirms a continuity with these liberating themes while broadening them into new cultural and historical contexts.

A related thread in the discussion addresses the lived reality of forgiveness, healing, and restoration. Scenes in the Gospels involving Zacchaeus, the paralyzed man, and others suggest that grace confronts not just individual wrongdoing but also structural harm. By linking forgiveness to social repair, the Son of Human Being underscores that real change includes economic restitution and renewed relationships.

One of the arguments presented is that Jesus's willingness to embrace the hardships of others challenges systems that favor the powerful. Rather than endorsing a distant messiah figure, the Gospels depict someone who associates closely with the poor, the ill, and those deemed unworthy by official religion. This association is not simply a momentary gesture of kindness; it is a consistent pattern demonstrating how the kingdom of God takes shape in tangible human contexts.

The chapter also highlights the importance of eschatological judgment in the teaching of Jesus, particularly where the Son of Human Being appears as the final judge. This imagery shows that divine evaluation is linked to concrete acts of mercy and solidarity with those who lack basic necessities. The outcome is a strong reminder that eternal life is not disconnected from people's actual circumstances but is intimately tied to how believers respond to social inequalities.

Alongside these themes, attention is paid to how the book of Acts carries forward the gawani spirit of Jesus's ministry. The earliest Christians share their possessions, support one another's needs, and transcend ethnic or cultural divisions. This collective life serves as a continuing example for today's congregations seeking a form of discipleship marked by justice, partnership, and mutual respect.

The portrayal of Stephen's martyrdom in Acts is interpreted as illustrating the cost of upholding a community ethic that stands against oppressive norms. Stephen's vision of the exalted Son of Human Being at the moment of his death links Christ's identity with unwavering commitment to truth. Modern churches can learn from this narrative about the courage required to persist in a shared ethic that liberates and empowers.

Throughout the chapter, there is an insistence that sin cannot be reduced to personal transgression alone. When social structures perpetuate dehumanization, silence about injustice can be complicit with wrongdoing. In the Son of Human Being, faith communities perceive a theological model that unites personal piety and collective accountability, leading to the dismantling of harmful systems.

Engagement with key figures in liberation theology reinforces these points, showing how social activism and spiritual devotion are integral to one another. The chapter draws parallels between Kang's gawani reading of Jesus and the work of theologians who underscore the holistic nature of redemption. The call is for a sustained approach, not isolated attempts, bridging worship and daily advocacy.

Worship itself is framed as a sphere where new relationships are formed in the image of the self-emptying Christ. The chapter suggests that when the church gathers, it must intentionally demonstrate equitable sharing and openness to all, rather than reinforcing social stratifications. Every sacramental act gains meaning when it propels believers to confront unjust structures beyond the sanctuary walls.

By affirming this connection between the altar and the public square, the narrative argues against a narrow religiosity that neglects the concerns of those on the margins. Jesus's example challenges communities to integrate compassion into civic responsibilities, economic decisions, and cultural expressions. The Son of Human Being thus stands as a critique of any faith stance that retreats from issues shaping people's quality of life.

Forgiveness in the Gospels, as described here, emerges as a social practice with far-reaching effect. It is not simply a matter of absolving guilt; it reclaims dignity for those labeled as outsiders. This focus on social reintegration and economic restitution ensures that grace is seen as restorative, mending rifts that undermine communal well-being.

Emphasis on the cross and resurrection deepens this reflection by underscoring that the struggle against oppressive forces meets resistance. Jesus's path, culminating in crucifixion, reveals the high cost of challenging societal hierarchies, yet the resurrection confirms a new horizon of possibility. The Son of Human Being thus symbolizes that the church can confront power and, through persevering faith, serve as an agent of communal renewal.

In practical terms, the chapter argues that congregations should adopt structures that promote transparency, shared governance, and tangible care for those who suffer. By incorporating gawani perspectives, believers avoid seeing mission purely as isolated philanthropy, choosing instead to engage in ongoing actions that dismantle exclusion. Such choices echo the early Christians who reshaped ordinary life patterns to align with the teachings and example of Jesus.

Another consideration is how theological education might incorporate these ideas. The text promotes an approach where future leaders learn to interpret biblical texts in ways that encourage broader social responsibility. Seminaries, study groups, and pastoral training programs can use gawani theology to form ministers prepared to shepherd faith communities that align devotion with systemic change.

In everyday congregational life, these themes prompt reflection on economic priorities, public advocacy, and pastoral care. The Son of Human Being perspective encourages believers to see that the spiritual and the material are interconnected realms. By fostering relationships that cross class, race, or cultural barriers, churches manifest a type of fellowship that mirrors the inclusive actions of Jesus.

The chapter does not reduce all theology to political engagement, but it insists that political and economic dimensions cannot be excluded from Christian practice. Jesus, in taking on a humble stance, shows how God identifies with those at the bottom rungs of society. His example challenges privileged groups to examine how their practices might perpetuate or dismantle cycles of marginalization.

Finally, the chapter concludes by noting that the Son of Human Being motif unifies both eschatological promise and immediate acts of mercy. By affirming Jesus's role in ultimate judgment while highlighting his real-time advocacy for the weak, the text portrays salvation as a process that involves both cosmic and local renewal. The result is a model of discipleship where the horizon of eternity motivates believers to engage vigorously in the temporal world, seeking the restoration of every neighbor's dignity.

7.

Embodying God's Kingdom Through Solidarity with Marginalized Communities

This chapter's opening section brings together distinct biblical narratives and theological frameworks to examine how material resources, social relationships, and spiritual commitments intersect in Christian discipleship. By focusing on the contrast between the wealthy official (Luke 18:18–30) and Zacchaeus (Luke 19:1–10), this introduction outlines the broader questions raised by gawani theology and minjung theology, as well as related liberationist approaches. Far from presenting a simplistic moral binary, these passages encourage readers to consider structural dimensions of wealth and inequality. This orientation sets the stage for an exploration of faith as an active engagement with society, challenging conventional boundaries between personal devotion and communal responsibility.

Biblical commentators have frequently noted that Luke's portrayal of the wealthy official suggests a person who fulfills religious duties but cannot relinquish his possessions when confronted by Jesus's directive to "sell all" and give to the poor (Luke 18:22). By contrast, Zacchaeus, the tax collector ostracized by his community, responds with a remarkable pledge to restore what he has taken unjustly and to share half of his property (Luke 19:8). These contrasting responses symbolize a larger pattern in Luke's Gospel, where those seemingly at the margins are often more receptive to transforming social bonds, while those with societal advantages may resist renouncing control. This chapter analyzes how these dynamics illuminate a vision of salvation that encompasses both tangible restitution and renewed fellowship.

Gawani theology enters this discussion by defining giving not merely as charity but as a shift in how individuals and communities handle power. According to Kang's view, gawani requires an ongoing willingness to reorient personal comfort for the benefit of others, thereby questioning the structures that isolate particular groups from communal life. Zacchaeus's decision to compensate fourfold those he has cheated exemplifies an integrative view of faith: it unites internal reformation with outward acts that address economic harm. In doing so, gawani challenges believers to see material possessions as shared resources, rather than private assets secured for personal interests.

Minjung theology offers another perspective by emphasizing the experiences of those systematically deprived of agency. Formed in the context of South Korea's industrialization under authoritarian governance, minjung theology critiques any form of Christian belief that remains aloof from real-life suffering. Ahn Byung-Mu's reflection on ὄχλος (crowd) in the Gospels highlights how Jesus aligns with people pushed aside by institutional power.[1] This chapter examines how minjung theology converges with gawani theology, urging the faithful to link spiritual convictions with public engagement. Both perspectives assert that the biblical call to love one's neighbor includes challenging oppressive frameworks, whether they involve political structures or entrenched economic inequities.

Additionally, this discussion builds on liberationist thought by scholars such as Gustavo Gutiérrez, who argues that salvation has ramifications for every dimension of human life, encompassing social, economic, and political spheres. Rather than limiting redemption to an internal or purely otherworldly experience, Gutiérrez's approach locates the gospel in contexts where poverty and exclusion persist. In parallel, gawani theology insists on the need to address how material wealth is accumulated and distributed, so that believers do not passively accept inequitable practices. This chapter's analysis contends that Luke's depiction of Zacchaeus and the wealthy official resonates with these liberationist

---

1. See Ahn, *Draußen*.

calls, demonstrating that a change of heart must manifest in social commitments and tangible forms of reparation.

A related area of inquiry involves James Cone's Black liberation theology, which underscores the role of race in systemic injustice, particularly in the North American context. Though the Luke 18–19 accounts do not directly speak to racial hierarchies, they illustrate how positions of privilege can hinder genuine discipleship by insulating individuals from the pain of others. Cone's critique—namely, that theology is incomplete if it does not address racism—parallels the warning in Luke 18 that one's possessions may become obstacles to authentic faith. This chapter applies that principle broadly, suggesting that any advantage—be it based on race, class, gender, or political favor—demands careful scrutiny in light of the gospel's ethic of social accountability.

Feminist theologians, such as Rosemary Radford Ruether, have likewise shown that patriarchal systems compound the challenges faced by many who already confront economic or social marginalization. The story of Zacchaeus underscores how an individual can realign priorities by dismantling exploitative practices, but it also invites examination of how gender inequities intersect with wealth distribution. For instance, women in various contexts may lack legal protections or financial resources, leaving them more susceptible to forms of exploitation often overlooked in standard readings of the Gospel. Integrating these feminist concerns helps situate gawani theology and minjung theology within a broader global discourse, where liberation is approached as a layered task involving multiple axes of inequality.

The connection between personal ethics and structural change stands out in this chapter as a central theme. In many congregations, acts of individual charity are lauded but rarely accompanied by organized efforts to reform exploitative systems. Gawani theology seeks to bridge that gap by urging the church to embrace economic sharing that is continuous and collective, rather than episodic. By highlighting Zacchaeus's moment of conversion as a catalyst for social repair, the text explores how modern believers might restructure entire patterns of ownership, housing, labor arrangements, and debt. When read together with minjung theology, these ideas emphasize that salvation involves an overlapping set of responsibilities: from intimate neighborly care to community-wide and even global advocacy.

Furthermore, this introduction clarifies that the call to "sell all" (Luke 18:22) is not merely about personal sacrifice but about resetting relational priorities. Whether in local cooperative housing or international campaigns for debt relief, gawani provides a frame for understanding that faith-based actions can challenge established norms. This process is not without complications; entrenched interests and longstanding social divisions pose hurdles. Still, the chapter will examine real-life applications, such as communal kitchens, shared facilities, and political lobbying, showing that these initiatives can expand the church's mission. Just as Zacchaeus's restitution restored a sense of dignity to those he had wronged, contemporary forms of giving can nurture trust and bolster community identity.

The subsequent sections will also discuss how these interpretations alter the classical notion of salvation. Rather than conceiving eternal life as purely future-oriented, Luke 19:9 and other passages reveal a broader horizon, were communities experience restoration here and now through just relationships. Liberation theologians often connect such concepts to biblical motifs like Jubilee (Lev 25), pointing out that social reordering stands at the heart of scriptural visions of divine deliverance. Gawani resonates with this outlook by treating giving as more than a personal choice; it serves as a hallmark of belonging to a reimagined community shaped by fairness and inclusivity.

A final point concerns the potential tension between personal piety and public transformation. Some readers maintain that the church risks diluting its spiritual essence if it ventures too far into political activism. Yet the text argues that Luke 19's depiction of salvation undermines this dichotomy. Zacchaeus's internal change is inseparable from his outward actions, and Jesus's proclamation that salvation has arrived emphasizes a fully integrated life of faith. This perspective aligns with minjung theology's insistence that doctrinal correctness alone cannot fulfill the gospel mandate unless it addresses ongoing hardships faced by the marginalized. As a result, this chapter's approach will affirm that worship, prayer, and sacramental practices can coexist—and indeed flourish—alongside efforts to overhaul unjust systems.

In sum, the upcoming discussion draws on multiple theological strands—gawani theology, minjung theology, and liberationist perspectives—to interpret the biblical accounts of the wealthy official and Zacchaeus as a combined narrative that highlights the stakes of embracing or resisting Jesus's kingdom ethic. The overarching argument is that a comprehensive reading of salvation includes economic justice, communal solidarity, and personal renewal, all which frame how believers should respond to possessions and power. By weaving together exegesis of Luke's Gospel with contemporary case studies, this chapter clarifies that the call to distribute to those who lack is neither a narrow rule nor an outdated principle, but a living invitation to reimagine communal life, making it more accountable and, ultimately, more faithful to the message of Jesus.

7.1. CONTRASTING THE WEALTHY OFFICIAL AND THE TAX COLLECTOR

Luke's Gospel sets up a resonant juxtaposition: one man is identified as a ruler (archōn), someone of considerable stature and financial advantage, while Zacchaeus is introduced as a tax collector bearing an untrustworthy reputation in his community (Luke 19:2).[2] The first figure, whose possessions and devout public image might suggest a revered status, ultimately rejects Jesus's call to divest his wealth and thereby restore bonds of solidarity. On the other hand, Zacchaeus, viewed by many as morally compromised—demonstrates a wholly different response when confronted with the possibility of ethical reorientation. In essence, Luke positions them side by side to show that, despite clear outward distinctions, both must decide how to address Jesus's invitation.[3] What makes this parallel especially important is that each man encounters Jesus from an entirely different social vantage. The ruler is frequently presumed to exhibit a blessed life, yet clings to personal control, Zacchaeus, though perceived as an outcast in moral and social terms, willingly resets his priorities by redistributing wealth. This choice inverts assumptions about who is deserving and indicates the wide scope of Jesus's mission. In effect, the Gospel frames salvation as more than private devotion; it reaches into the domain of material assets and the systems that shape them.[4]

Luke 19:1–10 clarifies how Zacchaeus's self-disclosure leads to a stark difference in outcomes relative to the official's refusal. Confronted by Jesus, he vows to give half his property to those in dire need and to compensate fourfold anyone he has cheated (Luke 19:8). This generous response moves beyond superficial repentance. It affirms that restitution and solidarity are inseparable aspects of a redeemed life. Jesus, noting

---

2. Luke 18:18 introduces the character as ἄρχων, commonly denoted "ruler," implying a respected or privileged station.
3. Cf. Friesen, *Imperial Cults*, 164.
4. Friesen, *Imperial Cults*, 164.

the authenticity of Zacchaeus's stance, proclaims, "Today salvation has come to this house" (Luke 19:9). Through that statement, Luke redefines salvation (sōzō) as a reality that must engage communal ties, not just personal assurance of a distant afterlife.[5] By demonstrating willingness to rectify tangible harm, Zacchaeus reframes the function of wealth, underscoring that Jesus's challenge to the well-placed official extends to each individual who wields resources and influence. The social ramifications are extensive: generosity becomes a unifying path that overcomes alienation and fosters an ethic of care within communities that once withheld acceptance.

Zacchaeus's Path of Renewal

The example of Zacchaeus portrays a redemption that fundamentally transforms the networks in which he participates. In relinquishing wealth to assist the vulnerable and reimburse the exploited, Zacchaeus rejects the notion that economic gain devoid of moral accountability can persist within faithful discipleship (Luke 19:8).[6] Such an action aligns with a holistic view of salvation, bridging interpersonal repair with public ramifications. The narrative depicts Zacchaeus as a figure who abandons patterns of exploitation in favor of forging new bonds with those formerly despised or victimized by him.[7] Jesus, upon seeing this dramatic turn, confirms that a new horizon of belonging has emerged within Zacchaeus's household, revealing that the impetus for genuine faith rests upon reconfiguring how assets are shared. This dynamic captures the impetus for social reformation embedded in the Gospel: wealth is not exclusively personal but is integrally related to community well-being. When Jesus announces that "salvation" has arrived, he underlines the interplay between private contrition and active steps to rebuild communal life.

Viewed more broadly, Zacchaeus's course of action suggests that any claim to follow Jesus cannot bypass the question of how resources are handled. Indeed, the official in Luke 18 cannot bring himself to sell all and join Jesus's band; in contrast, Zacchaeus chooses to restructure his life. Such a distinction shows that the invitation to spiritual renewal

---

5. The Greek term σῴζω (sōzō) conveys a holistic vision of salvation encompassing ethical and societal dimensions.

6. Cf. Friesen, "Poverty," 323–61.

7. Friesen, *Imperial Cults*, 188.

routinely intersects with systemic issues, pressing each disciple to evaluate what they owe their neighbors. The moral challenge of wealth, then, is that it can insulate certain individuals from the needs of the collective, restricting them from participating in the kind of inclusive fellowship Jesus inaugurates. Conversely, redistributing property and acknowledging past harms integrate personal contrition with structural adjustment—a pattern Luke's Gospel consistently highlights for believers who seek to enact the kingdom of God.

Expanding Gawani: Sacrifice and Freedom

Kang interprets Zacchaeus's conversion as an illustration of gawani), a theological practice that surpasses ordinary benevolence by restructuring social relationships from the ground up.[8] In this framework, gawani aligns with the Greek didōmi, signifying "to give," yet it embodies a deeper sense of offering, one that fosters outward-looking alliances rather than maintaining self-protection. Instead of relegating generosity to a solitary or sentimental gesture, gawani demands a decisive departure from self-focused comfort.[9] By articulating this concept, Kang emphasizes that giving is never marginal to discipleship but constitutes a hallmark of genuine faithfulness, paralleling Jesus's own decision to give himself in service of humanity. The objective is not fleeting charity but an ethic that can untangle oppressive systems and cultivate redeemed community.

Furthermore, gawani provides a constructive lens for addressing how personal spiritual transformation necessarily includes broader domains of life, including economic structures. Zacchaeus's pledge to distribute wealth arises from a newly recognized imperative to restore those he once defrauded. By reaffirming that possessions must not feed inequality, he shifts the center of moral accountability from ego-driven gain to collective flourishing.[10] Kang's vision of gawani highlights that the impetus for generosity is not vanity or coerced compliance, but instead an invitation to practice freedom from the anxieties that accompany material hoarding. In that sense, gawani fosters a reliance on communal ties that stand in contrast to cultures of hyperindividualism, where wealth often cements hierarchies.

---

8. Kang, *Theology of Gawani*, 14–17.
9. Moltmann, *Jesus Christ*, 10.
10. Cf. Friesen, "Poverty," 323.

Social Implications for Giving

This gawani ethic thereby weaves personal reorientation with disruptive critique of structural injustice. Zacchaeus's decision to repay fourfold the amounts he had unlawfully taken stands as a public renunciation of a revenue system operating at the expense of vulnerable neighbors (Luke 19:8). By offering restitution, he challenges assumptions that wealth accumulation can remain aloof from moral considerations. From that advantage, generosity functions not just as an internal shift but as a visible challenge to social order. Jesus's approval suggests that the power of salvation extends well beyond private relief, ensuring communal readmission for an individual once denounced for unscrupulous practices. As a result, gawani manifests a capacity to unify contrition with broad-scale reconciliation, bridging fractured relationships and redefining how property should be employed to sustain communal life.[11]

In parallel, the narrative linking Zacchaeus and the official underscores how two people confronted by Jesus can produce markedly different outcomes in spiritual and societal terms. One man, clinging to an idealized persona, eventually departs in sorrow because relinquishing social privilege feels too disruptive. Another, despised for exploitative behavior, turns around and channels his resources to serve common well-being, thus illustrating that inclusive fellowship is more plausible than it seems. This tension underscores the idea that redemption cannot avoid real-world implications. Zacchaeus's example may challenge anyone occupying a position of relative advantage to consider how a faith-based ethic demands reimagining the use of one's resources (Luke 19:10). All such transformations hinge upon whether individuals opt to "enter the kingdom" by adopting collaborative practices of gawani.

Rewriting Possessions and Power

Luke's exposition further clarifies that acquiring wealth or enjoying pious credibility is no automatic indicator of alignment with God's reign. Zacchaeus, who begins the story as an outcast, enacts a thorough realignment that disavows exploitation, whereas the official in Luke 18 is unable to break free from his comfort. The distinction between these two men exemplifies the Gospel's central message: reorienting wealth is integral

---

11. Novak, *Experience of Nothingness*, 22.

to participating in God's project of liberation. Faithfulness, then, does not hinge primarily on doctrinal correctness but on the readiness to join a network of reciprocity wherein possessions serve communal accountability.[12] Such an undertaking calls for an alternative approach to power willingness to lower personal security, trusting that new relationships can emerge in the context of shared responsibility.

By depicting Zacchaeus's significant decision, Luke implies that redemption—σῴζω (sōzō)—is not a detached condition but one that fosters a more inclusive social structure.[13] In that sense, the official's reluctance to surrender his fortune is not just an individual failing but also a failure to participate in the covenant's intention of justice. Zacchaeus, however, exhibits the capacity for tangibly restoring a social fabric once torn by greed. Gawani here operates as more than a spiritual principle; it points to a series of measures that enable individuals to step into a radically renewed sphere of communal trust. The final pronouncement of salvation that Jesus bestows recognizes that sincerity of generosity merges spiritual and social life into a cohesive practice of discipleship.

Cultivating Community Through Gawani

This emphasis on gawani resonates with a broader biblical motif that generosity can transform how entire groups function. In the feeding of the five thousand (Mark 6:30–44), Jesus invites his followers to enact gawani by providing nourishment for a large assembly, paralleling his own model of self-emptying.[14] The Johannine tradition likewise incorporates feeding imagery, connecting it to Jesus's "Bread of Life" discourse, to affirm that God's gracious act is not confined to abstract categories but materializes in actual distributions of bread. Early Christian communities that embraced such radical giving often found themselves knitting together networks of mutual care—an extension of Jesus's own mission. This underscores that gawani is not just a personal gesture but fosters a synergy that counters the rigid inequalities so prevalent in Roman society, thereby paving the way for a redemptive fellowship.[15]

---

12. Moltmann, *Jesus Christ*, 18.

13. Cf. Luke 19:9, describing the arrival of salvation in Zacchaeus's house.

14. Mark 6:30–44, John 6:1–13. See Waetjen, *Gospel*, 202, for a related perspective on feeding imagery.

15. Friesen, *Imperial Cults*, 188.

Kang's perspective of gawani likewise shows that generosity necessitates relinquishing one's self-enclosed posture, thus shifting the center of moral reflection from individual advantage to shared life.[16] By actively repudiating exploitative norms, believers open themselves to vulnerability but discover that their sense of community expands. The story of Zacchaeus reveals how love for one's neighbor is not ornamental; it redefines economic transactions and emboldens restitution. Put another way, self-emptying is not a symbolic aspiration, but a practice with the ability to challenge structures of oppression and usher in more hospitable patterns of life together.

Completing the Picture of Shared Life

When placed in conversation with the official's refusal, Zacchaeus's embrace of generosity clarifies a pivotal claim: those who assume they have little moral need may fail to grasp the call of Jesus, while those stigmatized by neighbors may prove more open to reimagining how wealth is utilized (Luke 18:18–30; 19:1–10). In the end, the Gospel narrative spotlights that any spiritual quest for eternal life can stagnate if individuals resist altering their economic assumptions. Where the official departs in sorrow, Zacchaeus epitomizes a renewed pattern of life, underscoring that gawani is central to embodying salvation. The challenge for modern readers emerges in recognizing that faith communities today can likewise enact gawani, unveiling a route to address structural inequalities by adopting an other-centered framework. Such an approach resonates with Moltmann's argument that Jesus unites sacrificial love with public transformation, thus calling for an ecclesial ethic that merges piety with inclusive justice.[17]

Ultimately, gawani underscores that the path to authentic discipleship encompasses social commitment and restitution on behalf of marginalized neighbors. By describing Zacchaeus's readiness to disperse his holdings, the Gospel narrative gives a vivid example of how trust in Jesus leads to decisive and public changes.[18] This does not trivialize spiritual devotion but insists that a profession of faith should intersect with how believers allocate resources. Over and over, Luke reveals that

---

16. Kang, *Theology of Gawani*, 15.
17. Moltmann, *Jesus Christ*, 18.
18. Luke 19:8–9. See also Frankl, *Man's Search for Meaning*..

Jesus's question "Will you sell all, or will you distribute to those who lack?" remains a continuing moral test. In adopting gawani, the community learns that salvation, far from a detached concept, emerges in lived expressions of generosity, bridging faith and day-to-day realities in ways that can truly reshape the social environment.

7.2. MINJUNG THEOLOGY AND GAWANI THEOLOGY: SHARED VALUES, DIFFERENT EMPHASES

Minjung theology and gawani theology both emphasize faithful practice oriented toward social equality, yet their approaches emerge from distinct contexts and highlight different dimensions of engagement. Minjung theology in South Korea arose within a climate of political oppression in the 1970s and 1980s, when impoverished citizens, laborers, and advocates for democratic reforms sought support from a church called to address structural injustice.[19] Drawing on the biblical portrayal of the ὄχλος (ochlos), Ahn Byung-Mu maintains that Jesus's deliberate association with powerless communities demonstrates that the gospel cannot be separated from the condition of those on the margins.[20] In practice, minjung theology urges believers to confront oppressive structures, holding that robust faith is actualized through public advocacy rather than confined to private piety. In this view, the kingdom of God is not a remote ideal but a present reality shaped by the collective efforts of those who assume responsibility for social and political transformation.

Gawani theology relates to this liberation-based ethos by emphasizing tangible acts of giving and the cultivation of interpersonal bonds.[21] In Kang's framework, giving transcends mere charity: it is a deliberate crossing of barriers that can unify diverse individuals. While minjung theology often addresses large-scale systemic concerns such as dictatorships, economic oppression, and cultural marginalization, gawani theology highlights how personal sacrifice sparks enduring communal collaboration. Yet the two bodies of thought do not contradict each other.

---

19. Moltmann, *Minjung Theologie*, 35. Contributors discuss how the church in South Korea arose in solidarity with labor activism and calls for systemic reform.

20. Moltmann, *Minjung Theologie*, 132. Ahn Byung-Mu argues that Jesus's bond with the ὄχλος (ochlos) embodies solidarity with the disenfranchised.

21. Kang, *Theology of Gawani*, 9–10. Kang, in close exegesis of Luke 19 and under the sign of χάρις that binds and looses, expounds the Zacchaeus scene as primal instance of gawani: giving that dismantles the acquisitive "I" and reconstitutes community.

Kang's writings explain that gawani fosters another-focused unity, so that structural work and individual generosity intertwine, forming a cohesive demonstration of the kingdom's presence.[22]

These parallel convictions echo the approach found in Latin American liberation theology, where Gustavo Gutiérrez advocates for the preferential option for the poor as a central gospel imperative.[23] Such theology critiques exploitation—be it political or economic—and contends that the church cannot remain neutral but must stand with grassroots campaigns seeking equity. James H. Cone's Black liberation theology likewise underscores that racism is a societal sin requiring active solidarity with Black communities; no account of Christ's ministry can be consistent if it ignores the reality of racial injustice or fails to join movements for systemic redress.[24] Comparable perspectives also manifest in arguments about dismantling entrenched racial hierarchies through community solidarity.[25] Gawani aligns with these liberation frameworks by affirming that sacrificial giving cannot be a passing gesture—it must shape the daily lives of believers and question systems that perpetuate poverty or exclusion. Kang shows that gawani's call to share possessions fosters both immediate relief and a broader challenge to stratified social orders.[26]

Individual and Institutional Applications

A recurring criticism in many congregations is that those with comfortable means often remain isolated from structural wrongs, believing that occasional charity or short-term volunteer projects suffice. Gawani theology refutes such assumptions by pointing out the necessity of boundary-crossing generosity.[27] The aim is not paternalistic charity,

---

22. Pieris, *Asian Theology*, 20. Pieris ties spiritual practice to social activism in various Asian liberation movements.

23. Gutiérrez, *Theology of Liberation*, 20. Gutiérrez states that an "option for the poor" is at the heart of the gospel's message.

24. Cone, *Black Theology*, 37. Cone maintains that confronting systemic racism is foundational to Christian faith in the American context.

25. See Carmichael and Hamilton, *Black Power*, 44. The authors stress how group solidarity can reshape the public order.

26. Kang, *Theology of Gawani*, 17–19. In deliberate proximity to Luke 6 and Acts 2, Kang (with an insistence reminiscent of Calvin's *instituta caritatis*) unfolds gawani as an economy of grace that exposes and overturns the possessive "I," thereby re-situating the community at the centre of Christian praxis.

27. Ahn, *Draußen*, 54. Ahn insists that theology attentive to the poor must push for

but genuine fellowship that recognizes the dignity of the oppressed and works collaboratively to transform oppressive norms. Churches might enact gawani in tangible ways by establishing budget transparency that prioritizes economically vulnerable households, forging alliances with labor or civil rights groups, or opening church facilities to grassroots activists who often lack safe gathering spaces.[28] In these contexts, gawani's emphasis on direct giving resonates with minjung theology's insistence on structural advocacy, culminating in a renewed communal ethic that reflects biblical ideals.

Such synergy broadens our grasp of liberation's scope. While minjung theology typically engages the question of how the church should oppose dictatorial regimes or predatory capitalism, gawani theology frames personal generosity as a catalytic practice for bridging social divisions. As James H. Cone has argued, a faithful theology must not only champion grand-scale reforms but also inspire local transformations, guided by compassion and sustained by daily acts of solidarity.[29] Kang likewise promotes an integrative approach, encouraging each faith community to pursue both policy-level advocacy and household-level giving that undermines everyday patterns of exploitation.[30] Minjung's large-scale perspective and gawani's focus on interpersonal change are thus interwoven dimensions of a shared pursuit.

Toward an Expanded Meaning of Salvation

Minjung theology maintains that the salvation Jesus offers must liberate people from real-world forces, such as political subjugation, economic subordination, and social marginalization.[31] It rejects reading the gospel exclusively through a spiritual lens that dismisses the necessity of reconfiguring existing institutions. Gawani theology concurs, contending that personal rescue should not be detached from communal reorganization.

---

genuine systemic change.

28. See Kittel et al., *Theological Dictionary*, 198, referencing "ὄχλος."

29. Cone, *Black Theology*, 37, argues that Christian thought without concrete confrontation of oppression falls short.

30. Kang, *Theology of Gawani*, 11–12. Reading the Son of a Human Being logia through the lens of gawani, Kang construes Jesus's self-designation as programmatic for "restorative sharing," a praxis that unmasks dehumanizing structures precisely by redistributing goods and dignity within the household of faith.

31. Ahn, *Draußen*, 54.

In short, redemption addresses the total well-being of people, including the structural contexts in which they live. Kang describes this as a deliberate self-questioning: "Do we, as believers, perpetuate or benefit from systems that deepen injustice?"[32] He suggests that gawani invites individuals to relinquish protective illusions—whether of wealth, social privilege, or moral exceptionalism—in favor of forging networks in which resources are openly shared. The reorientation of possessions within the church community exemplifies how biblical freedom is not a personal abstraction, but an ongoing confrontation with forms of oppression.

Furthermore, gawani's principle of boundary-crossing generosity implies that the faithful cannot merely rely on rhetorical affirmations of justice while retaining all material comfort. The church is thus reminded that Jesus's summons "sell what you have and follow me" carries implications for wealth distribution that remain unsettling to many.[33] Zacchaeus's example intensifies this point by showing how meeting Jesus compels radical acts that defy ordinary patterns of accumulation. Gawani does not claim these actions alone eradicate structural sin, but it does propose that authentic transformation must include altered uses of resources, bridging the private sphere and public activism.[34]

Uniting Social Structures with Personal Generosity

Critics might wonder whether individual philanthropic gestures can truly dismantle institutional injustices. Gawani theology stresses that personal giving, while fundamental, must be woven into organized initiatives that shape societal regulations, labor protections, and the protection of minority rights.[35] The logic is twofold: personal restitution or communal sharing is an immediate demonstration of solidarity, while broader mobilization harnesses collective power to overturn oppressive frameworks.[36] Churches, in turn, can cooperate with civic groups to en-

---

32. Kang, *Theology of Gawani*, 11–12, aligns the Son of Human Being theme with gawani's restorative aims toward the dehumanized.

33. Cf. Mark 10:45, which underscores Jesus's self-giving posture as foundational to discipleship.

34. Kang, *Theology of Gawani*, 12, observes that gawani, while personal, has social ramifications that invite believers to question norms of self-protection.

35. Cone, *Black Theology*, 37.

36. Gutiérrez, *Theology of Liberation*, 31, contends that personal generosity is insufficient unless it also transforms unjust social frameworks.

act policies that safeguard workers or to challenge discriminatory laws. By combining intimate generosity with large-scale activism, believers embody the full range of biblical freedom. As Kang observes, such unity fosters a new moral outlook that is both conscientious of everyday needs and deliberate in transforming public systems.[37]

In this respect, gawani also resonates with Asian liberation theology voices such as Aloysius Pieris, who sees the bridging of spiritual practice and social upheaval as central to genuine faith.[38] This bridging is more than a philosophical reflection; it is a pragmatic path that demonstrates how personal acts—like giving half of one's income or meeting urgent local needs—can complement more extensive alliances that address systemic oppression. Concretely, local congregations might adopt gawani-based budgets that allocate funds for education, family crisis aid, or legal advocacy for vulnerable populations. In doing so, they begin to approximate the fellowship that Luke portrays in Acts, wherein early believers reorganized their assets to ensure that no one among them suffered needless want.[39]

Biblical-Theological Foundations: The Son of Human Being and Gawani

Kang integrates the Son of Human Being motif, interpreting it as a scriptural foundation for gawani's transformative aim.[40] Mark 10:45 emphasizes that the Son of Human Being "came not to be served but to serve," guiding the church to connect cruciform love with collaborative relationships. Jesus's instruction—"sell what you have and follow me"—is not an isolated moral lesson but reflects a larger incarnational dynamic in which giving is essential to divine healing (Mark 10:45). Indeed, the wealthy man's reluctance to divest highlights how a fixation on possessions can deter genuine discipleship.[41] Consistent with minjung theology, gawani argues that thorough acceptance of the gospel mandates releasing attachments that sustain the subjugation of others. The cross is thus more

---

37. Kang, *Theology of Gawani*, 17–19.
38. Pieris, *Asian Theology*, 24.
39. Kang, *Theology of Gawani*, 17–19.
40. Kang, *Theology of Gawani*, 11–12.
41. Mark 10:22 shows how attachment to wealth prevents fully embracing the kingdom path.

than a theological symbol; it is a renewed standard of service and relinquishment, mirrored in how believers allocate resources and reposition themselves in relation to people lacking power.

Tensions and Convergences

Questions inevitably surface about gawani: Is it so heavily devoted to personal charity that it overlooks the structural blueprint of oppression? Kang insists that gawani is not a purely internal ethic but an assertion that self-renunciation, once placed in contexts of coercion, can become an agent of renewal.[42] Many liberation frameworks—including minjung theology—also argue that personal giving cannot stand alone if it fails to confront deeper social distortions.[43] Yet far from clashing, these perspectives converge to illustrate that complete liberation unfolds where sacrificial love integrates with strategic advocacy. Zacchaeus, upon returning what he stole, signals how personal change can reshape the entire community dynamics; the official, unwilling to cede wealth, illuminates how failing to engage the question of resources yields spiritual stagnation. Thus, minjung theology's stress on reorganizing sociopolitical structures resonates well with gawani's emphasis on sustained personal generosity, culminating in the kingdom's presence that is both communal and practical.

Concluding Reflections: A Shared Path Forward

Minjung theology and gawani theology ultimately uphold that discipleship entails more than cerebral convictions. Each tradition, in its own idiom, challenges believers to align spiritual commitments with economic practice and social activism. Minjung theology amplifies structural contestation, fostering solidarity with those oppressed by political tyranny or corporate dominance.[44] Gawani underscores relational closeness and giving across boundaries, emphasizing how private faith can manifest as sincere devotion to outcasts.[45] Their joint legacy assures that neither personal generosity nor public reform stands alone as sufficient;

---

42. Kang, *Theology of Gawani*, 12.
43. Gutiérrez, *Theology of Liberation*, 31.
44. Ahn, *Draußen*, 54.
45. Kang, *Theology of Gawani*, 9–10.

rather, they function in unity, reflecting the biblical witness that the gospel transforms souls and societies alike. As Aloysius Pieris reminds readers, it is fruitless to preach liberation if the faith community fails to meet practical needs.[46] Similarly, James Cone observes that a theology failing to address systemic oppression cannot faithfully represent the Jesus who stood with the least.[47]

Consequently, if congregations adopt gawani in tandem with minjung theology, they reinforce a church culture that offers not only charitable relief but also insists on dismantling oppressive structures. In so doing, they more fully practice Jesus's ministry, where Zacchaeus's restitution and the official's dilemma exemplify how wealth and privilege can either serve the kingdom or stand in its way. The synergy between collective advocacy and personal giving animates what liberation theologians since Gustavo Gutiérrez have advocated: a faith that upholds the inherent worth of all persons while challenging forces that undermine this worth. In the end, the continuing resonance of minjung theology and gawani theology lies in their insistence that the Christian calling is never abstract or static, but immersed in the living experiences of marginalized neighbors, always calling believers to break boundaries and practice a generosity that leads to shared redemption.

7.3. TOWARD AN EXPANDED UNDERSTANDING OF SALVATION

Many readers are accustomed to framing salvation as a personal state of moral or spiritual rescue. However, a gawani-oriented interpretation stresses that salvation encompasses broader social deliverance as well. Minjung theology, for example, contends that Jesus's salvific mission involves emancipation from structures of political subjugation and economic exploitation.[48] This perspective does not diminish personal spirituality, yet it cautions believers that real discipleship is incomplete if systemic injustices remain unchallenged. Whether individuals live in contexts of privilege or want, a gawani lens encourages communities to see how systemic forces—such as class hierarchies or political

---

46. Pieris, *Asian Theology*, 25.
47. Cone, *Black Theology*, 107.
48. Ucko, *People*, 155.

corruption—affect who suffers, how deeply they suffer, and whether that suffering persists.

For congregations in wealthier societies, the question arises: "In what ways do we perpetuate or benefit from oppressive systems?" Cone argues that believers in affluent contexts often remain unaware of how racial and economic inequalities linger within social structures.[49] In a similar way, gawani ethics demand a critical self-examination among those whose personal prosperity may come at the expense of underpaid laborers, displaced communities, or ecological destruction.[50] Recognizing this dynamic calls for a reevaluation of the standard charity approach, since piecemeal benevolence may soothe immediate need but can also deflect attention from the underlying systems that perpetuate disenfranchisement. The notion of gawani—an inclusive, participatory community bound by shared concern—pushes believers to see themselves as part of a tapestry of relationships shaped by power and inequality, requiring tangible steps toward reform.

Expanding the Scope of Shared Life

Minjung theology is known for its emphasis on the minjung, often translated as "the masses" or "the marginalized." Rather than regarding the crowd (ὄχλος) as a disorganized or homogenous throng, theologians like Ahn Byung-Mu have suggested reading the minjung in the New Testament as those who stand outside institutional or hierarchical power. Oppression is not merely an external fact but a force that fractures communal ties and keeps certain individuals voiceless.[51]

Gawani resonates with this perspective, revealing that authentic discipleship—like Jesus's association with outcasts—means actively restoring value and agency to those rendered invisible by dominant social orders. This leads to what some theologians call "social sanctification." Instead of treating salvation as a strictly personal rescue from sin, it highlights how entire networks—families, neighborhoods, economies, and legal systems—require transformation. If local families cannot afford healthcare, or if entire communities face gentrification and forced displacement, then

49. Cone, *God*, 37.
50. Kittel et al., *Theological Dictionary*, 583.
51. Ahn Byung-Mu's perspective on Heb 13:13 is cited in Ucko, *People*, 155. Ahn describes minjung as those "outside the camp," indicating solidarity with people excluded from institutional power.

to "save souls" in isolation from such realities would divorce the gospel from daily life. A gawani lens unites these domains, asserting that personal redemption unfolds more robustly where social systems allow dignity for everyone, particularly those often forgotten or exploited.

Integrating Social Structures and Personal Acts of Generosity

One of the hallmark examples frequently invoked when discussing gawani is the story of Zacchaeus. Zacchaeus exhibits repentance in concrete economic terms by offering to repay anyone he has defrauded, while also giving half of his possessions to the poor. Traditional readings might focus on his personal conviction, viewing Zacchaeus's gesture as a heroic, one-time choice to display generosity. Gawani-oriented readings, however, ask whether even this form of lavish giving can disrupt the systemic roots of injustice.[52] If financial inequities are reinforced by corrupt taxation or skewed property laws, how can any single act of restitution become part of a sustained movement for communal change?

Kang proposes that Zacchaeus's transformation, while catalyzed by a personal encounter with Jesus, highlights a principle of structural reorientation.[53] When that principle becomes embedded within networks—such as local churches partnering with nonprofits or grassroots organizations—individual generosity aligns with policy advocacy that addresses exploitation at the root. By bridging personal acts of charity with collective activism, believers avoid the danger of viewing repentance as merely private or symbolic. Instead, they participate in a broader reimagining of economic policies and social norms, thereby connecting spiritual growth with justice for those on society's margins.[54] In this synergy, moral agency is neither purely individual nor fully subsumed under collective action; it entails the intersection of both.

---

52. Luke 19:1–10. Zacchaeus's pledge to restore stolen funds demonstrates personal sincerity but does not single-handedly reform the tax system.

53. Kang, *Theology of Gawani*, 11. Here Kang uses the Zacchaeus story to show that personal conversion becomes authentic only when it triggers a tangible reordering of possessions and power relationships.

54. Kang, *Theology of Gawani*, 12. Kang insists that individual acts of generosity must be tied to collective critique of unjust structures, ensuring that gawani moves beyond symbolic charity toward concrete justice for people at society's margins.

Beyond Isolated Giving

Minjung theology and liberation theology consistently warn against an overreliance on charity. Gutiérrez argues that while benevolence can relieve immediate suffering, it does not systematically alter the mechanisms by which the poor remain impoverished.[55] Gawani thus calls believers to discern whether individual acts of giving inadvertently reinforce hierarchies in which the wealth continue to bestow while the impoverished remain perpetually dependent. This is why many faith communities, prompted by gawani insights, not only engage in soup kitchens or clothing drives but also lobby for just wages, equitable housing regulations, or environmental protections that benefit vulnerable populations.[56]

For instance, a church might consider using its real estate for affordable housing projects or might form a consortium that invests in local cooperatives. Members who take steps to minimize exploitative labor in their own workplace exemplify how personal ethics and community structures converge. Likewise, organizing financial workshops for low-income members and actively intervening in local policy debates to cap interest rates on predatory loans could be recognized as gawani praxis. Rather than conceiving generosity as a finite action—like cutting a check—communities deepen their commitment by addressing the entire ecosystem that perpetuates wealth inequality. By doing so, they collaborate in reshaping a more equitable social architecture, one in which personal charity complements and energizes systemic reforms.

Biblical-Theological Foundations: Son of Human Being and Gawani

Kang's exegesis of the Son of Human Being motif (ὁ υἱὸς τοῦ ἀνθρώπου) invests Jesus's identity with implications that extend beyond personal piety.[57] In Mark 10:45, Jesus reveals that this Son of Human Being came to serve rather than be served, offering his life to liberate many. The gawani

---

55. Gutiérrez, *Theology of Liberation*, xvii.

56. Gutiérrez, *Theology of Liberation*, 8. Gutiérrez's mention of Marxist thought underscores that genuine transformation requires concrete structural changes, not just individual acts of piety.

57. Kang, *Theology of Gawani*, 11, 18. Kang links the self-designation "Son of a Human Being" to Jesus' programmatic choice of service and to the birth of a "new humanity" that counters every dehumanizing power.

dimension here is significant because it portrays Jesus's mission as both sacrificial and community oriented. Service to others is not simply an add-on to personal devotion; it stands at the core of salvific action. Likewise, the cross becomes the ultimate illustration of solidarity with those dehumanized by Rome's colonial power or by local class divisions. To call Jesus the Son of Human Being underscores his empathy with, and commitment to, the struggles of humankind.

Incarnational Giving and the Jubilee Vision

Coupled with Jesus's sell what you have command in Mark 10:21, the emphasis on service and giving underscores the theological basis for integrating the cross's sacrificial dimension with reciprocal living in community. This synergy evokes an incarnational principle: God's presence dwells in human contexts, requiring not only personal devotion but also concrete steps to dismantle human-made injustices. Kang frames this incarnational aspect as part of gawani's invitation, calling all followers to adopt practices that counteract dehumanizing processes, be they economic, political, or social.[58]

In Luke's Gospel, Jesus announces the good news to the poor (Luke 4:16–20), sometimes referred to as Jesus's "Nazareth Manifesto," which references the Jubilee (Lev 25). Jubilee entailed the cancellation of debts, the liberation of slaves, and the return of ancestral land, promoting equitable restoration across Israelite society. Thus, Jesus's ministry is understood as continuing and expanding this Jubilee vision. When taken within a gawani framework, Jubilee is not a narrow concern for personal holiness alone but a dynamic call to rectify broader injustices related to land tenure, labor exploitation, and wealth concentration.[59] In a modern context, it could prompt churches to question the global debt crisis, ecological degradation, or exploitative supply chains.

---

58. Kang, *Theology of Gawani*, 12. Kang stresses that Jesus's self-giving must translate into concrete, community-shaping gawani rather than remain a private sentiment.

59. Luke 4:16–20 references Isa 61 and Lev 25, framing Jesus's public ministry as embodying Jubilee.

Tensions in Appropriating Gawani

Some critique gawani-inspired readings for concentrating too narrowly on acts like selling possessions or distributing wealth to the poor, worrying that these readings might encourage a purely voluntary, patchwork approach to systemic problems.[60] Yet Kang clarifies that such personal gestures form an entry point rather than the entire solution. Gawani aims to demonstrate how personal generosity, when oriented by a communal consciousness, initiates relationships of trust and restitution. At the same time, minjung theology and liberation theology underscore that if personal benevolence does not challenge oppressive structures, then any transformation remains incomplete. In short, gawani does not replace structural activism; it energizes it by anchoring economic justice in the concrete acts of ordinary believers.

The Zacchaeus Paradigm and the Persistence of Social Transformation

The story of Zacchaeus exemplifies how a single person's economic decision can pivot social relationships, restoring communal bonds and redeeming reputations (Luke 19:1–10). When Zacchaeus acknowledges his wrongdoing and seeks to compensate for those he cheated, he interrupts the cycle of distrust and exploitation. Yet the text also implies that deeper social systems allowed him to amass wealth in the first place, pointing to a network of tax collectors and political alliances. Gawani highlights that effective restitution moves beyond Zacchaeus as an individual case; it challenges others in similar economic arrangements to reconsider the ethics of their participation. As Gutiérrez insists, real liberation arises where personal change and collective reordering converge.[61]

Moreover, the motif of Son of Human Being enters the Zacchaeus narrative through Jesus's self-understanding as the one who seeks and saves the lost (Luke 19:10). This searching and saving extends the gawani impulse: to restore all who have been socially and spiritually alienated. Minjung theology underscores how the lost can be both those crushed by poverty and those who benefit from oppressive systems yet forfeit

---

60. Kang, *Theology of Gawani*, 18. Kang situates the Pentecost scene as the genesis of a Jubilee-shaped community, insisting that individual acts of sharing gain theological weight only when they unsettle the entrenched logics of possession and exploitation.

61. Gutiérrez, *Theology of Liberation*, 66.

their true humanity in the process. The dual dimension of liberation thus involves the poor regaining access to life's resources, and the privileged relinquishing unjust advantages. Gawani fosters a community where both these movements occur simultaneously, healing social fragmentation from multiple angles.

Practical Extensions: Church and Society

An increasing number of congregations adopt gawani-like approaches, aiming to weave personal devotion with structural transformations. Some devote resources to economic empowerment programs, such as microloans or job training, ensuring that acts of charity feed into lasting opportunities. Others engage with local government to propose ordinances limiting predatory lending or guaranteeing tenant rights. In regions dealing with the vestiges of colonial injustice, churches might align with indigenous communities seeking legal recognition of land claims. Such initiatives echo a gawani commitment to preserving human dignity by ensuring communities can steward their resources fairly.

Educational Outreach and Theological Training

Another way gawani manifests is through theological education. Seminaries and church-based study groups may develop curricula examining how biblical texts address economic oppression or communal ethics. Workshops can highlight historical struggles—such as the South Korean minjung movement, Latin American base communities, or Dalit theology in India—to illustrate how local believers have fused faith with activism. This historical awareness strengthens the argument that gawani is not a newly invented category but a retrieval of biblical and early church models in which property-sharing and mutual aid were central (Acts 2:44–45, 4:32–35).

Additionally, some instructors encourage critical reflection on how Jesus's injunction to "deny yourself, take up your cross, and follow me" intersects with global capitalism, consumer habits, and the ecological crises that disproportionately harm low-income communities. Believers are led to see that the cross is not an abstract theological idea; it symbolizes concrete solidarity with those suffering, often because of systemic greed or environmental exploitation. The gawani vision thus becomes a vital resource for prompting sustained engagement with injustice, challenging the assumption that faith is primarily an individual matter of private morality.

Gawani, the Son of Human Being, and Eschatological Hope

Kang suggests that Jesus's resurrection inaugurated a "new exodus community," which signals that God's reign does not await a distant future but emerges in the present whenever communities practice shared life (κοινωνία).[62] In this sense, the Son of Human Being points to a collective recreation of humanity, an eschatological transformation lived out in everyday relationships. The earliest Christian communities, as depicted in Acts, practiced economic sharing so extensively that Luke mentions it twice, demonstrating the significance of communal solidarity in the fledgling church.[63]

From a gawani perspective, that early Christian ethos stands as a template for modern disciples, urging them to move away from individualistic consumerism and to embrace a culture of "living together."[64] Yet the narrative of Ananias and Sapphira warns how greed or dishonesty can quickly undermine collective trust. A gawani reading sees this as highlighting the vulnerability of communal solidarity when individuals, under pressure from self-interest, withhold resources or conceal their motivations. While these tensions arise in every generation, gawani theology encourages believers to persist in building networks of transparency, stewardship, and mutual care.[65]

Conclusion: Holistic Liberation and the Call to Embodied Discipleship

A gawani approach to salvation expands theological horizons, showing that liberation from sin requires concurrent liberation from oppressive

---

62. Kang, *Theology of Gawani*, 18–19. Kang links Pentecost to the new exodus community, reading Acts 2 and 4 as a Jubilee-shaped κοινωνία whose shared life signals God's reign breaking into present structures.

63. Acts 2:44–45, 4:32–35.

64. See Bonhoeffer and Wells, *Life Together*. Bonhoeffer's *Gemeinsames Leben* resonates with gawani's emphasis on shared practices.

65. Acts 5:1–11. Ananias and Sapphira's deceit contrasts sharply with the transparency that fosters community trust.

structures. Jesus's call to "sell what you have and follow me," when read through gawani, becomes an invitation to abandon illusions of moral or economic neutrality and to embrace relationships oriented around mutual flourishing.[66] Minjung and liberation theologies reinforce this dimension by underscoring that faith communities cannot fulfill their mission if they neglect real-world injustices that continually impoverish and marginalize many.[67]

In practical terms, gawani-minded congregations may adopt both personal acts of generosity and collective strategies that challenge unjust laws or market mechanisms. By weaving together these personal and structural components, the church models a new way of sharing life where charity transitions into covenant. Discipleship entails a willingness to surrender cultural habits that prioritize self-protection, investing instead in corporate well-being. Such a transformation does not come without cost; yet it reflects the pattern of the Son of Human Being, who exemplified servanthood and collective restoration.

In sum, gawani compels believers to see that the cross, the resurrection, and the call to communal life are not separate threads but a single tapestry. Service, justice, and restored fellowship weaving together in a manner that challenges the status quo. Even everyday actions—like how one invests money, shops for goods, or votes in local elections—take on new significance within this shared vision of liberation. Where personal repentance is integrated with systemic advocacy, and where sacrificial love becomes a daily discipline, the community's life discloses the presence of God's ongoing redemption. As gawani interpreters note, salvation is not a passive end-state but an active, relational process by which the dehumanized regain their voice and the privileged learn to relinquish oppressive advantages, enabling the entire body to flourish together.

7.4. MINJUNG THEOLOGY'S INSIGHT FOR GLOBAL CHRISTIAN PRACTICE

Minjung theology has contributed to rethinking how Christianity can respond to sociopolitical hardships, particularly in contexts defined by class disparities and authoritarian power structures. Its foundational premise

---

66. Mark 10:21. The wealthy man's reluctance indicates how love of possessions can block genuine discipleship.

67. See Cone, *God*, 37, and Gutiérrez, *Theology of Liberation*, 8, both urging believers to confront social structures that perpetuate suffering.

is that the gospel must address the real-life conditions of people who have been pushed to society's margins, whether they are manual laborers, rural farmers, or individuals under governmental repression. Rather than situating theology in an abstract sphere of doctrinal statements, minjung theology contends that a proper understanding of Christ's teachings emerges from solidarity with those who endure systematic forms of deprivation.[68] This claim aligns with gawani, which likewise advocates a faith expression rooted in genuine communal sharing and reorients believers toward transforming structures that perpetuate inequality.

Historical Evolution and Core Themes of Minjung Theology

Minjung theology arose in South Korea during the 1970s, a period marked by rapid industrialization and repressive military regimes. Many workers found themselves under harsh labor conditions, with low wages, little job security, and minimal legal protection. As they organized strikes and public demonstrations against these injustices, theologians such as Ahn Byung-Mu and Suh Nam-Dong recognized that the Christian message spoke directly to these events—not merely as an abstract call to charity but as an invitation for believers to stand with the suffering.[69] In this setting, minjung referred to the marginalized populace, systematically denied legal, social, or economic power.

By pairing minjung with biblical motifs, these theologians questioned theological perspectives that seemed detached from local struggles. For instance, Ahn Byung-Mu reexamined the biblical term "ὄχλος" (crowd), discovering parallels with the minjung in Korea who lacked institutional clout.[70] Such readings challenged traditional interpretations that focused on spiritualized dimensions of salvation, urging churches to align their ministries with the oppressed. More explicitly, minjung theology understands Christ's incarnation as a sign that God takes sides with the forgotten of society, weaving spiritual redemption together with liberation from exploitative arrangements. By highlighting this holistic approach, minjung thought fosters an understanding that the faith community cannot be silent in the face of economic or political maltreatment.

---

68. Kim, *Theodizee als Problem*, 152.
69. Kim, *Theodizee als Problem*, 153.
70. Kim, *Theodizee als Problem*, 153.

The Critique of Universalizing Tendencies

One of minjung theology's notable contributions is its critique of "universal" theological claims that often mirror the perspectives of dominant cultural or political groups. Historically, Western mission agencies or local church elites formulated theological statements without involving those most affected by social injustices. Minjung voices call this tendency into question, claiming that theology done from above risks overlooking the lived realities of exploited populations.[71] Instead, minjung theology advances an approach from below, in which grassroots knowledge and experiences inform the reading of Scripture. This reflexive method resonates with gawani's principle that faith must manifest in tangible acts of justice, moving beyond personal piety toward communal responsibility.

Furthermore, minjung theology emphasizes that local contexts—such as the plight of factory workers or rural peasants—are not peripheral to the Christian message but integral to understanding the fullness of salvation. When groups suffer under repressive systems, it is insufficient for believers to offer generic promises of "heavenly reward." Real solidarity means reconfiguring how resources and powers are shared, ensuring that marginalized neighbors are granted an active role in both ecclesial leadership and broader social advocacy. Such steps place minjung theology in alignment with other movements—like liberation theology and certain strands of postcolonial theology—that press for structural reforms, not simply moral or spiritual uplift.

Gawani and the Emphasis on Sharing Resources

Gawani, similarly, challenges affluent believers to relinquish their grip on wealth and status in a manner that visibly benefits those at a disadvantage. Although private generosity is a valuable trait, gawani reminds Christians that addressing systemic injustices demands collective, organized responses. Even if an individual donates half of their possessions, systemic injustice may continue unless institutions, laws, and social customs are recalled serving the common welfare.[72] This perspective echoes minjung theology's conviction that liberation is not a single act, but an ongoing process tied to economic and political engagement.

---

71. Kim, *Theodizee als Problem*, 154.
72. Kim, *Theodizee als Problem*, 153.

For instance, in Korean contexts, minjung-oriented churches have mobilized around fair labor practices—pushing for legislation that protects workers from exploitation. They have facilitated legal aid for those unjustly imprisoned and built educational programs to empower local families. Gawani strengthens this model by underscoring the necessity of communal sharing. Rather than confining charity to acts of individual goodwill, gawani calls believers to pool resources, support cooperatives, and partner with grassroots movements that amplify the voices of those who rarely reach political decision-making arenas.[73] Such practices illustrate how personal transformation merges with structural change, reinforcing the biblical idea that genuine discipleship entails reshaping social conditions for collective flourishing.

People's Movements: Biblical Imagery and Social Transformation

Minjung theology's engagement with biblical stories like the exodus demonstrates the potency of combining scriptural narratives with the lived realities of oppressed groups. In the Exodus account, God's intervention liberates the Israelites from oppressive pharaohic rule; minjung theologians parallel this to modern struggles for freedom from unjust rulers or exploitative economies. Instead of conceiving these biblical episodes solely as ancient history, they interpret them as symbols of God's ongoing commitment to rescue the marginalized in every generation.[74]

Through this lens, people's movements become contemporary enactments of the exodus, with gawani urging participants to see faith not as a private transaction but as a communal phenomenon. Thus, local church leaders who adopt minjung theology often preach messages that underscore solidarity with strikers, protestors, or disenfranchised communities. This reorientation compels believers to view their worship gatherings and theological reflections as incomplete unless they engage the realities of homelessness, wage theft, gender inequity, or militarism. Gawani complements this stance by insisting that wealth and status, where present, be redirected to support those who cannot otherwise secure justice. Shared life is no longer an optional addendum to discipleship; it becomes the essence of what it means to follow Jesus.

---

73. Ucko, *People*, 158.
74. Kim, *Theodizee als Problem*, 154.

A Broader Framework: Postcolonial and Feminist Theologies

The synergy between minjung perspectives and postcolonial theology emerges from their common concern about how imperial or colonizing forces have shaped Christian doctrine. Historically, many regions in Asia, Africa, and Latin America experienced missionary enterprises that carried Western cultural assumptions. Postcolonial theologians such as Kwok Pui-lan contend that these assumptions often silenced local voices, treating them as objects of evangelization rather than valid sources of theological reflection.[75] Minjung theology resonates with such critiques, having itself arisen as a local expression in the face of outside influences—especially North American and European theological models that lacked direct acquaintance with Korean sociopolitical problems.

In a postcolonial framework, the distribution of interpretive authority is a key question. Who decides how to read Scripture, set liturgical practices, or define orthodox belief? Gawani supports a reallocation of this authority by acknowledging that those on the underside of history often uncover biblical meanings overlooked by privileged interpreters. Rather than token inclusion, postcolonial readings demand that local communities generate their own theological discourse, consistent with minjung's argument that theology belongs to the people, not solely to professionals or scholars.[76]

Feminist theology also connects with minjung viewpoints by pointing out that patriarchal structures often amplify economic and political oppression, especially for women. Rosemary Radford Ruether argues that Christian theology must unmask how hierarchical social norms disadvantage women, whether through limited leadership opportunities or systemic underpayment.[77] Within a minjung context, female factory workers sometimes endure dual layers of marginalization: as laborers exploited by corporate owners and as women restricted by cultural stereotypes.

By combining minjung and feminist readings, one sees that addressing oppression demands a full acknowledgment of how power intersects along multiple axes: class, gender, race, and more. Gawani, similarly, calls for an inclusive approach to resource sharing, ensuring women are not mere recipients of aid but coshapers of community priorities. Indeed, if

---

75. Kwok, *Postcolonial Imagination*, 20.
76. Kwok, *Postcolonial Imagination*, 22.
77. Ruether, *Sexism*, 105.

gawani aims to restore collective well-being, it must intentionally confront the ways patriarchy restricts both the moral agency and the material security of women within the church and beyond.[78] Without such deliberate attention, theology risks perpetuating the same domination it seeks to dismantle.

Expanding the Understanding of Eternal Life

Minjung theology redefines salvation by linking it to earthly liberation, contending that authentic discipleship demands engagement with social realities rather than a focus solely on personal afterlife concerns.[79] Gawani extends this discourse by illustrating that eternal life takes shape in communal relationships that embody equity and mutual care. If believers isolate personal salvation from practical involvement in lifting up marginalized neighbors, they hollow out the transformative core of the Christian message.

Thus, an understanding of eternal life shaped by minjung and gawani frameworks goes beyond the promise of heaven to highlight communal regeneration in the present. Churches that embrace this perspective integrate spiritual disciplines (prayer, Bible study, sacraments) with direct engagement in structural change—such as advocating legislation for worker protections or constructing communal funds to provide emergency relief. Seen in this light, "the people of God" ceases to be a static label or privileged in-group; it evolves into a dynamic collective that actively addresses imbalances in power and resources.[80]

Ongoing Tensions and Critiques

Despite these strengths, critiques do arise. Some warn that minjung theology might romanticize the people, overlooking internal divisions—such as ethnic or gender biases—within marginalized communities themselves. Similarly, critics worry that fervor for social activism may overshadow central Christian doctrines like the divinity of Christ or sacramental worship. For minjung theologians, however, these core doctrines gain new relevance when read through the lens of the oppressed.

78. Ruether, *Sexism*, 144.
79. Kim, *Theodizee als Problem*, 153.
80. Ucko, *People*, 162.

Christ's incarnation, for instance, signifies God's alignment with real human suffering, prompting a theological focus on liberation from tangible oppression.[81]

In parallel, certain churches may show reluctance to adopt gawani's radical call for structural redistribution, arguing that their traditions emphasize personal morality over systemic critique. Yet gawani underscores that personal virtue and social transformation operate together. If personal morality does not extend to the reorganization of exploitative systems, it can reinforce complacency. Hence, gawani advocates bridging personal repentance and communal action, reflecting minjung theology's ethos that love for God must encompass love for the socially excluded.[82]

Practical Extensions: Strengthening Global Christian Engagement

Educational Programs and Seminary Curricula

Seminaries can design courses that explore minjung theology and gawani as part of broader contextual theological studies. Encouraging students to conduct field research in underprivileged neighborhoods fosters direct engagement with those who face daily struggles, prompting emergent theologians to integrate biblical study with grassroots observation. Curriculum might also cross-pollinate with postcolonial and feminist discourse, ensuring that future church leaders appreciate the complexity of real-world challenges.

Local Church Solidarity Committees

Building on minjung theology's impetus, congregations might form committees dedicated to connecting with labor unions, supporting political detainees, or working with community organizers. Gawani's contribution lies in prompting these committees to address resource sharing actively. For example, church budgets could allocate a substantial portion to cooperatives that create stable income avenues for unemployed or underpaid workers.

---

81. Kim, *Theodizee als Problem*, 153.
82. Kim, *Theodizee als Problem*, 153.

Inclusive Leadership Models

Gawani's emphasis on collective ownership implies that church leadership structures should represent the diversity of the congregation. Feminist perspectives reinforce this by calling for an end to patriarchal patterns that sideline women's voices. Drawing on minjung theology, committees can prioritize direct participation from those at society's edges, ensuring that the shaping of pastoral priorities arises from a wide spectrum of experiences, not just an elite group.

Dialogue with International Partners

Since many regions share comparable struggles—i.e., colonial legacies, oppressive labor regimes, patriarchal constraints—churches influenced by minjung theology can align with global networks pursuing similar ends. These collaborations might involve shared research projects, cultural exchanges, or cohosted conferences that advance the notion of liberation as a global Christian imperative. Such partnerships confirm that the local focus of minjung does not limit its scope; rather, it offers a template for worldwide ecclesial movements toward justice.

Public Advocacy for Policy Reform

Gawani posits that personal acts of generosity, while commendable, cannot rectify entrenched social problems on their own. Consequently, churches can mobilize around specific policy proposals—like fair wage legislation, protections for migrant laborers, or antidiscrimination statutes—echoing minjung theology's longstanding tradition of confronting repressive authority. Emphasizing that believers have an ethical duty to engage civic processes, these movements ground their activism in biblical convictions about communal well-being.

Reframing the Mission of the Church

When minjung theology, gawani principles, postcolonial analysis, and feminist concerns converge, the church's mission is reimagined as an all-encompassing endeavor that addresses individual hearts and public frameworks. Rather than treating spiritual formation and social change as competing objectives, these theological streams illustrate how they interlock. Salvation is not only about personal repentance or eschatological hope but also about reshaping social structures that have inflicted harm on vast populations.

Minjung theology, in particular, challenges believers to ask "Who benefits from our theological statements, and whose voices are absent?" By placing the experiences of laborers, peasants, and the oppressed at the heart of biblical interpretation, it underscores that the mission of God resonates with concrete struggles for dignity. Gawani affirms this orientation by reminding believers that wealth or social privilege can be redeemed only if it is channeled into processes of restoration for those historically deprived of power.[83] Viewed together, these theologies suggest that eternal life is not an escape from the world but a call to cultivate relationships of shared justice and reconciliation within it.

Conclusion: Toward an Encompassing Vision of Liberation

Minjung theology's local roots in Korea illuminate broader questions about how the gospel speaks to oppressed communities worldwide. Its commitment to reading Scripture from below, articulating the concerns of factory workers, rural farmers, and political prisoners, reveals a dynamic model of contextual theology that resonates with gawani. Both approaches press the church to embody tangible solidarity, renouncing superficial charity in favor of system-level transformation. Alongside postcolonial and feminist theologies, minjung and gawani amplify an inclusive perspective on salvation—one that merges personal faith with public reform.

In practice, this synergy challenges Christian communities to reevaluate their priorities, ensuring that worship services and institutional policies alike serve the cause of liberation. Congregations might foster educational initiatives, sponsor advocacy campaigns, and implement inclusive leadership structures that reflect a truly communal ethic. When theology is anchored in the lived experiences of those historically excluded from power, the message of Christ takes on renewed depth and vigor, showcasing that grace does not stand aloof from the realm of human injustice.

Consequently, a holistic view of salvation emerges—one that is neither merely spiritual nor exclusively political but wholly woven into

---

83. Ruether, *Sexism*, 226.

people's material conditions and shared existence. Such a perspective invites believers to see redemption as a cooperative mission, grounded in collective responsibility and nourished by the biblical witness that God sides with the afflicted. In so doing, minjung theology, gawani, postcolonial, and feminist approaches converge into a rich tapestry of faith dedicated to the well-being of all. Churches that embrace these combined insights stand better equipped to testify credibly about God's liberating love, manifest in both human hearts and transformed social frameworks.

7.5. CASE EXAMPLES AND CONTEMPORARY APPLICATIONS

Extending Gawani Beyond Occasional Giving

Churches informed by gawani theology typically move beyond short-term charity events to cultivate more permanent alliances aimed at alleviating structural inequalities. Instead of hosting infrequent donation drives or limited volunteer programs, these communities seek to reshape how members invest resources, organize their social networks, and formulate public witnesses. The guiding idea is that giving is not merely a momentary gesture of benevolence; it is a lifestyle embedded in ongoing relationships of solidarity.[84] In many settings, these relationships shift the focus from top-down giving to mutual partnerships, emphasizing the cocreation of new systems in which economic and social disparities gradually diminish.

Such practices underscore that Christian discipleship, under a gawani perspective, necessitates sustained economic initiatives. Whether by challenging exploitative labor policies, establishing communal support structures, or engaging debt-relief campaigns globally, these churches redefine the scope of conventional charitable outreach. They challenge members to rethink how personal salvation and communal transformation intersect, contending that spiritual renewal materializes most vividly when believers cooperate in acts of restitution and rebuilding, both locally and internationally.

---

84. Davies, *Urban Food Sharing*, 25. Davies describes how food sharing initiatives transform conventional models of charity into collaborative frameworks that address structural inequalities.

Communal Kitchens and Cooperative Food Sharing

An illustrative example of gawani in action lies in communal kitchens. Unlike sporadic soup kitchens that rely on donor-driven provisioning, gawani-based communal spaces assemble resources from multiple social strata. Wealthier participants contribute land, facilities, or consistent funding, while neighbors who face food insecurity bring specialized cooking skills or volunteer labor.[85] In this arrangement, service ceases to be a one way transaction; it becomes an interdependent partnership. The shared kitchen becomes a living environment where participants collectively manage ingredients, coordinate meal planning, and sometimes even cultivate gardens to supply fresh produce. In the process, typical distinctions between giver and recipient begin to dissolve, replaced by a shared commitment to stability and well-being.

This dynamic resonates with biblical imagery of shared meals. In many gospel narratives, Christ's ministry pivots on the significance of eating together, revealing an ethic that erodes social boundaries. Within gawani theology, communal kitchens serve as modern analogs, illustrating how equitable food sharing can undermine class segregation. Because people from varied backgrounds collaborate daily, they engage one another's stories, forging bonds of empathy that purely episodic charity seldom fosters. The outcome is a network of reciprocal support, lessening isolation and promoting ongoing empowerment.[86]

Cooperative Housing and Integrated Neighborhoods

Alongside communal kitchens, some gawani-oriented congregations develop cooperative housing projects designed to break the cycle of displacement that many low-income families endure. Instead of segregating individuals who have limited financial means into marginal urban zones, a collective fund—often supplemented by church member donations—supports housing complexes where residents comanage facilities. These multipurpose complexes may include shared childcare areas, communal gardens, and mixed-income apartments. Such arrangements exemplify

---

85. Davies, *Urban Food Sharing*, 25. Communal kitchens often involve multidirectional sharing, challenging hierarchical assumptions about who gives and who receives.

86. Bantekas and Lumina, *Sovereign Debt*, 13, illustrates how local programs can intersect with broader debt cancellation movements to reduce systemic burdens on vulnerable nations.

the principle that gawani is not simply about donating money; it reshapes how believers inhabit physical spaces with others.

Participants frequently describe a significant change in perspective after coliving arrangements begin. Individuals used to comfortable housing situations discover the realities of precarious living conditions, seeing firsthand how easily a lost job or sudden medical bill can push families toward eviction. Meanwhile, those who formerly experienced housing instability gain a stronger sense of agency by serving as co-owners or comanagers of their living environment.[87] This balanced synergy deepens the theological premise that generosity flows in multiple directions, challenging the belief that the poor are always the beneficiaries. As a result, everyone involved experiences a shift in identity: from being passive churchgoers to active collaborators in creating forms of community that reflect shared responsibility.

Advocacy for Global Debt Relief

While local programs address neighborhood-level economic struggles, gawani-minded churches also engage in national and international issues, notably the movement to reduce or cancel burdensome foreign debts faced by economically disadvantaged nations. Over decades, movements such as Jubilee 2000 and subsequent debt cancellation campaigns have underscored that crippling debt obligations can perpetuate underdevelopment by siphoning resources away from vital sectors like healthcare, education, or infrastructure.[88] Congregations inspired by gawani regard this problem not as a distant geopolitical concern but as an extension of biblical calls for debt remission (e.g., Lev 25, Deut 15). In their view, societies that claim to follow Christ's teachings must practice systemic forgiveness of debt when it suppresses life and well-being.

Practical involvement may include petitioning global financial bodies like the International Monetary Fund or the World Bank to reevaluate interest rates and repayment schedules. Some congregations host educational events explaining why certain nations struggle with inherited debt from past regimes, or how punitive interest compounds over time.

---

87. Gutiérrez, *Theology of Liberation*, 20, argues that preferential care for the poor should shape church priorities, calling for practical demonstrations of solidarity.

88. Kröger, *Die Befreiung des Minjung*, 50; cf. Gutiérrez, *Theology of Liberation*, xlii, 90, 139. Both underline that genuine solidarity with the poor must include systemic remission of debts that "suffocate life."

By highlighting these realities, church members become aware that their own economic stability is sometimes tied to exploitative financial arrangements abroad.[89] Gawani theology thus transforms moral conviction into political activism, urging believers to adopt an expansive outlook on neighborly obligation. Rather than limiting neighborly love to personal acquaintances or local communities, they extend it to entire regions that suffer from institutionalized injustice.

Gutiérrez's Perspective on Preferential Commitment

Gustavo Gutiérrez famously argues that the church's identity includes prioritizing the welfare of those caught in oppressive social conditions.[90] Gawani theology intensifies this stance by demonstrating how local philanthropy and global advocacy form a coherent witness of faith. If liberation theology challenges believers to address the root causes of poverty, gawani adds an operational mechanism for sustained resource sharing and restructured relationships. Instead of seeing preferential concern for the poor as an abstract principle, these communities embed it in tangible ventures: fair hiring practices, equitable housing, and macrolevel economic reforms.

Moreover, gawani theology bolsters Gutiérrez's argument that Christians do not merely help the marginalized but encounter them in ways that transform all parties. This convergence resonates with the Zacchaeus story, where economic restitution simultaneously leads to spiritual awakening. Believers in affluent contexts engage not just in paternalistic giving but in reciprocal encounters that break down stereotypes and realizing priorities. Gawani prompts a mutual journey of renewal, hinting that the greatest spiritual growth often transpires among those who dismantle unjust arrangements on behalf of others and, in the process, discover liberation from their own attachments to privilege.

---

89. Luke 19:6 notes Zacchaeus's joy upon welcoming Jesus, implying that material generosity deepens relational restoration and personal freedom.

90. Cone, *Black Theology*, 29, emphasizes that love must be expressed through contesting structural injustice, not merely through empathetic feelings.

Spiritual Growth and Psychological Release

Another dimension of gawani practice revolves around the inner or psychological liberation that emerges when believers relinquish protective attitudes toward wealth or status. Congregations that devote extended resources to communal programs frequently discover heightened solidarity within their fellowship and an increased sense of ethical clarity.[91] Because individuals are no longer divided by economic stratification, they experience more trusting relationships, lowering anxieties that often stem from materialistic pressures or consumerist norms.

This process aligns with Luke's account of Zacchaeus in 19:1–10, where the tax collector finds joy after voluntarily giving half his possessions to those in need. His transformation is not just a moral realignment but a social reconciliation, altering how he interacts with neighbors who once despised him. In a similar vein, gawani-minded church members testify that sharing assets in a structured, sustained manner fosters emotional release from the burdens of competition and isolation.[92] They gain new friendships with people from different class backgrounds and collectively affirm the scriptural principle that genuine community life thrives on generosity rather than hoarding. The outcome, as depicted in Luke 19:6, is genuine gladness and renewed belonging.

Deepening the Zacchaeus Paradigm

The Zacchaeus narrative spotlights how restitution reshapes personal identity and community ties. Traditionally ostracized, Zacchaeus had functioned within exploitative tax-collection systems. However, once he encounters Jesus, he not only abandons that system but also reconfigures the social bond between himself and those he defrauded. Gawani theology sees this realignment as a blueprint for contemporary believers, suggesting that faithful commitment requires rectifying exploitative structures at personal, local, and public levels. In other words, a

---

91. Friesen, *Imperial Cults*, 190, demonstrates how scriptural themes of liberation encourage faithful communities to challenge sociopolitical dominance in all its forms.

92. Bantekas and Lumina, *Sovereign Debt*, 13, reflects the rationale behind linking local activism with larger-scale economic reforms, showing that global financial systems often perpetuate local poverty.

Zacchaeus-like gesture is not confined to giving partial wealth away; it entails forging fresh alliances rooted in justice.[93]

Modern analogs can be found in churches that actively challenge predatory lending practices in their cities. Instead of limiting themselves to private charity for individuals caught in debt cycles, these communities pressure local councils to enact fair lending regulations. They may host legal clinics offering free consultations or set up microfinance initiatives that serve as an alternative to high interest payday lenders. These systemic interventions mirror Zacchaeus's restoration pledge by addressing the root processes that generate economic oppression. Through each step, the mission of the church transcends a mere spiritual message and becomes intertwined with tangible structural reform.

Love and Justice in the Public Sphere

James Cone contends that any theology grounded in love must confront underlying social oppression, including racism, sexism, and class-based discrimination.[94] Gawani theology echoes this conviction by highlighting that sincere love requires persistent, visible engagement with local and global injustices. Congregations functioning under this paradigm collaborate with labor unions, push for living wage laws, advocate for comprehensive healthcare, and endorse political measures aimed at rectifying systemic imbalances. The impetus is to move beyond rhetorical claims of care toward pragmatic interventions that shape social systems.

What distinguishes gawani from many standard social gospel approaches is the insistence that giving is not an optional add-on to faith. Rather, it is an intrinsic aspect of discipleship that weaves together devotion and public activism. Prayer, scripture reading, and worship rituals do not stand apart from policy discussions or economic campaigns; they nurture the moral vision and relational capacity that fuel committed engagement. Thus, churches that practice gawani do not treat activism as a mere sideline. They integrate it into congregational life, encouraging every member to consider how their personal professions, civic roles, and investments could be harnessed for the broader welfare. The interplay of

---

93. Davies, *Urban Food Sharing*, 25, discusses shared land, cooking space, and skill exchanges that promote community cohesion.

94. Cone, *God of the Oppressed*, 29. Cone argues there that authentic love necessarily expresses itself in active resistance to racism, sexism, and class oppression.

love and justice becomes a hallmark of kingdom ethics, manifested in both spiritual and material realms.

The Expanded Definition of Eternal Life

Luke 19 and Mark 10 indicate that when Jesus speaks of eternal life, he often links it to ethical realignments such as wealth reallocation and neighborly solidarity. This synergy resonates with gawani theology, which views "salvation" as a comprehensive term encompassing spiritual renewal, relational healing, and social equity. By establishing cooperatives, canceling oppressive debts, or redistributing land and housing, believers actualize a foretaste of the kingdom in which abundance is shared. Salvation, therefore, is not restricted to personal piety or a distant eschatological promise; it emerges in the community's capacity to treat all neighbors with dignity and fairness.

From a gawani perspective, personal conversion is incomplete if it fails to address the structures that keep many in poverty. When individuals donate a portion of their income or time to communal kitchens but neglect, for example, the unjust wage policies in their own companies, they risk upholding the very disparities they claim to remedy. The unwavering commitment to bridging love and justice transforms gawani from an inspirational idea into a theological posture demanding consistent social action. In that sense, the measure of a gawani community's faith is witnessed in how effectively it reshapes daily life—both private and public—to reflect the upside-down kingdom ethic heralded by Jesus.

Sustaining Partnerships Amid Obstacles

Churches aiming to sustain gawani practices inevitably encounter obstacles. Some members worry that structural engagement diverts attention from prayer and worship. Others fear potential conflicts with local authorities or business interests when championing fair wages or debt relief. Financial constraints also pose challenges, as sustained communal programs require ongoing contributions, volunteer support, and professional expertise. Congregations might initially rally around a shared vision, only to find enthusiasm waning when faced with complex legal hurdles or the slow pace of policy reform.

Nevertheless, gawani theology posits that these struggles can deepen faith precisely because they compel the church to rely on collective discernment, resource pooling, and solidarity building with broader civic organizations. For instance, a congregation that faces resistance while advocating rent control may forge stronger partnerships with neighborhood coalitions, discovering that their witness becomes more impactful through collaboration rather than operating in isolation. Pastoral leaders often encourage members to view setbacks not as signs of defeat but as invitations to sharpen their understanding of communal discipleship. Over time, repeated involvement in such efforts can foster robust networks of trust spanning religious and secular divides.

Overcoming Skepticism and Nurturing Hope

Critics sometimes argue that local faith communities lack the requisite expertise or legislative influence to shape large-scale socioeconomic issues. Gawani theology, however, frames such critiques as reminders that the church must continuously learn, train leaders, and expand its alliances. Though congregations might not solve every structural problem alone, they can meaningfully contribute by raising moral awareness, exemplifying alternative economic models, and building momentum for broader reforms. This incremental approach recalls biblical themes of a small seed growing into a sizable tree, suggesting that minor acts of faithful partnership can yield significant outcomes over time.

Hope emerges as a guiding force: believers trust that even modest but consistent efforts—like hosting communal meals, endorsing living-wage campaigns, or dialoguing with global debt networks—reflect the transformative love at the heart of the gospel. Gawani communities often rely on liturgical elements (prayer services, communal blessings, testimonies of shared breakthroughs) to sustain morale. In these gatherings, participants reaffirm that their struggle is not merely a political or economic endeavor but an embodiment of divine compassion seeking to heal fractured relationships. This perspective helps them face practical hurdles without relinquishing the broader vision of a more equitable, grace-filled society.

Conclusion: Gawani as Holistic Transformation

In sum, gawani theology illustrates how Christians can integrate faith and social action through deliberate, enduring commitments to sharing wealth and power. Case studies range from communal kitchens and cooperative housing to global alliances for debt cancellation, showing that gawani is neither confined to local charity nor restricted to policy activism. It encompasses both, insisting that personal generosity complements structural reforms. By embracing biblical images of Zacchaeus's joyful restitution, worshipers discover that genuine discipleship emerges where moral conviction meets institutional advocacy, forging new avenues of justice.

Equally, gawani fosters relational bonds that transcend class distinctions and produce inward liberation for those who previously clung to material privileges. Through sustained collaborations with secular nonprofits, labor organizations, and international campaign networks, congregations expand their witness beyond Sunday services. Indeed, love and justice converge in tangible acts of transformation, testifying to the integrated nature of salvation advanced by gawani. Far from a marginal emphasis, it recovers the biblical tradition that anchors worship in daily practice, culminating in a communal vision of eternal life characterized by fairness, compassion, and shared well-being.

7.6. SUMMARY AND FORWARD-LOOKING REFLECTIONS

This concluding section illustrates the chapter's central argument that an authentic Christian community requires more than private religiosity; it must manifest in real-world economic and social engagements. By contrasting the wealthy official's reluctance (Luke 18:18–30) with Zacchaeus's readiness (Luke 19:1–10), the chapter underscores that discipleship involves reorganizing resources for the well-being of others. This reinterpretation of familiar narratives signals a broader call to integrate faith commitments with structural change, bridging moral conviction and everyday practice.

A prominent topic in this conclusion is that personal transformation alone cannot address systemic barriers. Zacchaeus's repentance goes beyond an internal turnaround; his dedication to repaying and distributing wealth has communal implications. Such a model of restitution compels believers to contemplate how faith-driven ethics might shape housing, labor policies, education funding, and other spheres where resources are determined. The wealthy official's unwillingness to "sell all" (Luke 18:22) offers a telling contrast, reminding readers that the most devout individuals can still resist altering power arrangements that advantage them.

Another point of emphasis is the role of gawani theology, which interprets giving as an expansive, continuous practice rather than an occasional act of charity. Building on the Greek concept of "didōmi," Kang portrays generosity as a process that unravels exploitative norms and nurtures alternative bonds in society. This theology posits that if Zacchaeus's transformation is viewed only as private moral renewal, then the greater social ramifications may be overlooked. Gawani thus preserves the link between personal faith and community welfare by urging a constant willingness to cross economic and social boundaries.

Minjung theology likewise contributes a perspective that situates Christian responsibility within the struggles of those who are marginalized. Since it arose in South Korea during periods of industrial strife and dictatorship, its call for structural advocacy complements Zacchaeus's willingness to address the harms he caused. Minjung theologians argue that the church should not remain a bystander when workers, farmers, or minority groups endure oppression. Instead, these theologians claim that each congregation's mission demands tangible solidarity with disenfranchised neighbors—an outlook echoed in the Zacchaeus story, where restitution merges with renewed fellowship.

A third thread connects these frameworks to liberationist conversations around the world, including those by Gustavo Gutiérrez, James Cone, and others who emphasize that Christian salvation involves relief from political, economic, or racial forms of subjugation. Cone's critique of white churches' complacency in the face of racial injustice, for example, parallels Luke's critique of wealth-based privilege: believers cannot assume that superficial acts of charity will undo systemic sin. Instead, a reorganization of resources—like Zacchaeus's fourfold repayment—becomes essential to bridging divisions that privilege certain groups while excluding others.

The theme of restitution recurs as a practical expression of turning away from oppressive structures. While many theological approaches stress repentance, this chapter insists that repentance includes addressing material or relational injustices. Zacchaeus's example informs contemporary scenarios in which individuals, institutions, or churches acknowledge historical or present injustices—such as exploitative labor practices or discriminatory lending—and work to rectify them through structured compensation or policy reform. These acts of restitution anchor spiritual devotion in verifiable community outcomes, highlighting that salvation fosters new social ties.

Another theme involves the church's capacity to develop communal systems as alternatives to inequitable models. Cooperative housing initiatives, communal kitchens, and microfinance ventures illustrate ways that faith communities can emulate Zacchaeus's reorientation at an institutional level. Rather than relying solely on state apparatus or market-driven solutions, local congregations can pool resources and expertise, thereby modeling relationships founded on mutual care. This resonates with the Acts vision (2:44–45) of believers sharing all things, reinforcing the biblical aim of forging unity across class divides.

The chapter also underscores the importance of forging partnerships between churches and civic organizations. Gawani theology advocates direct involvement in policy discussions, labor movements, and anti-poverty campaigns. Likewise, minjung theology encourages congregations to stand with workers and citizens who struggle against authoritarian structures. In many contexts, these alliances challenge the church to adopt a more public role, pursuing laws or regulations that protect vulnerable populations. Through such actions, faith-based communities transition from offering isolated acts of charity to pursuing systemic reforms that echo Zacchaeus's bold realignment.

The interplay between personal sacrifice and broader social transformation forms a repeated focal point. Zacchaeus and the wealthy official represent two divergent paths: one that clings to status, and another that invests in reconciliation. Contemporary believers, likewise, face a choice: either cling to advantages conferred by class or racial privilege, or distribute assets in ways that ensure communal fairness. By demonstrating how such redistributions can inspire lasting change, the chapter warns against superficial self-righteousness while endorsing a discipleship that uproots destructive systems.

A related area is the chapter's discussion of wealth's seductive power. The wealthy official initially appears faithful but departs sorrowful, unable to break from comfort. This outcome warns that sincere religious devotion may stall when confronted by Jesus's instruction to let go of possessions. In parallel, many contemporary Christians avoid confronting systemic inequities if it requires renouncing certain economic benefits.

This cautionary tale invites ongoing self-assessment within congregations that enjoy economic security, calling them to reevaluate the line between personal piety and shared responsibility.

Kang's interpretation of gawani also reframes the notion of communal care by emphasizing the psychological and spiritual liberation that can occur when economic hoarding diminishes. Just as Zacchaeus experiences joy (Luke 19:6), local churches may find stronger unity and lowered anxiety when they shift from insular habits to collective generosity. This dimension underscores that liberating others from oppressive conditions can also free wealthier believers from isolation and fear. Thus, gawani emerges as a reciprocal process, in which everyone gains when generosity becomes an intentional lifestyle.

Another branch of reflection underscores the potential tensions that arise when faith groups openly challenge entrenched power structures. Some church members fear that activism distracts from worship or evangelism. However, the chapter cites biblical passages indicating that worship stands incomplete if it ignores the material needs of neighbors. Zacchaeus's conversion story ends with Jesus declaring that "salvation has come to this house" (Luke 19:6), linking spiritual affirmation with the decision to redistribute wealth. Contemporary applications similarly blend prayer, teaching, and public engagement, bridging sacred rituals and daily justice.

Feminist and postcolonial approaches also enrich this conclusion by highlighting how broader injustices—patriarchy, racial discrimination, and economic imperialism—intersect. Following minjung theology, these perspectives affirm that no theological reflection is neutral, and that ignoring certain voices can perpetuate marginalization. The Zacchaeus narrative underscores the potential for transformation across social boundaries, a motif that resonates with calls to dismantle not just class privileges but also gender and racial hierarchies that structure the global church.

A further point explores the notion of eternal life as relational and collective, rather than solely an individual afterlife promise. In Luke 18 and 19, the kingdom ethic emerged in communal reciprocity and inclusive fellowship. Gawani theology clarifies that salvation happens when believers reorganize their economic interactions, not just their internal beliefs. This approach encourages readers to reinterpret eternal life as an ongoing quality of relationship sustained by fairness, love, and

EMBODYING GOD'S KINGDOM THROUGH SOLIDARITY   149

cooperative arrangements. The church thus becomes a living arena where God's reign is partially demonstrated here and now.

To reinforce these arguments, the chapter references multiple historical and contemporary examples—from the progressive reforms initiated by certain Korean congregations influenced by minjung theology to church alliances with debt relief coalitions in various parts of the world. These cases spotlight how theological convictions, when paired with consistent organizing, can challenge oppressive tax codes, land ownership norms, and exploitative labor practices. By echoing Zacchaeus's stance, these congregations reaffirm that systematic injustice need not remain unchallenged.

Another angle addressed is the formation of ecclesial identities that welcome relationships across classes rather than isolating affluent members from poorer neighbors. When believers codevelop solutions—such as shared meal programs or supportive housing—those with abundant resources and those in need become partners rather than benefactors and beneficiaries. Gawani insists that this partnership approach fosters more dignifying connections, mirroring the shift in Zacchaeus's life from unscrupulous tax collector to an agent of reconciliation within his own city.

The notion of continuous moral reflection emerges as well. While some may attempt a single philanthropic gesture, the Zacchaeus story models a far-reaching shift in how resources are acquired and allocated. This impetus for ongoing ethical review suggests that churches should periodically evaluate their financial priorities, facility usage, and philanthropic strategies. The chapter encourages communities to ask whether they inadvertently benefit from oppressive systems—such as reliance on low wage labor or ignoring local housing crises—rather than simply relying on personal acts of kindness.

A significant portion of the conclusion also deals with the pastoral dimension. In counseling and preaching, ministers can highlight Zacchaeus's story as an example of how spiritual freedom often involves letting go of deeply ingrained attachments to material wealth. Drawing on gawani, pastors might urge congregants to see radical giving as a path toward discovering new communal bonds and an enriched sense of purpose. By incorporating Luke's emphasis on restitution, pastors can guide individuals to find ways of offering both apology and tangible compensation to those they have harmed.

The chapter proposes that the church's mission calls for an explicit willingness to cross the threshold into difficult public issues like corporate greed, predatory lending, or environmental exploitation. Whereas some might prefer a purely spiritual emphasis, the Zacchaeus narrative reveals that kingdom values must challenge any realm of injustice. The gawani perspective affirms that such challenges, though controversial, align with the biblical witness of Jesus turning over tables in the temple, a demonstration that worship and justice cannot be neatly separated.

Another section explains that theological education plays a pivotal role in disseminating this integrated approach. Seminaries and training programs can adopt courses that combine scriptural exegesis with sociological awareness. By inviting future church leaders to reflect on Luke 19 alongside contemporary socioeconomic data, theological institutions can prepare graduates to interpret biblical mandates in light of urgent social questions. Embedding gawani and minjung angles in the curriculum ensures that future congregational leaders grasp how divine grace relates to reimagined economic life.

The possibility of interfaith collaboration emerges as a subsequent theme. While Zacchaeus's example is distinctively rooted in Christian thought, the principle of rectifying economic exploitation may resonate with Jewish, Muslim, Buddhist, or secular organizations as well. The chapter notes that forging coalitions with groups that share common goals can amplify the church's capacity to address injustice. Gawani's emphasis on boundary-crossing generosity provides a basis for working across religious lines without sacrificing core gospel commitments.

An additional reflection highlights the emotional impact of these initiatives. Zacchaeus's joy (Luke 19:6) exemplifies the release from shame and isolation. In modern contexts, believers often speak of relief from guilt and renewed hope when they engage in philanthropic or systemic efforts that rectify historical damage—such as paying reparations to communities previously harmed by discriminatory practices. This emotional dimension reminds us that financial and structural changes frequently lead to healing of relationships, which extends beyond mere financial transactions.

The discussion also addresses how personal faith journeys can be enriched by communal accountability. Zacchaeus presumably did not keep his pledge hidden; his vow to repay fourfold was publicly known (Luke 19:8). Similarly, gawani theology suggests that congregations might hold members accountable for ethical business operations, fair wages, and nonexploitative investment strategies. This accountability fosters an environment where the church embodies Jesus's ethic rather than treating it as an unattainable ideal.

The analysis of entering the kingdom in Luke 18 and 19 is relevant here. The official's sorrow at not relinquishing wealth, contrasted with Zacchaeus's reception of salvation, clarifies that the kingdom entails material consequences. The chapter underscores that Jesus's repeated statements about wealth and the poor are not rhetorical flourishes but urgent imperatives to rectify economic imbalances. Gawani theology interprets these imperatives as community guidelines—reminders that possessions are entrusted to believers for just stewardship rather than personal indulgence.

Another underlying question is how to sustain these commitments over time. The conclusion indicates that many faith-based movements start strong but can lose momentum. Gawani advocates a long-term perspective, integrating policy advocacy, continuous education, and shared practices in weekly life, so that efforts do not remain transient. By referencing examples of successful cooperatives or campaigns that endured for decades, the chapter underlines the feasibility of sustained generosity, provided believers commit to consistent action.

The theme of unlearning oppressive habits also arises. If Zacchaeus's career in tax collection taught him to exploit his own people, his transformation involved unlearning that pattern. Congregations that benefit from exploitative supply chains or real estate speculation might require a similar process of unlearning. The practical steps can include shifting procurement policies, facilitating ethical investment funds, or forming alliances with fair-trade organizations to ensure that daily church activities no longer reinforce systemic injustice.

The chapter offers a reminder of how local context shapes the ways these biblical lessons are applied. Minjung theology in South Korea emerged under militarized conditions, and gawani-inspired projects may adapt to contexts shaped by different political or cultural pressures. Nonetheless, the essence is consistent: local communities interpret the call to reconfigure economic relationships, taking into account their unique challenges. Such contextual adaptation demonstrates the elasticity of Luke's message, bridging first-century Jericho and modern societies around the globe.

Some might argue that these practices are overly idealistic. However, the discussion notes that Luke's Gospel itself extends a bold vision, urging the rich to lay aside their advantages (Luke 18:22). Scholars like

Ahn Byung-Mu, James Cone, and Rosemary Radford Ruether have similarly maintained that radical generosity is not optional but integral to the gospel's social dimension. The chapter defends the practicality of such teachings by citing case studies in which local churches successfully collaborated to enact relevant reforms.

The final paragraphs reiterate that worship, when disconnected from social responsibility, risks hollowing out the gospel's transformative core. Zacchaeus's joyful acceptance serves as a concluding narrative portrait, indicating that heartfelt devotion converges with decisive action. In the same way, modern faith communities that heed gawani and minjung calls for restitution embody the biblical pattern: their prayers and hymns resonate more fully when accompanied by a shared ethic of accountability and compassion. This synergy releases new capacities for healing fractured societies.

In summary, this chapter's overarching conclusion is that the path modeled by Zacchaeus—namely, the willingness to reallocate personal wealth for communal flourishing—provides a rich paradigm for interpreting and practicing discipleship. Gawani theology, minjung theology, and various liberationist approaches converge on the belief that genuine salvation touches social and economic realities. By dismantling harmful structures, fostering networks of equal partnership, and ensuring that spiritual renewal includes restitution, the church enacts Luke's vision of a kingdom that honors every neighbor's dignity. It is in this expansive framework, simultaneously spiritual and material, that Christian communities can bear a faithful witness to the Messiah who declared salvation for even the most marginalized members of society.

8.

Toward a Gawani-Feminist-Black Liberation Ethos

Reimagining Community and Resource Sharing

Communities grounded in early Christian traditions have long sought to embody economic sharing, gender justice, and racial equity. This pursuit, however, has not always been integrated, resulting in fragmented efforts that address one form of oppression without examining others. Recent discussions suggest that a holistic approach emerges when gawani theology, feminist critiques, and Black liberation priorities come together, challenging ecclesial practices that ignore how economic, racial, and gender-based injustices overlap.

One central theme is the value of shared responsibility. While many churches affirm principles of giving, gawani theology points to more structured collaboration in resource allocation. Feminist theology draws attention to how these economic practices either overlook or empower women, highlighting that any community project must address caregiving work and inclusive leadership. Black liberation movements link property ownership, wages, and financial transparency to ongoing struggles against systemic racism. Their combined voices urge congregations to reevaluate whether existing budgets, pastoral roles, and neighborhood partnerships function in ways that bring tangible support to marginalized neighbors.

A second theme is the reenvisioning of ecclesial authority. Traditional hierarchies often concentrate power in the hands of a few, leaving women, people of color, and economically vulnerable individuals on the periphery. Gawani theology, referencing early Christian models, promotes shared oversight of finances and leadership roles. Feminist theology underlines the urgency of dismantling paternal patterns in decision making, while Black liberation thought stresses that concentrating leadership in privileged circles neglects systemic racism. This joint emphasis urges churches to adopt governance structures that incorporate a range of voices from the very outset.

A third area involves examining how faith communities engage their surrounding culture. Local congregations commonly operate within systems shaped by capitalist norms, patriarchal assumptions, and racial biases. Gawani approaches call on churches to invest in cooperatives, transparent budgeting, or communal housing projects, but feminist and Black liberation voices remind us that without attention to who benefits—and who remains excluded—these initiatives risk reinforcing existing inequalities. Broad-based coalitions, partnering with grassroots movements and advocacy groups, provide a channel for churches to address issues like living wages and fair housing in a systematic way.

A fourth theme explores the role of worship and language in shaping priorities. Feminist theology highlights how naming God exclusively in male terms can reinforce the same authority patterns congregations seek to undo. Churches adopting gawani ideals can integrate inclusive language, ensuring that both resource sharing and spiritual language align with communal values. Black liberation perspectives further push worship contexts to include the realities of race-based oppression, linking liturgical practices to social resistance.

A fifth consideration centers on how practical engagement with real-world challenges can unite gawani, feminist, and Black liberation frameworks. Congregations that transform budget committees into spaces of shared discernment often see new opportunities for outreach. They can develop mutual aid funds, childcare cooperatives, and advocacy platforms that specifically include women and racial minorities in both planning and execution. Such direct collaborations prevent a narrow focus on one demographic or on purely symbolic statements of equality.

A sixth point addresses the tension between broad commitments and localized realities. Gawani theology references Acts 2 and 4 as guiding texts, but urban congregations in rapidly gentrifying neighborhoods or rural communities lacking economic infrastructure encounter unique problems. Black liberation scholars note that historical legacies of segregation persist even in seemingly post-racial contexts, while feminist leaders emphasize how class and cultural factors compound barriers for women. These varied concerns underscore the need for adaptable models that anchor resource sharing in the particulars of each community.

Finally, a seventh theme highlights the creative possibilities that arise when churches intentionally combine elements of gawani, feminist, and Black liberation thought. Instead of operating in silos, congregations can revisit Scripture, reframe leadership roles, and set shared priorities for budget allocations and local partnerships. These changes involve ongoing self-examination, where believers acknowledge that neither spiritual growth nor social justice stands in isolation. In doing so, a more integrated ethos emerges—one that not only counters economic disparities but also addresses racial bias and patriarchy through concrete, communal practices.

8.1. THE DELAY OF THE PAROUSIA AND THE EMERGENCE OF THE GAWANI ETHOS

In the earliest stages of the Christian movement, there was a widely held assumption that Jesus's return would occur within a short historical window. This belief drove many initial practices, including communal sharing of possessions, a high level of mutual accountability, and a pronounced sense of urgency in evangelistic missions. Over time, however, as the anticipated consummation did not take place in the immediate manner early believers had expected, theological questions arose regarding how the church should conduct its life, distribute its resources, and maintain hope. The tension between an imminent parousia and ongoing historical developments became especially visible in the writings attributed to Luke—namely the Gospel of Luke and the Acts of the Apostles.

These texts offer a distinctive vision for how the Christian community might negotiate the passage of time without losing sight of eschatological conviction. Instead of succumbing to apathy or disillusion, the Lukan narrative highlights practices that channel an eschatological outlook into the material realities of daily life. Out of this framework emerges what contemporary interpreters have termed the gawani ethos, encompassing a set of values and behaviors oriented toward fellowship, stewardship of resources, and the cultivation of inclusive relationships. By probing the delayed parousia through the lens of Luke-Acts, one encounters an insistence that the final chapters of salvation history are still in progress, even as the church continues to operate in a world not yet fully reconciled to God's reign.

The following pages explore, at expanded length, how these convictions shaped Christian communities both in antiquity and in later periods, touching on themes of economic justice, communal life, and theological reflection that persist into modern contexts. Particularly notable are the ways Luke reframes eschatological hope so that, rather than diminishing activism, the delay serves as a catalyst for ethical engagement and relational depth within the church. This perspective resonates through subsequent monastic movements, liberation theologies, and postcolonial readings that seek to integrate spiritual aspiration with tangible social change.

8.1.1. Eschatological Expectations in Early Christian Thought

Immediate Anticipation and Its Communal Consequences

During the first generation following Jesus's earthly ministry, many believers assumed they stood on the brink of an imminent cosmic event: the parousia of Christ.[1] Early kerygmatic preaching underscored urgency, as seen in passages like Acts 2:14–36, where repentance and baptism were portrayed not just as ethical choices but as a preparation for the swift arrival of God's reign. This posture informed communal structures, pushing individuals to relinquish personal comforts in favor of collective well-being. The letters attributed to Paul, such as 1 Thessalonians, reinforced this message, expressing that believers should remain watchful because the day of the Lord would come unexpectedly.

Yet as time lapsed, communities began to grapple with a paradox: they had oriented much of their communal and spiritual energy around the belief that God's final intervention was near, but that definitive moment was not unfolding in the manner initially anticipated.[2] While some

---

1. Moltmann, *Theology of Hope*, 27. Moltmann underscores how the early church's horizon was dominated by an expectation of imminent consummation, influencing its ethical and communal expressions.

2. Moltmann, *Theology of Hope*, 31. This portion addresses the growing awareness that historical progression was outstripping immediate prophetic hopes, prompting

Christians remained steadfast in their convictions, others feared that the community's foundational hope had been misplaced. This concern led to new exegetical endeavors and pastoral strategies, including a reevaluation of what it meant for the church to be the eschatological people of God.

Reassessing the Delay of the Parousia

Over time, leading figures in the church offered interpretations that reframed the delay as part of God's redemptive program.[3] Texts like 2 Pet 3:8–9 spoke of divine patience, suggesting that what appeared to be a postponement was, in fact, an expression of mercy, giving humanity a broader opportunity for repentance. Such an approach signaled a shift from urgent expectation to faithful perseverance, holding that the end was certain but not strictly predictable according to human timetables.

Luke's writings, though not always explicitly addressing the question of eschatological postponement, consistently interweave a motif of sustained communal life marked by hospitality, sharing, and sensitivity to marginalized persons. This narrative strategy points to the idea that living in the in-between time—after Jesus's resurrection but before his return—need not undermine fervor or resolution. On the contrary, it creates a context for believers to develop practices that demonstrate the kingdom's character, even if historical consummation remains open-ended.

8.1.2. Luke's Historiographical Approach and Theological Agenda

Investigative Method and Narrative Construction

Luke's prologue (Luke 1:1–4) underscores the author's effort to compile an "orderly account," suggesting a particular sensitivity to historical veracity and coherence.[4] By pairing the Gospel of Luke with the Acts of the Apostles, the author sets forth a two-volume narrative that moves from the story of Jesus to the unfolding witness of the early church. This

---

revised theological frameworks.

3. Moltmann, *Theology of Hope*, 227. Here, Moltmann considers how leaders of the nascent church reinterpreted the delay as part of a divine timeline, preserving communal dynamism.

4. Wright et al., *Surprised by Hope*, 40. This text clarifies Luke's meticulous approach to his sources, noting that historical investigation grounds the theological message in concrete realities.

approach situates Christian origins within a continuity that implies ongoing divine activity, extending beyond the time frame many might have initially assumed for the eschatological climax.

In effect, Luke crafts a narrative arc that underscores divine faithfulness across historical moments. The method does not treat eschatological hope as an isolated phenomenon; instead, the presence of the Spirit and the formation of Christian community serve as signs that God's salvific plan remains operative.[5] Luke's editorial choices—particularly the emphasis on shared life, the spread of the gospel to various cultural groups, and repeated references to communal solidarity—signal that even though the final consummation is delayed, the church is to persist in manifesting kingdom realities in every generation.

Reinterpreting Fulfillment through Praxis

A distinguishing mark of the Lukan perspective is the emphasis on how God's promises are partially realized in the active faith of believers. For instance, Jesus's reading of Isaiah in Luke 4 recontextualizes prophetic themes of liberation by insisting that they are "fulfilled in your hearing." (v. 21). This wording highlights that divine fulfillment is not exclusively reserved for a terminal moment of cosmic upheaval; it also surfaces in the ongoing embodiment of justice and mercy among God's people.[6]

By extension, Acts carries this logic forward, illustrating how the earliest believers, led by the Spirit, structure their shared life in a way that addresses economic and social inequalities (Acts 2:44–45; 4:32–35). In Luke's scheme, the "delay" of Jesus's return becomes less a source of doctrinal crisis and more an occasion for the community to live faithfully in the present.[7] Each narrative segment—whether focusing on table fellowship, communal prayer, or practical service—reinforces the notion that divine fulfillment can be tasted in real communal experiences, even while the ultimate promise remains pending.

---

5. Wright et al., *Surprised by Hope*, 47, points out how Luke's depiction of ongoing divine activity encourages readers to see eschatological hope as intertwined with practical discipleship.

6. Trible, *Rhetoric of Sexuality*, 22. Trible examines Luke 4:16–20, emphasizing how Jesus's appropriation of Isa 61 situates liberation as an active, present concern.

7. Cone, *Spirituals*, 36. Cone contends that the reality of waiting did not nullify the impetus for transformation, drawing analogies with African American spiritual traditions.

TOWARD A GAWANI-FEMINIST-BLACK LIBERATION ETHOS 159

8.1.3. The Nazareth Manifesto and Its Implications

Reading Isaiah in the Synagogue (Luke 4:16–20)

Luke 4:16–20 stands out as a pivotal scene in which Jesus identifies himself with the anointed figure described in Isa 61:1–2.[8] The text emphasizes release for captives, sight for the blind, and liberation for the oppressed, situating Jesus's ministry within a tradition of prophetic advocacy. Scholars often refer to this moment as the "Nazareth Manifesto," because it frames Jesus's mission in social and economic terms, not simply spiritual or apocalyptic ones.

Of relevance to the delayed parousia is how Luke highlights that these promises of release and liberation are recognized as present realities. This orientation challenges any inclination to treat salvation purely as a future event, insisting instead that the earliest disciples saw a foretaste of God's reign in the immediate reordering of social and economic relationships. The same impetus, recast in Acts, underpins how the postresurrection community continues Jesus's liberative agenda even when the eschatological horizon remains unconsummated.

Socioeconomic Transformations Considering Delay

As the church absorbed the message of the Nazareth Manifesto, it encountered multiple contexts—urban centers, rural landscapes, Jewish synagogues, Gentile households—in which the question arose: how should believers demonstrate that liberation in an era before the final restoration of all things? Texts such as Luke 6:20–26 and parallel admonitions echo Jesus's concern for the vulnerable, suggesting that the church's credibility would hinge on its alignment with such priorities.[9]

Given that the second coming might not be imminent, the call to embody these transformative values became more pressing rather than less. Communities wrestling with poverty, slavery, or disenfranchisement found in the Nazareth Manifesto a rationale for sustained action, grounded in the conviction that the Spirit remained active among them,

---

8. Trible, *Rhetoric of Sexuality*, 74–75. Trible's further commentary on the social dimensions of the Nazareth Manifesto, linking Isaiah's prophecy to economic and cultural restructuring.

9. Cone, *Spirituals*, 66. Highlights how Lukan ethics, including the Beatitudes, function as a call to align communal resources with marginalized populations' needs.

empowering them to practice and advocate for social healing. Thus, Luke's emphasis on liberation was never relegated to a remote eschatological future but served as a benchmark for current ecclesial conduct, pointing toward the continuing presence of God's kingdom among those who are marginalized.

8.1.4. Pentecost as a New Exodus: Gawani Community in Acts

Typological Resonances of Exodus

Acts 2:1–13 situates the birth of the Christian church at Pentecost, drawing parallels to Israel's foundational event of the exodus. In Exodus, Israel transitions from enslavement to covenant community; in Acts, the disciples receive the Spirit and transition from a scattered group to a spiritually empowered assembly.[10] This thematic link underscores that the church's identity is not an interim arrangement waiting passively for the end, but a renewed people committed to reflecting God's liberative design in their daily structures.

By coupling exodus imagery with the outpouring of the Holy Spirit, Luke suggests that just as the Israelites were not merely rescued but formed into a covenant people, so too the Christian community is formed for a specific vocation: to demonstrate, in real and tangible ways, that God's salvific energies are at work. This theological vision helps reframe the delay of Christ's return as a period in which believers can incarnate the values of the new covenant, rather than a time of doctrinal uncertainty or ethical complacency.

Economic Sharing as a Mark of Spiritual Authenticity

Acts 2:44–45 and 4:32–35 repeatedly highlight that believers hold possessions in common, selling personal property and distributing the proceeds so no one would lack essential needs.[11] Interpreters differ on whether this communal economy was absolute or primarily a spiritual

---

10. Schüssler Fiorenza, *In Memory*, 100. Schüssler Fiorenza discusses parallels between the exodus motif and Luke's Pentecost narrative, arguing that a covenant identity extends to all believers.

11. Schüssler Fiorenza, *In Memory*, 115, notes that repeated emphasis on communal unity in Acts suggests Luke viewed shared possessions not merely as an isolated event but as an ongoing norm.

symbol of unity, but its central placement in the narrative suggests that Luke attaches substantial importance to how believers handle wealth.[12]

This pattern—often called gawani living—goes beyond philanthropic gestures. It instead represents a restructuring of communal relations that reflects the jubilee principle of canceling debts and restoring equity. Such a method of distributing resources confronts typical social stratifications by witnessing a reality in which believers, though living in a world riddled with inequality, actively shape a countercultural system. The impetus to share arises from the conviction that the Spirit is reversing oppressive trends, forging a society aligned with the ethos Jesus himself proclaimed.

Ananias and Sapphira: A Test of Gawani Integrity

Acts 5:1–11 underscores the gravity of this communal commitment through the cautionary tale of Ananias and Sapphira, who conspire to deceive the assembly about the proceeds of a property sale.[13] The narrative depicts this deception as a disruption of the Spirit-shaped fellowship. Their fate illustrates that hidden self-interest and lack of transparency can corrode the core of communal life. Although harsh to modern readers, the punishment met out underscores Luke's conviction that authentic stewardship and honesty are nonnegotiable for a community seeking to embody the new exodus ethic.

In many ways, the scene stands as a direct contrast to the positive examples in Acts 2 and 4. Where others freely gave, Ananias and Sapphira hoarded. Where Spirit fosters unity, their duplicity prompts fracture. The rhetorical impact of this account presses home that the gawani ethos is not an optional add-on but a defining trait of what it means to be an assembly guided by the risen Christ's Spirit.

---

12. Walton and Swithinbank, *Poverty*, 43. The authors explore how property sharing confronted stratified economic structures within the early church, offering a model for resource reallocation.

13. Walton and Swithinbank, *Poverty*, 44, stresses that the punishment of Ananias and Sapphira underlines the gravity of undermining fellowship through deception, highlighting sincerity as essential.

8.1.5. Historical and Institutional Transitions

From Apostolic Dynamism to Imperial Church

As centuries passed, the institutional church underwent profound transformations, especially after Constantine's conversion and the subsequent legitimization of Christianity within the Roman Empire.[14] While official endorsement brought about greater stability and broader cultural influence, it also led to adjustments in how communal life was practiced. Ecclesiastical hierarchies replaced some forms of grassroots fellowship, and large-scale structures often overshadowed the more intimate communal patterns depicted in Acts.

This shift did not entirely erase the memory of early Christian sharing, but it did confine such radical practices to the margins or to specific movements like monasticism. Monastic communities, including those founded by Pachomius or guided by the *Rule of St. Benedict*, revived aspects of gawani living—such as communal property or a vow of poverty—for spiritual formation. However, these efforts frequently unfolded in cloistered environments, differing from the broader society-wide communal economy Acts envisions.

Monastic Reappropriation of the Gawani Ethos

Throughout medieval Christianity, the monastic ideal provided a haven where property sharing, rigorous accountability, and humble service retained some continuity with the Acts model.[15] These contexts often emphasized collective dedication to prayer, manual labor, and communal welfare, grounded in the conviction that the body of believers should function as an extended household.[16] In doing so, monastics sought to

---

14. Kang, *Theology of Gawani*, 17–18, examines how, after Constantine, the intimacy and radical nature of the earliest Christian communal ethos gradually gave way to formalized ecclesial systems. Kang links the Pentecost narrative (Acts 2 and 4) to a new exodus community, whose Jubilee-shaped sharing challenges later imperial patterns of church life.

15. Moltmann, *Church in the Power*, vii, discusses the persistence of communal ideals in monastic communities, relating them to the Acts vision of shared life and mutual care.

16. Moltmann, *Church in the Power*, xv, addresses the historical variety of monastic communities, noting how they selectively adopted or adapted the resource sharing ethos for spiritual discipline.

TOWARD A GAWANI-FEMINIST-BLACK LIBERATION ETHOS   163

reconcile the constraints of feudal or imperial realities with the longing for a social expression of the gospel that mirrored the earliest church.

Yet monastic movements were by no means uniform. Their motivations ranged from ascetic retreat to evangelistic outreach, and practical commitments to economic justice could vary. Nevertheless, the fact that even partial forms of gawani sharing persisted across centuries underscores the enduring influence of Luke's narrative, particularly for those seeking to integrate contemplative devotion with tangible moral responsibilities.

8.1.6. Liberation Theology, Postcolonial Hermeneutics, and Broader Social Engagement

Liberation Theology and Acts 2–4

In the modern period, liberation theology—originating in Latin America and spreading globally—revitalized interest in Acts 2:44–45 and 4:32–35 as paradigms for addressing systemic inequities and political oppression.[17] By asserting that the Holy Spirit galvanizes believers to confront injustice, liberation theologians read Luke's account as a call for collective economic transformation, not merely personal charity.[18] This perspective interprets the gawani ethos as an enduring mandate, pushing contemporary faith communities to adopt practices that challenge exploitative social structures.

Through this lens, the delay of Christ's return accentuates the duty to address real suffering. If the parousia is not happening imminently, the church has a responsibility to engage robustly with oppressive systems, forging alliances with marginalized groups and advocating policy changes.[19] The Acts model, thus, supplies theological grounding for endeavors that move beyond local fellowship to influence social, economic, and even governmental spheres. Believers are urged to see that eschatological

---

17. Boff and Boff, *Introducing Liberation Theology*, 7. Liberation theologians often reference Acts 2–4 to demonstrate that socioeconomic renewal is grounded in the earliest Christian witness.

18. Boff and Boff, *Introducing Liberation Theology*, 44. Argues that communal property practices manifest the gospel's call to stand against systems perpetuating poverty, shaping both church life and broader society.

19. Boff and Boff, *Introducing Liberation Theology*, 46. Maintains that because Christ's final advent remains pending, believers must actively transform present conditions, aligning them with kingdom values.

hope neither allows resignation nor fosters fatalism but instead motivates a tangible reorientation of resources toward those on society's periphery.

Postcolonial Critiques and Cultural Diversity

Postcolonial hermeneutics similarly appropriates Luke-Acts, especially the Pentecost narrative, to illuminate how God's work transcends linguistic and cultural boundaries. Acts 2 underscores the Spirit's capacity to unify diverse peoples, suggesting that an authentic ecclesial identity must remain open to intercultural exchange and shared accountability.[20] Interpreters in this field note that Luke's portrayal contains subversive elements regarding imperial and economic domination, illustrating how early believers formed a countercultural collective that challenged status driven norms of the Roman world.

These insights hold practical significance for contemporary churches seeking to address legacies of colonialism or ongoing global inequalities. The gawani ethos can be adapted in contexts where historical exploitation persists, encouraging faith communities to dismantle barriers related to race, ethnicity, and class.[21] By reaffirming mutual responsibility, Luke's narrative provides a theological scaffold for reconciling the postcolonial quest for justice with core Christian commitments, even when political structures remain resistant.

8.1.7. Contemporary Expressions of the Gawani Ethos

New Monasticism and Intentional Christian Communities

New monastic communities represent one of the most visible modern efforts to reinstate something akin to the gawani ethos.[22] These groups, often operating in urban or economically disadvantaged neighborhoods, practice shared income, collective decision-making, and a profound

---

20. Bonhoeffer and Wells, *Life Together*, 48. Bonhoeffer's view of Christian community underscores how fellowship transcends cultural divisions, suggesting a blueprint for inclusive ecclesial life.

21. Bonhoeffer and Wells, *Life Together*, 49, highlights that economic cooperation and shared life are key hallmarks of authentic community, bridging linguistic, cultural, and class differences.

22. Bonhoeffer and Wells, *Life Together*, 50, documents contemporary new monastic experiments, which adapt traditional monastic commitments to urban contexts and emphasize social engagement.

sense of local mission. Their organizational models are intentionally small-scale, seeking to cultivate honest relationships and genuine accountability. Although these communities are not always large or widespread, they illustrate that the Acts model can be reappropriated in the present, challenging mainstream consumer culture by emphasizing stewardship and hospitality.

Such intentional communities typically ground their activities in worship rhythms that link spiritual practices—prayer, biblical reflection, liturgy—to outward-focused service. Believing that the indefinite extension of time before Christ's return is no excuse for complacency, they see shared economic structures as an antidote to rampant individualism.[23] Internal tensions can arise, including questions of sustainability and leadership, yet many participants argue that these tensions are opportunities to refine ethical commitments and ensure that the gawani ethos remains authentic.

Broader Congregational Movements and Social Advocacy

Outside of new monastic contexts, numerous congregations have integrated gawani-like practices into standard parish life. Food cooperatives, shared housing initiatives, microlending programs, and communal funds for crisis relief offer examples of ways church members pool resources to address the needs of both congregants and neighbors in distress.[24] These projects echo to Luke's emphasis on building a socially just community that transcends socioeconomic barriers.

Various denominational networks—Methodist, Catholic, Lutheran, Presbyterian—have likewise sought to institutionalize a preferential option for the poor, reminiscent of the gawani model. By tying theological convictions to structured programs of advocacy and mutual support, these churches demonstrate that the impetus to replicate Acts 2 and 4 persists as more than an academic ideal; it is a living movement influencing real-life economic and policy choices. This orientation frequently intersects with philanthropic or governmental initiatives, forging alliances

---

23. Moltmann, *Church in the Power*, xviii. Moltmann notes that certain congregations engage directly with civic initiatives, mirroring Luke's communal approach on a broader social scale.

24. Moltmann, *Theology of Hope*, 227, returns to Moltmann's theme that the church, during the in-between time, should be an active agent of divine reconciliation and justice.

between faith-based groups and broader social movements seeking reform in housing, healthcare, and labor rights.

8.1.8. Reframing the Delay of the Parousia: Theological and Practical Dimensions

Eschatological Expectation as an Ongoing Motive

The apparent postponement of Christ's return, historically a challenge to the earliest Christian worldview, emerges in Luke's writings as an occasion for proactive engagement rather than defeat or cynicism.[25] In effect, the church's identity coalesces around the notion that believers are to embody the kingdom's priorities—care for the marginalized, stewardship of resources, inclusive fellowship—throughout an indefinite temporal stretch. Far from diminishing the force of eschatology, this approach intensifies it, insisting that hope for Christ's return saturates every aspect of communal life, from the distribution of food to the forging of cross-cultural relationships.

Such a posture can also unite diverse theological perspectives. Whether within liberationist circles or evangelical assemblies, the principle that the not yet status of the parousia should energize rather than paralyze fosters a shared commitment to transformative practices. Engaging in gawani ideals, then, becomes a collaborative endeavor: believers witness to the reality of God's reign even as they await its future consummation.

8.2 SUSTAINING THE GAWANI VISION IN MODERNITY

In contemporary contexts, sustaining the gawani ethos meets various obstacles, including consumerism, political polarization, and global economic pressures. The example of the first church, however, continues to challenge communities toward cooperation, responsibility, and hospitality. By consistently referring back to passages like Acts 2:44–45 and 4:32–35, churches can remain vigilant against pressures that erode unity and service.

---

25. Wright et al., *Surprised by Hope*, 40, concludes that the Acts model remains a touchstone for contemporary believers, reinforcing that waiting for Christ fosters, rather than negates, committed service.

Furthermore, theological education and leadership training have begun incorporating these principles, teaching future pastors and lay leaders to balance institutional demands with the radical ethic Luke depicts. Course offerings in seminaries often include modules on Christian community development, drawing from the Acts narratives to shape comprehensive approaches to social ministry. In some regions, this has led to innovative partnerships between churches and non-faith-based organizations, broadening the application of gawani-like ideals to tackle systemic issues such as income inequality or environmental degradation.

8.1.9. Conclusion

Luke's two-volume work offers a consistent message that communal practices—particularly economic sharing, transparent accountability, and socially inclusive relationships—represent a tangible manifestation of the kingdom of God. Although the earliest believers assumed a rapidly approaching culmination, the subsequent historical reality necessitated a theology suitable for an extended interim. Luke's solution was not to dilute eschatological expectancy but to position the church as a constant sign of divine in-breaking, whether or not Christ's return occurred imminently.

The gawani ethos stands as a concise reference to this pattern of life: a collective prioritizing reciprocity, empathy, and economic justice. Its relevance transcends the apostolic era, surfacing repeatedly in monastic communities, theological reformations, liberation movements, and emerging intentional communities. Each iteration testifies to the enduring power of Luke's depiction: if the Spirit truly animated the church, believers will find themselves drawn into forms of fellowship that challenge conventional norms.

In the contemporary world, marked by wide-reaching inequalities and shifting cultural landscapes, the gawani ethos offers both spiritual impetus and practical templates for renewal. Whether through reconfiguring local church finances or launching larger-scale advocacy efforts, those who embrace Luke's narrative find a coherent mandate to align their ministries with God's reconciling agenda. Ultimately, the delay of the parousia is neither a doctrinal embarrassment nor a reason for inaction; rather, it is an open vista for the church to embody the compassion, generosity, and unity that foreshadow the final restoration of all things.

8.2. BLACK THEOLOGY AND GAWANI THEOLOGY: CONVERGENT AIMS, DISTINCT EMPHASES

Black theology and gawani theology each propose community-centered ways of living out faith that confront oppressive social structures. Despite arising from different historical contexts, they share a commitment to reshaping how the church engages with both resource distribution and marginalized voices. By addressing systems that perpetuate inequality, these approaches challenge believers to move beyond personal piety and toward communal practices aimed at restoring dignity. They both aim to strengthen fellowship through collective responsibility, but their specific emphases—one focusing on racism, the other on economic imbalance—yield complementary yet distinct visions.

Black theology, formed during intense struggles against segregation and discrimination, embeds its perspective in the lived reality of African American communities. It contends that any proclamation of the gospel must tackle the sin of white supremacy and the social arrangements that sustain it. This tradition frames liberation as inseparable from the fight for civil rights, linking biblical motifs of exodus and redemption to real-world campaigns for equity. Consequently, its leaders have historically urged churches to become active agents of social reform, underscoring the biblical call to defend and uplift those who have been cast aside by racial hierarchies.

Gawani theology, on the other hand, directs attention toward shared economic stewardship within faith communities, drawing on passages in Acts where believers voluntarily held goods in common. Though still at an early stage of articulation, it proposes that local congregations question ownership models and design collaborative structures for mutual provision. This call to reorganize economic life stands in sharp contrast to popular notions of personal success and competition, prompting churches to enact policies that mirror the fellowship ideals of the early believers. In such a framework, collective oversight of finances, property, and daily sustenance is viewed as an outgrowth of the gospel's transformative power.

Taken together, Black theology and gawani theology encourage a church that addresses multiple layers of injustice. While Black theology underscores the urgency of dismantling racism, gawani theology highlights the need to reassess communal finances. Their shared vision asserts that the pursuit of justice should shape worship, leadership, and

The Roots of Black Theology

Black theology emerged in earnest during the civil rights era of the mid-twentieth century, positioning itself as a direct confrontation against the legacy of slavery, segregation, and systemic racism in the United States.[26] Churches and theologians within African American communities rooted their ideas in a tradition that fused biblical motifs, emotionally charged preaching, and the cultural expressions of spirituals and gospel music. This heritage shaped a collective understanding of faith as a catalyst for both spiritual resilience and tangible social change.[27] Indeed, many early proponents insisted that the Christian gospel, if disconnected from real-world liberation, would be incomplete and ethically compromised.

One of the pivotal architects of Black theology was James H. Cone, who argued that Jesus's ministry cannot be severed from the struggles of those most severely oppressed.[28] By associating the crucifixion with the traumatic realities of lynching and segregation, Cone posited that God's solidarity extends into contexts of bodily violence and systemic subjugation. The resurrection then signals that oppressive structures lack ultimate dominion and that the divine will stand firmly on the side of the marginalized. On this basis, Black theology contends that racism is not merely an unfortunate social phenomenon; it constitutes a denial of the gospel's core affirmation that all persons are created and redeemed for full participation in God's reign.

From its inception, Black theology also maintained that the church must not limit itself to spiritual consolation but must campaign for

---

26. Styron, *Confessions of Nat Turner*, 48. Styron addresses the historical currents of enslavement and yearning for freedom, connecting them to the theological underpinnings of African American interpretations of Scripture.

27. Cone, *Spirituals*, 37. Cone references the cultural tapestry of spirituals and blues as vital forms of resistance, linking them closely to biblical motifs of liberation.

28. Russell, *Feminist Interpretation*, 16. Russell contends that racism constitutes a structural distortion of Christian liberation, emphasizing that communities must address race-based hierarchies with the same urgency as other forms of oppression.

widespread structural reform.²⁹ Racial hierarchies are sustained by legal codes, economic barriers, and cultural narratives that demean Black life; thus, any authentic witness of the church demands a forceful critique of such arrangements. Among the varied manifestations of this stance, one finds local congregations organizing voter registration, hosting literacy classes, and pooling communal resources to address daily hardships. Ultimately, this tradition wove together biblical study, sociopolitical analysis, and public advocacy in ways that refused to isolate religion from the broader quest for justice.

Furthermore, Black theology understands cultural outputs—especially spirituals—as more than aesthetic artifacts. They serve as coded messages, revealing the communal longing for deliverance in contexts where open resistance was severely curtailed.³⁰ These songs channeled biblical themes of exodus, exile, and restoration, casting them in an African American idiom that spoke directly to the harsh realities of bondage and segregation. Such a cultural-theological synergy offered more than emotional uplift; it instilled a robust sense that God is intimately present in ongoing struggles for dignity. In this sense, the spiritual dimension intersects continually with concrete battles against systemic injustice.

The Intersection with Gawani Ethics

Gawani theology, grounded in the Acts narrative of communal living, emphasizes solidarity through shared resources and mutual accountability.³¹ By focusing on the earliest Christian practice of "having all things in common" (Acts 2:44–45), gawani theology highlights how discipleship extends into economic arrangements, challenging believers to form communities that transcend prevailing norms of material competition. Although initially formulated with an eye toward economic inequities, gawani theology also aligns with broader liberative approaches—such

---

29. Russell, *Feminist Interpretation*, 33. Russell also argues that denominational bodies endorsing or tolerating racist practices undermine the gospel's liberating scope; ecclesial reform becomes an immediate consequence of genuine conversion.

30. Fanon, *Black Skin, White Masks*, 86. Fanon discusses how cultural expressions serve as coded strategies of communal affirmation, linking artistic forms to broader projects of emancipation.

31. Engels, *Origin of the Family*, 166. Engels's socioeconomic critiques provide a lens for understanding how communal ownership can arise, aligning with gawani theology's emphasis on shared resources.

as Black theology—that view social reform as an integral component of Christian faith.

In African American history, forms of communal assistance—such as pooling wages, rotating childcare, and establishing cooperative banks—functioned as strategies of survival amid hostile legal and social environments.[32] These practices resonate with the gawani premise that Christian ethics must be lived out collectively, rather than relegated to private piety. Within both the Black and gawani traditions, the Holy Spirit is understood not simply as a provider of emotional solace, but as a catalyst for reconfigured relationships and systemic interventions. Thus, a Black church organizing economic cooperatives in an inner-city context and a modern gawani-inspired collective challenging corporate profiteering may share an underlying theological logic: the gospel mandates a radical reorientation of communal life.

Black theology and gawani theology likewise converge in their insistence that salvation surpasses an inner spiritual event, demanding tangible demonstrations of unity and care across social boundaries. For Black theology, this involves actively opposing racist structures that deny the full personhood of African Americans.[33] Gawani theology locates parallel urgency in reshaping how property and power are distributed, contending that faith without equitable stewardship remains truncated. Each tradition asserts that to follow Christ is to realign human communities in a manner that disrupts oppressive hierarchies.

Yet they differ in specific focal points. Black theology zeroes in on the sin of white supremacy, revealing how racial hierarchies distort the church's claim to universal fellowship. Gawani theology addresses the sin of unchecked economic disparity, pushing believers toward shared ownership and participatory governance. Despite these diverse emphases, both traditions foster an expanded vision of redemption that extends beyond soul-saving to include the transformation of relational, political, and economic frameworks.

---

32. Isasi-Díaz, *La Lucha Continues*, 269. Isasi-Díaz reflects on the ways marginalized communities employ cooperative practices for survival, suggesting that such practices mirror the biblical impetus for shared living.

33. Cone, *Spirituals*, 66. Cone posits that racism not only devalues persons but also contradicts Christ's mission, compelling Christians to address racial subjugation as an immediate theological concern.

Sustaining Communities of Resistance

Both Black theology and gawani theology uphold communities of resistance, local fellowships that embody the gospel by challenging exclusionary norms and cultivating shared practices of care.[34] Historically, the Black church functioned as a base of operations for civil rights activism: congregations organized educational forums, provided food and shelter, and hosted planning meetings for protest marches. In this context, spiritual formation was inseparable from sociopolitical engagement. The church did not merely gather for worship services; it also fostered the communal coherence required to confront voter suppression, job discrimination, and segregated schooling.

Gawani theology underscores a similar dynamic by foregrounding the necessity of forging cohesive economic relationships under the Spirit's guidance.[35] Drawing on the Acts motif of believers who sold their possessions and goods and distributed the proceeds to all, gawani proponents argue that Christian discipleship envisions a reordering of material resources for the common good. Echoing the historical Black church's emphasis on practical justice, gawani theology insists that without systemic accountability and communal policies, the ideal of fellowship remains rhetoric. Faith communities thus need to implement cooperative structures—such as communal banks, shared housing arrangements, or group-owned businesses—to dismantle entrenched power differentials.

Because many African American churches had to navigate entrenched racism while also contending with poverty, their lived experience offers valuable lessons for gawani-oriented congregations. In particular, the ways that Black churches balanced worship, social education, and mutual support highlight the integration of spiritual and structural dimensions. Gawani experiments, ranging from urban Christian co-ops to rural land trusts, can glean insights from these precedents, ensuring that their pursuit of economic solidarity is not colorblind nor inattentive to additional layers of oppression. Where gawani theology addresses property and wealth, Black theology reminds us that racial biases remain embedded in broader societal institutions and must be actively confronted.

---

34. Townes, *Womanist Ethics*, 3. Townes frames communities of resistance as those challenging the production of oppression in cultural norms, echoing both gawani's and Black theology's impetus to restructure relationships.

35. Cone, *Spirituals*, 92. Cone highlights the necessity of forging material solidarity, rather than restricting the Holy Spirit's work to personal consolation.

Conversely, theologians shaped by Black traditions can reference gawani's New Testament foundation to illustrate how communities resist a dualistic split between spirit and matter.[36] The Acts narrative, culminating in scenes where believers care for each other's needs and break bread in egalitarian fellowship, furnishes a model for bridging racial divides with economic sharing. Some Black theologians propose that reparations or social programs aimed at correcting historic injustices mirror the biblical principle of restitution integral to communal wholeness. From this angle, gawani theology and Black theology reinforce each other in calling for a dual transformation: overcoming racist mindsets and economic exploitation through proactive communal policies.

Collaborative Dimensions and Wider Applications

When Black theology's commitment to challenging white supremacy meets gawani theology's emphasis on redistributive community life, the result is a framework in which Christian discipleship becomes a vehicle for both racial equity and economic justice.[37] In practical terms, a congregation that already addresses racism can integrate gawani strategies by implementing shared funds for emergency housing or cooperatives for job training. Meanwhile, groups already practicing gawani-style collective finances can adopt Black theology's approach to analyzing and dismantling biases that shape membership, leadership, or resource allocation.

This synergy resonates in academic settings as well. Seminaries or Christian colleges aiming to cultivate holistic ministry training might develop courses that pair exegetical study of Acts with African American theological texts discussing race, power, and embodiment. Students could explore how early Christian communal patterns speak to contemporary racial wealth gaps, or how the beatitudes inform movements for civil rights. In effect, such cross-pollination can form leader's adept at addressing the complexities of oppression that link class-based injustices with racial ones.

---

36. Styron, *Confessions of Nat Turner*, 49–50. Styron documents how believers bridged daily economic needs with a faith-based impetus for unity, hinting at a biblical rationale for combined spiritual and material fellowship.

37. Russell, *Feminist Interpretation*, 25. Russell suggests that addressing race and class inequities jointly expands the scope of ecclesial responsibility, paralleling Black theology's anti-racist focus with gawani's economic reorientation.

Beyond academic circles, the alignment between Black theology and gawani theology extends to worldwide contexts dealing with various forms of marginalization. Indigenous movements struggling for land rights, for instance, can be illuminated by gawani theology's stress on communal stewardship, while Black theology's articulation of structural sin intersects with global critiques of racial prejudice. Churches that wrestle with anti-immigrant sentiment or internal cultural biases can likewise find guidance in a theology that prioritizes equitable resource-sharing, grounded in biblical narratives and historically tested activism.

Such collaboration also fosters a broader cultural shift in how the church understands mission. Rather than seeing outreach as mere charity, it becomes an invitation to reimagine both economic and racial systems so that all members of society partake in shared decision-making. This requires rethinking leadership structures: ensuring that those from historically marginalized groups hold positions of influence in shaping community direction. In parallel, it necessitates examining how property laws, zoning regulations, and tax policies might disadvantage certain populations—a realm where gawani theology's emphasis on structural equity merges with Black theology's anti-racist moral urgency.

Conclusion

Black theology, born from African American resistance to white supremacy, and gawani theology, emerging from a fresh reading of the Acts community, converge on the insistence that authentic Christian witness envisions radical transformation of oppressive institutions and systems.[38] Both traditions challenge believers to affirm that God's reconciling power applies to every layer of society, not just individual spirituality. In the Black tradition, this entails confronting racial hierarchies that have historically relegated communities of color to the margins; gawani theology underscores the equally pressing demand to reform economic relations in light of the earliest Christian practices of solidarity.

Neither approach confines salvation to a matter of personal faith or moral exhortation. Instead, they portray salvation as communal healing—a shift in how power is exercised, how property is shared, and how marginalized voices are recognized. This alignment of aims does not

---

38. Russell, *Feminist Interpretation*, 46. Russell notes that a robust soteriology covers both individual morality and systemic liberation, resonating with the core claims of Black and gawani theologies.

TOWARD A GAWANI-FEMINIST-BLACK LIBERATION ETHOS 175

eliminate the distinctions in their core emphases but highlights a shared conviction that the Spirit's presence induces communal reconfigurations, from the local church to the wider civic sphere.[39] By holding spiritual devotion and systemic reform in tandem, Black and gawani theologies lay claim to a version of the gospel that reverberates in struggles for justice across racial and economic boundaries.

Historically, Black congregations combined public advocacy with liturgical celebration, revealing that theological reflection can guide and energize social movements. gawani theology, referencing the Acts model, likewise pushes congregations to embrace concrete communal ownership and accountability. Where they intersect, believers are invited to affirm that the fight against racism and the pursuit of economic fairness serve as complementary dimensions of Christ's liberating mission. The result is an all-encompassing witness that refuses to neglect racial hierarchies on one side or economic injustices on the other.

By fostering communities of resistance, forging collaborative strategies, and reimagining ecclesial practices, the synergy of these two traditions leaves room for profound hope—one anchored not in shallow optimism but in the conviction that God's reign disrupts every system of exclusion. Even as many churches remain hesitant to overhaul their current structures, the joint perspectives of Black theology and gawani theology continue to prompt rigorous self-examination. Each tradition underscores that faith communities must embody mercy and equity in ways that are outwardly observable, thereby confirming the biblical claim that "faith without works is dead." This unified call ultimately beckons the broader church to enact an expansive, justice-oriented discipleship responsive to the complexities of race, economics, and human dignity.

8.3. FEMINIST THEOLOGY: GENDER, LIBERATION, AND COMMUNAL PRAXIS

Feminist theology and gawani theology have emerged within Christian thought as two frameworks that challenge conventional assumptions about power and participation in church communities. They question the ways in which gender roles and economic structures can undermine

---

39. Fanon, *Black Skin, White Masks*, 124. Fanon's critique of internalized structures of oppression illustrates how transformative praxis must penetrate societal frameworks, corresponding to the mission-based perspective in each theological tradition.

the unity and equality often proclaimed in Christian teaching. Each one contends that social norms, whether patriarchal patterns or inequitable resource control—must be reexamined if the church hopes to embody genuine fellowship. Instead of viewing faith as merely personal belief, both feminist and gawani approaches emphasize communal responsibility, insisting that worship language, leadership models, and stewardship practices align with a commitment to human dignity.

Feminist theology critiques how male-focused traditions, clerical hierarchies, and limiting references to God have minimized women's experiences. It shows that patriarchal interpretations have shaped biblical scholarship and congregational practices, leading to the exclusion of women from crucial leadership roles. By reconsidering not just texts but also worship and governance, feminist theology highlights the need for language that includes female representations of God and for decision-making structures where women's voices are recognized. It calls the church to connect doctrinal ideals of unity with tangible reforms that honor the contributions of all members, upholding a fellowship of service rather than status.

Gawani theology, while still at a preliminary stage, adds another element by focusing on economic relationships within Christian congregations. Inspired by passages describing shared possessions in the Book of Acts, it suggests that resource distribution should reflect a wider ethos of communal care. Local communities with limited means demonstrate how mutual support can combat systemic inequalities. Yet gawani thinkers have not fully detailed how to integrate these convictions into each facet of church life. Instead, they offer a guiding principle that questions individualistic ownership and advocates a shared approach to finances, property, and charitable endeavors.

Feminist and gawani perspectives converge when they demonstrate that neither economic aid nor inclusive language alone can transform a congregation if deeper assumptions remain unchanged. Each framework encourages believers to question the customs and hierarchies that prioritize certain voices—often male or financially privileged—over others. By jointly stressing the significance of collective oversight and participatory leadership, they point to a more expansive view of church renewal. Rather than offering quick fixes, both traditions propose continuous communal reflection, encouraging structures and practices that promote equity in stewardship, language, and governance. Through these complementary visions, a path emerges for congregations to adopt reforms that address the many facets of injustice and move toward authentic fellowship.

The Emergence of Feminist Theology

Feminist theology arose as part of broader feminist movements that examined how religious traditions often contained patriarchal norms, sidelining women's voices and relegating them to subordinate roles.[40] By the mid-twentieth century, theologians recognized that doctrinal formulations, biblical scholarship, and church practices typically assumed male experiences as universal, effectively neglecting the perspectives of women.[41] Mary Daly insisted that exclusive reliance on masculine terms for God, along with male-dominated institutional structures, contradicted the gospel's promise of liberation.[42] Her critique alerted many churches to the possibility that worship language and leadership patterns might inadvertently reinforce unjust hierarchies.

Another major influence was Rosemary Radford Ruether, who argued that historical theology frequently attributed rationality, authority, and spiritual insight only to men.[43] Ruether contended that male-biased discourse permeated seminaries, pastoral training, and official pronouncements, thus inhibiting women's intellectual and ministerial potential. In response, feminist scholars began systematically uncovering how women had contributed to the expansion of early Christianity and shaped theological debates, even though they rarely received official acknowledgment. This recovery work aimed to rebalance a tradition that too often excluded or minimized the very experiences shaping half of humanity.

---

40. Ruether, *Sexism*, 60. Ruether argues that any attempt to formulate a Trinitarian model with fixed gender roles ultimately reproduces patriarchal structures and fails to represent a liberative vision of God.

41. Ruether, *Sexism*, 100. She maintains that Christian theology has historically privileged male reason and spiritual authority, denying women equal participation in theological discourse.

42. Russell, *Feminist Interpretation*, 13. Russell traces the rise of feminist hermeneutics to critiques like Mary Daly's, which exposed how patriarchal norms have governed scriptural interpretation and church life.

43. Ruether, *Sexism*, 135. According to Ruether, traditional theology frequently relegated women to second-class status in both creation and redemption, necessitating a critical reappraisal of Christological claims.

Elisabeth Schüssler Fiorenza advanced these aims by reexamining early Christian materials, challenging established interpretations that portrayed women as mere onlookers in the apostolic age.[44] She pointed to figures like Mary Magdalene, who announced the resurrection message, and to various Pauline references indicating that women "labored in the Lord."[45] Schüssler Fiorenza proposed that patriarchal exegetical habits had eclipsed the more inclusive realities of the earliest Jesus communities. In so doing, feminist theology reshaped church historiography, insisting that an egalitarian ethic is intrinsic to Christian origins rather than a late modern invention.

Moreover, feminist theology reevaluated certain scriptural passages that appear to endorse women's subordination or to condone forms of violence against them.[46] Old Testament laws and narratives, for instance, sometimes depict women as male property or condone forced marriages. Feminist interpreters contended these texts reflected the patriarchal culture of the day, not the enduring will of God.[47] By confronting problematic stories, they sought to distinguish the liberating message at Scripture's core from cultural biases embedded in ancient contexts. This distinction underscores that believers can affirm biblical authority without uncritically preserving oppressive conventions.

The Communal Praxis and Hermeneutical Shift

Beyond the boundaries of historical revision, feminist theology introduced a new hermeneutical framework frequently described as a "hermeneutics of suspicion," which critically examines biblical interpretations

---

44. Schüssler Fiorenza, *In Memory*, 35. Schüssler Fiorenza argues that feminist theological critique must recover not only women's oppression in the biblical text but also their agency as bearers of divine revelation.

45. Schüssler Fiorenza, *In Memory*, 164–166. In this section, she examines Rom 16—especially verses 6 and 12 ("ἐκοπίασεν πολλὰ ἐν Κυρίῳ / labored much in the Lord")—together with Phil 4:3, demonstrating that Paul lists several women (Mary, Tryphaena, Tryphosa, Persis, and others) as co-workers who "labored in the Lord," thereby challenging later patriarchal interpretations that cast early Christian women as mere bystanders.

46. Schüssler Fiorenza, *In Memory*, 107. She contends that Mary Magdalene functioned as an apostolic witness to the resurrection and not merely as a marginal figure, challenging patriarchal reconstructions of early Christianity.

47. Trible, *Rhetoric of Sexuality*, xii. Trible criticizes how certain biblical narratives—particularly those involving sexual violence—have been interpreted to legitimize male dominance rather than expose systemic harm.

that appear to sustain male authority or downplay women's contributions.[48] This perspective does not limit itself to textual analysis alone; it challenges the entire interpretive process, asking who reads Scripture, in what context, and under which assumptions. Feminist theologians underscore that interpretive power is often bound to social authority, so they advocate readings intended to empower contemporary communities—especially women in settings marked by injustice—to claim biblical themes of liberation.[49]

Within worship and communal life, this hermeneutical shift encourages believers to reevaluate language, ritual leadership roles, and theological metaphors. One frequent observation is that speaking of God primarily as "Father" or "Lord" may reinforce cultural ideas that leadership rests exclusively in male hands, whereas supportive or subordinate roles are delegated to women.[50] To counter these imbalances, feminist theologians propose inclusive or female images for God, suggesting that such references can affirm that women, too, bear the divine image and hold essential roles in faith communities. This shift also fuels practical changes in worship, prompting congregations to recenter women's narratives and leadership so that stories of biblical women no longer remain at the margins.[51] Such efforts question any liturgical or communal structures that overlook or silence women's voices, highlighting the importance of open dialogue and shared authority in shaping faith experiences.

In addition, this framework expands the conversation about ecclesial governance. Feminist theologians observe that how decisions are

---

48. Oduyoye, *Daughters of Anowa*, 96. Oduyoye addresses how Western patriarchy, combined with preexisting paternal authority, constrained matrilineal heritage and muted women's opportunities for spiritual leadership. Her analysis demonstrates why a hermeneutics of suspicion becomes vital for examining embedded hierarchies in cultural and religious contexts.

49. Oduyoye, *Daughters of Anowa*, 170. Here, Oduyoye stresses that "voicing" is indispensable for women to articulate their realities. She notes that when African women speak out about patriarchal oppression and seek leadership opportunities, they often face resistance, making collective strategies essential for genuine change.

50. Johnson, *She Who Is*, 11. Johnson advocates inclusive and female-affirming metaphors for God, arguing that the persistent use of paternal language can reinforce hierarchical structures. She suggests that adopting expansive images for the divine contributes to a more equitable faith practice.

51. Oduyoye, *Daughters of Anowa*, 183. Oduyoye observes that some Christian communities discourage or marginalize women's protest against patriarchal norms. She highlights examples of women founding new churches where they can exercise their leadership callings more freely, revealing how essential it is to integrate women's narratives into the core of worship and community life.

made affects the entire fabric of church life. If authority for defining doctrine, interpreting Scripture, or distributing resources is restricted to ordained men, then the biblical message of unity and freedom remains incomplete.[52] Feminist thinkers connect their critiques of centralized, male-only governance with the broader concerns of liberation movements, arguing that whenever interpretive or managerial power is concentrated in the hands of a single group, marginalization arises.[53] This stance resonates with scriptural motifs of Spirit-filled fellowship in the book of Acts, where the outpouring of the Spirit fosters a community marked by shared participation and collaboration, transcending cultural legacies of male domination.

By highlighting how language about God and leadership structures can nurture or inhibit equitable community, feminist theologians point to the need for continual reexamination of customary practices. In worship contexts, inclusive imagery that features female dimensions of God not only broadens theological language but also reminds congregations that they are called to serve collaboratively rather than revert to hierarchical habits. This is particularly urgent in communities where women's experiences have been systematically overshadowed or suppressed, often under the guise of tradition.[54] The introduction of new liturgical materials, such as prayers and sermons that center women's experiences, can reshape the collective memory of faith and empower women who may otherwise believe their insights are irrelevant to official church teaching.

Moreover, feminist approaches contend that genuine liberation in the church requires a transformation of decision-making structures so that all members, women and men, exercise active roles in discerning spiritual and organizational directions.[55] Some feminist scholars link this emphasis

---

52. Althaus-Reid, *Indecent Theology*, 11. Althaus-Reid questions how ecclesial power structures are configured, underscoring that a community proclaiming liberation must reimagine who holds decision-making authority. She emphasizes that theology and governance become intertwined, necessitating an openness to voices that traditional hierarchies have often neglected.

53. Althaus-Reid, *Indecent Theology*, 13. Building on her broader critique of grand narratives, Althaus-Reid explores how ecclesial institutions can perpetuate exclusion if only one interpretive perspective is recognized. She contends that innovative theological reflection emerges when diverse viewpoints are honored rather than suppressed.

54. Oduyoye, *Daughters of Anowa*, 170.

55. Althaus-Reid, *Indecent Theology*, 16. Arguing that theology engages not merely abstract doctrine but the real-life power structures of religious communities, Althaus-Reid proposes that inclusive decision-making is fundamental for a church committed to social and spiritual transformation.

on collaborative leadership to other liberationist theologies, such as those in Latin America or Africa, where power imbalances often manifest in both cultural and religious systems. In these contexts, reinterpretations of biblical passages dealing with economic oppression, gender-based exclusion, and spiritual authority gain traction as tools for empowerment. The aim is not simply to redistribute ecclesial authority but to embody the biblical ideal of mutual service and solidarity, dismantling systemic barriers that have confined women's leadership to the margins.

Additionally, feminist theology challenges the assumption that tradition inevitably supports patriarchal norms. By reading Scripture considering women's stories, experiences, and community practices, feminist scholars recover narratives that emphasize shared ministry and mutual care. They show that the New Testament offers multiple examples of women exercising spiritual leadership. Yet, such examples have often been minimized by institutional practices.[56] Feminist readings underscore the complexity of biblical texts, urging an interpretive stance that considers context, power dynamics, and the living reality of contemporary believers. Where some might argue that masculine language for God is merely symbolic, feminist perspectives call attention to how symbolic language shapes social attitudes, influencing everything from personal spirituality to denominational policies.

Ultimately, this hermeneutical and liturgical progression intersects with questions of social responsibility. Feminist theologians claim that churches cannot fully embody justice-oriented faith if they disregard the experiences of those who have been silenced. Reconsidering biblical passages that endorse shared decision-making, and equitable leadership becomes essential for shaping a community that reflects scriptural themes of unity and freedom. In practice, this may mean revising church constitutions, reforming clergy training to be more inclusive, and crafting worship resources that enable women to articulate their perspectives on Scripture openly and confidently.[57] Such steps seek to move beyond theoretical acceptance of equality and direct congregations toward lived expressions of justice and communal well-being.

---

56. Althaus-Reid, *Indecent Theology*, 17. Althaus-Reid notes that colonial history frequently imposed patriarchal frameworks while erasing alternate forms of communal authority. She suggests that by reclaiming overlooked biblical models of shared ministry, faith communities can pursue liberated ways of worship and governance.

57. Oduyoye, *Daughters of Anowa*, 183.

Feminist theologians, in conversation with broader liberationist discourses, also encourage a larger global dialogue. Many emphasize that the experiences of women in African, Asian, or Latin American churches offer critical perspectives on the intersection of culture, economy, and religion. By examining how colonial powers reinforced patriarchal patterns while simultaneously introducing Christian beliefs, scholars reveal why a hermeneutics of suspicion is pivotal for unveiling hidden injustices.[58] This reevaluation entails not only rereading Scripture but also reevaluating theological education, liturgical formation, and congregational leadership practices, so that ecclesial communities worldwide can align themselves more faithfully with biblical calls to liberation. Through these measures, feminist theology proposes a reconfigured communal praxis, where both women and men contribute to interpreting Scripture and implementing the church's mission. In doing so, it challenges long-standing assumptions about gender, power, and the nature of faith itself, indicating that the quest for liberation demands both critical self-reflection and a committed communal response.

Points of Convergence with Gawani Theology

Feminist theology and gawani theology converge in their premise that Christian discipleship compels the faithful to transform social systems, not merely hearts or individual behaviors. Gawani theology, rooted in Acts 2 and 4, draws attention to how early believers pooled resources and practiced mutual care, exemplifying a communal ethic that challenges economic exploitation. Feminist theology complements this perspective by underscoring that sharing material goods cannot be separated from ensuring that women wield equal influence in communal processes.[59] A fellowship that distributes financial resources fairly but neglects women's leadership or discards their distinct voices perpetuates hidden inequities.

Both traditions center on the principle that authentic liberation requires rethinking traditional assumptions. Gawani theology questions capitalist norms of private ownership, whereas feminist theology interrogates the paternal constructs embedded in church language and

---

58. Oduyoye, *Daughters of Anowa*, 96.

59. Russell, *Feminist Interpretation*, 44. Russell points out that communal economics, reminiscent of Acts, fail unless they also dismantle norms that position women as secondary or invisible.

organization.⁶⁰ Each approach demands that the church embody tangible signs of equality: from how property is managed to how worship speaks of God. By merging these concerns, an integrated community might champion economic justice alongside a thoroughgoing critique of patriarchal customs. For example, while reading about the apostolic community sharing goods, leaders might address how cultural patriarchy restricts women's property rights, thus forging a more holistic expression of Christian solidarity.

Furthermore, feminist theology broadens the notion of the oppressed, acknowledging that women, especially those at the intersection of racial, economic, or cultural marginalizations, experience compounding vulnerabilities.⁶¹ Gawani's vision of inclusive fellowship is enriched when it adopts such an intersectional perspective, thereby avoiding an oversimplified dichotomy between rich and poor that might obscure the layered nature of women's oppression. If women cannot access communal resources or shape communal decisions because of entrenched biases, gawani's goal of equitable distribution remains unfulfilled.

Reimagining Ritual, Language, and Leadership

Feminist theology has long underscored the importance of reexamining how churches craft liturgies, address God, and share authority, noting that language and symbolism can either reinforce or undercut communal fairness.⁶² Historically, depictions of God as "Father" or "King" have sometimes converged with male-focused leadership patterns, limiting women's engagement in corporate prayer and sacramental functions. By introducing language for God such as "Mother," "Wisdom," or "Creator," which transcends gender categories, feminist theologians outline an avenue for honoring the scriptural theme that every person, regardless of gender, is formed in God's image. Such an emphasis fosters an environment where all believer's talents are recognized, so that teaching

---

60. Ruether, *Sexism*, 88. Ruether underscores the interconnectedness of wealth sharing and gender equality: ignoring one dimension undermines the full realization of justice.

61. Phiri, *Women, Presbyterianism and Patriarchy*, 59. Phiri describes how women's oppression is compounded by cultural, class, and colonial legacies, requiring multifaceted liberation strategies.

62. Johnson, *She Who Is*, 76. Johnson points out that paternal language can blend with hierarchical clerical structures, often inadvertently restricting women's potential roles. She suggests inclusive images of God as a way to reframe worship and leadership.

and Eucharistic leadership are not confined to a particular group. When exclusively masculine language is left unchallenged, it may preserve systemic inequities, especially for those who have encountered exclusion over time.[63] Consequently, feminist perspectives highlight the necessity of reevaluating established terminology and encouraging women to help shape congregational life.

Meanwhile, some emerging discussions tentatively link gawani theology with a focus on inclusive expressions of faith and communal stewardship. It must be emphasized, however, that gawani theology is still at a formative stage—without official publications—and it is thus premature to draw firm conclusions regarding its views on worship language or leadership structures.[64] Although parallels have been suggested between feminist models of equality and a gawani emphasis on shared resources, no verified texts confirm whether gawani thinkers indeed assert that worship language exerts broad effects on congregational programs. In this sense, any proposed correlation between gawani theology and linguistic inclusivity should be approached cautiously, to avoid overstating claims unsupported by definitive sources.[65] Still, the possibility of blending collective resource-sharing with an inclusive vision of God deserves measured consideration if the tradition develops in ways compatible with feminist theological principles.

Furthermore, both feminist theology and provisional interpretations of gawani theology draw attention to the makeup of leadership committees. If women's voices are limited to a nominal capacity, genuine equality remains elusive.[66] Feminist scholars, for instance, have long argued that women should assume substantive roles in determining doctrine, administering finances, and interpreting Scripture's contemporary applications. Though gawani theology's trajectory remains largely speculative, there are suggestions that it, too, may stress the need for balanced authority

---

63. Chopp, *Power to Speak*, 3. Chopp argues that language used in ritual settings shape's collective identity, sometimes upholding biases that disadvantage marginalized groups, including women.

64. No official gawani publication exists to date. Any reference to gawani positions remains speculative, requiring further documentation or research.

65. Chopp, *Power to Speak*, 4. Chopp observes that egalitarian ideals must be demonstrated not only in shared resources but also in how the community references and engages the divine.

66. Althaus-Reid, *Indecent Theology*, 8. Althaus-Reid notes that committees often appear inclusive in principle yet remain controlled by male decision-makers in practice, thereby limiting transformative possibilities.

in communal decision-making. In any scenario, excluding women from central discussions can foster a gap between a stated commitment to shared ownership and the undercurrent of male-directed leadership.[67] Thus, feminist perspectives and potential gawani concepts both advocate participatory governance reminiscent of early Christian fellowship, urging that no single faction monopolize ecclesial control or hermeneutical power.

Moreover, feminist theologians emphasize the influence of worship language on discipleship, education, and general spirituality. Relying solely on masculine titles for God might subliminally position women's contributions as secondary, regardless of public declarations of gender equality.[68] In contrast, inclusive language can broaden the space for women's active engagement, reflecting the idea that all members' insights are vital to the church's communal life. If future gawani thought ultimately aligns with this perspective, it would encourage the same practice of integrating collective ownership with references to God that encompass all believers. Still, these possibilities remain hypothetical until gawani theology solidifies through published works or sustained scholarly dialogue. Consequently, while feminist theology critiques both economic and linguistic inequities, any statement claiming that gawani thinkers definitively do the same must be treated with caution. As these approaches develop, they may help shape a church environment where liturgical speech, resource sharing, and leadership formation converge in affirming the dignity of every participant.

Broadening the Liberation Paradigm

Feminist theology has long insisted on examining not only the distribution of economic resources but also the cultural practices that aggravate disparities for women. In numerous regions, women bear heavy household obligations, often with restricted access to inheritance rights or formal education, which intensifies their vulnerability to various forms

---

67. Althaus-Reid, *Indecent Theology*, 16. The author critiques hidden power mechanisms within ecclesial systems, arguing that real liberation demands transparency and equal participation in all organizational spheres.

68. Chopp, *Power to Speak*, 9. Chopp cautions that even unspoken patterns of patriarchal language can steer congregational culture toward undervaluing women's leadership and spiritual gifts.

of exploitation.⁶⁹ Phiri points out that these constraints are frequently sanctioned by both unwritten social codes and religious expectations, so rectifying material imbalances alone is insufficient.⁷⁰ In other words, a faith community committed to justice should look beyond material equity to confront the subtle norms that limit women's autonomy, thereby recognizing that patriarchy is a comprehensive system encompassing social, familial, and religious domains.⁷¹

A gawani-inspired church, if it concentrates solely on communal wealth sharing, risks overlooking the diverse ways patriarchal assumptions infiltrate daily interactions and decision-making processes. For instance, congregation members might collectively pool resources for projects yet still relegate women to subordinate roles when it comes to leadership or determining program priorities. Such an approach leaves the mandate of Acts—where the faithful hold possessions in common— only partially realized, as gawani theology aims to unify economic stewardship with genuine equality across gender lines. Oduyoye proposes that societies often embed patriarchal systems within religious traditions, making it imperative for communities to review their entire cultural framework if they wish to achieve holistic liberation.⁷² She observes how women's voices have historically been muted, suggesting that without explicit attention to gender-based disadvantages, economic reforms alone cannot fully dismantle long-standing hierarchies.⁷³ Indeed, cultural transformation must accompany financial redistribution, lest women merely exchange one form of marginalization for another.⁷⁴

---

69. Phiri, *Women, Presbyterianism and Patriarchy*, 28. Phiri identifies how cultural norms, and religious constructs jointly limit women's agency, underlining that improvements in economic conditions alone do not necessarily enable genuine empowerment.

70. Phiri, *Women, Presbyterianism and Patriarchy*, 32. Phiri observes that patriarchy persists when institutional structures remain uninterrogated, revealing the necessity of explicit interventions aimed at correcting imbalances in authority.

71. Phiri, *Women, Presbyterianism and Patriarchy*, 41. Phiri discusses the transformations in familial and communal power dynamics, suggesting that effectively advocating for women's rights requires alterations in how both church and society assign responsibility.

72. Oduyoye, *Daughters of Anowa*, 33. Oduyoye critiques the deep-seated cultural assumptions that undermine women's efforts to claim social or religious authority, emphasizing the need for systemic change.

73. Oduyoye, *Daughters of Anowa*, 83. Here, Oduyoye explains that patriarchal practices are often perpetuated through societal mores that cast women in caretaking roles while preserving male privilege in decision-making.

74. Oduyoye, *Daughters of Anowa*, 88. Oduyoye elaborates on how economic

Such perspectives find concrete illustration in the Pentecost narrative, where the Holy Spirit's empowerment extends equally to "sons and daughters," thus urging a community that welcomes women's public roles (Acts 2:17–18). Ruether underscores that when scriptural texts highlight shared prophetic ministry, it becomes contradictory for churches to confine women to peripheral spheres.[75] She further proposes that the prophetic impulse in Christianity mandates a critical analysis of social norms, including those that justify sexism under the guise of tradition.[76] By combining gawani theology with feminist readings of Acts, believers can acknowledge that resource allocation must align with inclusive leadership structures, forging a culture that encourages women to speak, minister, and guide the community's trajectory. Ruether describes this integrative endeavor as an extension of biblical faith, whereby the church deepens its commitment to justice by refusing to segment gender equity from other social issues.[77]

From a practical standpoint, this synergy of feminist and gawani perspectives prompts churches to reevaluate daily customs. For instance, men might historically dominate church councils or finances, while women remain relegated to caregiving tasks or supportive roles. A gawani community, on the other hand, would insist on designing collaborative committees that ensure women's voices are integral to planning and budgeting. By structuring fellowship around consistent participation of women, the church moves closer to the biblical ideal of a shared life, emphasizing interpersonal respect and cooperative management of assets. Kang contends that this interconnectedness is not purely symbolic; it has tangible effects on how believers view property, charity, and economic responsibility.[78]

---

improvements unaccompanied by a reevaluation of cultural traditions can perpetuate inequalities beneath a veneer of prosperity.

75. Ruether, *Sexism*, 24. Ruether notes that biblical accounts featuring women's prophetic engagement undermine the notion that women should remain passive in ecclesial settings.

76. Ruether, *Sexism*, 31. Ruether argues that the ecclesial community is compelled to evaluate social norms that have historically used religious justification to exclude women from positions of leadership.

77. Ruether, *Sexism*, 33. Ruether underscores the urgency of linking gender equality to the broader framework of liberation theology, ensuring that the struggle against oppression encompasses women's distinct challenges.

78. Kang, *Theology of Gawani*, 17. Kang contends that gawani theology involves both spiritual and administrative elements, calling for shared resources, inclusive leadership, and a commitment to uplifting marginalized voices.

Additionally, feminist theology broadens how congregations approach worship, insisting that corporate expressions must include laments for the harm caused by patriarchy. Services might begin with a collective acknowledgment of historical injustices that have marginalized women, inviting both men and women to reflect on how these cultural patterns persist.[79] Such practices mark a significant step in fostering repentance that transcends emotional regret. They also pave the way for reformed church policies, such as adopting transparent voting procedures or rotating leadership assignments, that address ongoing inequalities. As Phiri underscores, any effort to empower women must tackle the practical realities of how authority and resources are distributed rather than relying solely on rhetorical commitments to unity.[80]

Moreover, integrating gawani principles with feminist liturgical insights can stimulate imaginative forms of celebration. Congregations might honor significant biblical women—e.g., Mary Magdalene, Miriam, or Lydia—thereby connecting scriptural precedents to contemporary issues of representation and leadership. In tandem with gawani's emphasis on collective stewardship, these observances encourage the entire assembly to examine how funds are allocated, whether women have an equal voice in determining their use, and how symbolic or ritual changes reinforce broader shifts toward egalitarian fellowship. Through such holistic engagement, the church's confession moves beyond symbolic humility into structured reforms that actualize shared authority and mutual service.[81]

Feminist scholars also highlight the instructive value of narrative examples, where women's stories serve as catalysts for renewing theological discourse. Phiri's work reveals that, in certain contexts, women once held recognized authority in matrilineal lines but later encountered eroding autonomy due to shifting political economies.[82] In these scenarios, biblical calls to communal solidarity cannot be adequately fulfilled unless the restoration of women's decision-making power becomes an explicit goal. Within gawani theology, addressing these imbalances offers a chance for the church to exhibit unity that is substantiated by concrete steps, rather than relying on abstract professions of equality. Consequently, an

---

79. Oduyoye, *Daughters of Anowa*, 83.
80. Phiri, *Women, Presbyterianism and Patriarchy*, 32.
81. Phiri, *Women, Presbyterianism and Patriarchy*, 41.
82. Phiri, *Women, Presbyterianism and Patriarchy*, 28.

ethics of common property transforms into a commitment to champion women's leadership in committees, ministries, and educational ventures.

Finally, both feminist and gawani approaches converge in illustrating how spiritual transformation is inherently linked to social practices. While theological reflection may stress repentance or communal love, it is in tangible policies and day-to-day relations that these convictions achieve real significance. As Ruether argues, any form of liberation theology flounders if it fails to scrutinize entrenched biases that assign power unevenly between men and women.[83] A gawani-inspired congregation seeking to hold all things in common must therefore verify that no hidden inequalities persist in worship language, organizational charts, or resource oversight. When these elements align with an ethos of inclusivity, the biblical narrative of the Spirit-infused community becomes a lived reality, shaping how faith communities practice justice, care for one another, and present a credible witness to society.[84]

Relevance of Contemporary Churches and the Imperative of Structural Equity

Contemporary churches frequently navigate a range of challenges that include leadership diversity, equitable compensation, and conscientious language usage. While some congregations attempt to address these concerns only at a surface level, a more comprehensive approach recognizes the cultural patterns that have historically marginalized women. If worship services, policy guidelines, or theological curricula uphold male-centered assumptions, then congregations risk preserving hierarchies rather than promoting inclusive participation. Feminist theology provides a valuable lens for scrutinizing these subtle, and sometimes overt, paternal structures. It especially focuses on how language and interpretive criteria can reinforce gender biases when they remain unquestioned.[85]

Yet language is only one dimension of the wider institutional landscape that must be examined. Gawani theology emphasizes a systematic reconfiguration of financial priorities, property management, and salary structures. Without an honest appraisal of economic practices, including

83. Ruether, *Sexism*, 33.
84. Kang, *Theology of Gawani*, 17.
85. Russell, *Feminist Interpretation*, 14. Russell examines the marginalization of women in biblical studies and interprets collaboration among feminist and liberation scholars as an impetus for exploring alternative methods of interpretation.

salaries for staff, resource allocation for community outreach, and operational budgets, churches cannot fulfill their ethical commitments. Indeed, it is insufficient to rely solely on egalitarian rhetoric if church assets continue to be directed in ways that sustain disparities. By critically evaluating who decides budgetary priorities and how property is utilized, gawani theology insists that congregations embrace shared responsibility rather than confining women to supportive or peripheral roles. When implemented together, feminist theology and gawani theology extend beyond conceptual discussions, propelling real changes in local church environments.

Addressing Gender Biases through Feminist Theology

Feminist theology has highlighted the complex ways patriarchal presumptions manifest in sermons, worship bulletins, and biblical studies. This call for inclusive discourse not only critiques the content of sermons but also challenges the interpretive norms that have historically placed women on the margins of theological debate.[86] Through decades of scholarship, feminist theology has argued that church communities need to rethink fundamental assumptions about how women's experiences shape biblical interpretation. In one setting, women's scholarship served as a catalyst to reevaluate the mainstream methodological approaches and to ask how interpretations might shift when read through a lens attentive to gender-based exclusion.[87] For instance, reexamining biblical narratives can reveal how certain passages have been framed to uphold a viewpoint that benefits men while reducing women's involvement to a supplementary function. Moreover, early American feminists suspected that traditional interpretations entailed a deliberate marginalization of women.[88] Hence, feminist theology calls for reading scripture and practicing worship in ways that amplify women's perspectives, reinforcing that both men and women are bearers of equal dignity.

86. Russell, *Feminist Interpretation*, 15. Russell contends that feminist hermeneutics must question the foundational criteria for biblical interpretation and move beyond superficial adjustments.

87. Russell, *Feminist Interpretation*, 18. On this page, Russell outlines how liberation perspectives that highlight female figures—mothers, wives, or other roles—help reframe biblical texts in a way that challenges prevailing patriarchal attitudes.

88. Russell, *Feminist Interpretation*, 23. Early American feminists like Sarah Grimké and Antoinette Brown argued that interpretations of Scripture deliberately marginalized women, calling for new scholarly efforts.

Nonetheless, no matter how diligently a church may seek to implement inclusive language, progress remains limited without tangible shifts in governance. A purely rhetorical approach can result in frustration if women remain excluded from synods, presbyteries, or session meetings. In contexts where leadership forums remain largely male-dominated, lip service to feminist ideals does not address systemic exclusion. From a feminist theology standpoint, rethinking biblical interpretation and worship language must be accompanied by structural reforms, such as revising membership criteria for executive committees, approving training programs for future female leaders, and creating open discussion platforms where women's concerns are addressed sincerely. Congregations that implement such changes begin to see how reexamining language and interpretive frameworks fosters a more equitable environment overall.

Gawani Theology and the Restructuring of Economic Priorities

Gawani theology, as it currently stands, does not claim to be a complete practical theology with a thoroughly systematized framework. Rather, it offers a preliminary perspective emphasizing communal sharing (gawana) as an ethos directed toward restoring human relationships in socioeconomic contexts.[89] While this approach draws on certain theological patterns—such as reordering power or valuing the perspectives of marginalized people—it refrains from presenting a fully articulated ecclesial method or parish-level blueprint. Instead, it highlights that church communities need to engage in meaningful exchange of resources to address economic inequities that persist within congregations, thereby revealing a broad trajectory rather than a definitive program.

Despite its early stage of development, gawani theology raises pointed questions about who holds authority over church budgets, property, and compensation structures. Kang describes how gawani arises from the realities of hardship lived, where families develop an ethic of sharing as a means of survival.[90] For churches, this emphasis on sharing invites reflection on the ways philanthropic programs can sometimes overlook deeper systemic issues. Leaders may disburse charity funds without investigating

---

89. Kang explains that gawani theology is still in a preliminary stage, highlighting "sharing" as an organizing theme while acknowledging it has yet to develop a full practical framework. Kang, *Theology of Gawani*, 4.

90. Kang describes how Gawana arose from real-life contexts of scarcity, illustrating how an ethic of sharing emerged as a survival strategy. Kang, *Theology of Gawani*, 3.

whether wage imbalances or property rights remain skewed in ways that disadvantage certain members—often women or other historically underserved groups. If gawani theology is to extend beyond an initial concept, future theological work could propose specific avenues for committees, ministry teams, or even denominational bodies to undertake structural changes. In this regard, gawani theology highlights economic fairness as a critical dimension of church mission, even if it has not yet supplied detailed strategies for implementing such fairness.

When examining how power is distributed in congregational life, the gawani concept underscores the importance of broad-based participation. Traditional governance models, in which pastors or elders unilaterally manage assets and ministries, often restrict the input of those whose voices are most needed.[91] Gawani theology posits that genuine community emerges when all believers, regardless of social standing, can have a role in deciding how resources are allocated. However, Kang acknowledges that at present, gawani theology does not put forth a fully established set of steps to achieve this. Rather, it gestures to the need for committees to reexamine who decides salaries, who sets terms of property usage, and how philanthropic outreach might be reorganized to foster more inclusive participation.

One central theme in this preliminary theology is that helping can inadvertently become paternalistic if structural inequalities remain unaddressed.[92] For instance, if a congregation directs funds to assist low-income families but never questions how wages are determined for certain staff or volunteers, it risks reinforcing a dynamic in which some individuals permanently occupy a precarious economic position. Gawani theology thus points to the possibility of shared oversight—what it names as "forgoing individualism" and choosing a cooperative way of life.[93] Yet it stops short of prescribing specific governance models. Rather than setting out a step-by-step plan, gawani theology calls attention to the necessity of conversation and discernment, suggesting that future studies

---

91. The emphasis on broad-based governance and the questioning of hierarchical asset control is a recurring motif, although gawani theology does not detail the precise means to implement these changes. Kang, *Theology of Gawani*, 3.

92. Kang stresses that philanthropic efforts can unintentionally uphold inequality if they fail to address underlying wage or property disparities. Kang, *Theology of Gawani*, 3–4.

93. Kang, *Theology of Gawani*, 18.

TOWARD A GAWANI-FEMINIST-BLACK LIBERATION ETHOS   193

might shape these broad convictions into more detailed frameworks that local congregations can adopt.

Such an approach aligns loosely with other theologies that also demand practical steps, including strands of liberation theology and certain progressive ecclesiological movements. However, Kang clarifies that gawani theology is not merely a reiteration of these perspectives but seeks to incorporate them into its guiding vision of shared resources.[94] This vision stems from the everyday experiences of those facing economic hardship, reminiscent of the Malawian communities described in Kang's field observations. Recognizing that gawana, a localized ethic of sharing, helped families endure oppressive conditions, the theology of gawani encourages churches elsewhere to consider how such a principle might translate into contexts where wealth is often unevenly distributed.

Beyond economics, gawani theology also urges believers to view themselves as interdependent, resisting the impulse to see mission purely as top-down charity. According to Kang's narrative, the core idea is that faith communities begin to encounter the significance of "sharing love" by practicing mutual reliance.[95] However, since gawani theology remains nascent, it offers few detailed protocols on how to integrate this ethos into ministerial planning or theological education. Future refinement might involve collaboration with Christian educators, pastoral leaders, and lay ministers who could translate the concept of communal sharing into programs on the ground—ranging from budgeting processes to leadership development and property management.

In sum, gawani theology, while still an emerging and not yet codified practical theology, calls attention to resource disparities in church life and proposes that shared oversight be seen as a core practice. Nevertheless, it does so by focusing on a fundamental conviction about community, rather than articulating a comprehensive set of policies. By acknowledging that sharing everything together is no simple matter, it poses a challenge to congregations that continue to operate with hierarchical authority structures and unexamined economic practices.[96] Rather

    94. Kang identifies ways in which gawani draws from or parallels other theological movements while maintaining an independent direction shaped by local experiences. Kang, *Theology of Gawani*, 1.
    95. The notion of "sharing love" features prominently as gawani theology's guiding value. Kang, *Theology of Gawani*, 1.
    96. Kang's text characterizes this notion of "sharing everything together" as important for building authentic fellowship but notes the difficulty in translating this ethos into concrete policies. Kang, *Theology of Gawani*, 4.

than deliver a finalized template, gawani theology underscores the need for further theological reflection, possibly leading to an expanded model of ecclesial life that values inclusive governance. Churches seeking to adopt these broader principles may find themselves inspired to test new forms of economic collaboration and communal leadership. In so doing, they might move toward a more consistent alignment between faith claims and material realities, living out a transformative sense of gawani that fosters solidarity across social divisions.

Confronting Domestic Violence and Social Inequities

One of the most urgent areas where feminist and gawani theologies converge is the church's response to domestic violence. Feminist theology clarifies that spiritual counsel, while crucial, does not suffice if material conditions prevent survivors from leaving a harmful household.[97] Churches that assume moral authority must evaluate whether they provide practical assistance—such as referrals to safe housing, partnerships with legal aid organizations, or direct financial support. Without these measures, laudable theological language remains abstract. In societies where women are discouraged from pursuing independence or from resisting patriarchal expectations, pastoral counseling must be accompanied by concrete resources.[98]

Moreover, certain traditions may see limited involvement of women in decision-making bodies, leading to situations where their experiences with abuse remain unvoiced. In such cases, a congregation might formulate responses to domestic violence that fail to address root causes. By collaborating with professionals who specialize in trauma and financial planning, the church can broaden its approach, ensuring that survivors are met with informed empathy and sustainable strategies. This involves reevaluating not only the structural composition of pastoral teams but also the philosophical underpinnings that have historically undervalued women's autonomy.[99] Through these efforts,

---

97. Phiri, *Women, Presbyterianism and Patriarchy*, 76. Phiri shows how leadership transitions in the Nkhoma Synod affected women's influence, pointing out that financial dependence remains a crucial barrier to women's liberation.

98. Phiri, *Women, Presbyterianism and Patriarchy*, 102. Women's inability to attend central decision-making sessions illustrates the structural exclusion that can undermine churches' claims of egalitarian theology.

99. Phiri, *Women, Presbyterianism and Patriarchy*, 104. Phiri notes that inadequate

ministries can move from a stance of passive consolation to proactive involvement that empowers survivors.

The Role of Educational and Leadership Training

Many pastors and lay leaders receive minimal training in addressing both economic injustice and patriarchal norms. Indeed, theological education has often underscored spiritual formation or biblical literacy without devoting comparable attention to gender equity or institutional economics. In some cases, denominational leadership dissuades women from pursuing advanced theological studies, thereby limiting the number of women prepared to assume pivotal roles.[100] Churches that wish to champion truly inclusive leadership must, therefore, incorporate specialized workshops and courses on financial advocacy, conflict resolution, and trauma care. These training programs help leaders recognize that social inequalities are intertwined with theological convictions, and they prepare both men and women to enact structural changes that support liberation.

Crucially, the presence of women who have undergone theological and pastoral training can influence how administrative and spiritual guidance is conducted within a congregation. For instance, if women are consistently encouraged to marry early or step aside from formal education, they may lose opportunities to cultivate theological discernment that could eventually enrich church leadership.[101] A gawani-informed approach, which insists on equitable salaries and educational access, alleviates the pressure on women to choose between spiritual calling and economic stability.

---

theological education for women often arises from cultural pressures, hindering their capacity to shape ecclesial strategies.

100. Phiri, *Women, Presbyterianism and Patriarchy*, 105. Expectations that women marry early or assume subservient roles obstruct their pursuit of extended education, impacting their ability to engage in leadership positions.

101. Phiri, *Women, Presbyterianism and Patriarchy*, 106. Phiri proposes that congregations need to encourage women's theological advancement so that when ordination or expanded leadership opportunities arise, capable female candidates are available.

Reimagining Church Governance and Hermeneutical Frameworks

Additionally, the governance structures of many denominations still reflect patriarchal conventions. Certain traditions bar women from serving as elders or otherwise restrict their influence on doctrinal stances. A feminist theology perspective would urge congregations to dismantle these restrictions, pointing out that the marginalization of women's voices not only compromises equity but also hampers the church's ability to respond creatively to emerging social concerns.[102] Put differently; by limiting women's input, churches may remain tethered to outdated exegetical practices that fail to respond to contemporary injustices.

In parallel, a gawani-informed approach highlights how budget committees, capital campaigns, and routine expenditures can either replicate gender disparities or promote communal well-being. Leadership circles often determine the day-to-day financial reality of ministries, deciding whether women receive adequate reimbursement for their labor or if community outreach primarily focuses on certain demographics. By intentionally including women's perspectives at each stage of the budgetary process, churches can foster a shared sense of accountability for how resources are used.

Engaging Postcolonial Narratives and Cultural Realities

Further complexity arises when one sits in church structures within postcolonial contexts. Some African congregations, for instance, have inherited economic systems, interpretive strategies, and leadership models shaped by Western colonial frameworks.[103] As a result, well-intentioned development projects may fail if they do not honor local gender norms or if they apply foreign templates without adaptation. Dube, Mbuvi, and Mbuwayesango stress that the legacy of colonization continues to influence contemporary theology, leading to tensions between imported

---

102. Phiri, *Women, Presbyterianism and Patriarchy*, 137. Reevaluating the Genesis creation story in light of African women theologians underscores how perceptions of women's inherent "inferiority" inform church leadership restrictions.

103. Dube et al., *Postcolonial Perspectives*, 1. The introduction discusses how biblical interpretation in Africa is shaped by postcolonial contexts, which requires attention to how power operates in religious spaces.

doctrines and indigenous practices.[104] An approach that unites feminist and gawani theologies acknowledges these layers, urging congregations to critically evaluate how historical imbalances can remain embedded in present-day finances and leadership patterns.[105]

In many instances, external missionary work initially introduced hierarchical structures that positioned men as cultural mediators, while women were assumed to be secondary participants. By intentionally confronting these legacies and enabling local communities—especially women—to articulate priorities for worship, leadership, and social engagement, churches transcend mere paternalistic oversight. This approach recognizes that true transformation requires listening to and elevating the experiences of all community members, ensuring that local dynamics are neither trivialized nor overshadowed by imported organizational strategies.

Language, Liturgy, and Symbolic Representation

Language choices in worship and Christian education deeply affect whether women feel truly acknowledged as equal partners. If they are consistently depicted as supporters or assistants rather than cocreators, then underlying assumptions about their subservient role in the church remain unchallenged. Russell argues that an inclusive linguistic approach forces a fresh reevaluation of how biblical texts are read and applied.[106] Congregations might, for example, revise standard liturgical language to affirm women's leadership, incorporate biblical women's voices more thoroughly in sermons, or rewrite educational materials that previously treated women's experiences as tangential. This shift not only pertains to pronouns for God but also extends to how female biblical figures are interpreted and taught in Sunday schools or adult education classes.

---

104. Dube et al., *Postcolonial Perspectives*, 2. The authors propose a critical review of historical theories, urging the adoption of new themes and postcolonial frameworks that address colonial impositions in African biblical studies.

105. Dube et al., *Postcolonial Perspectives*, 3. By tracing the "Scramble for Africa," the authors reveal how missionary work often introduced patriarchal structures that sidelined women's roles in local church contexts.

106. Russell, *Feminist Interpretation*, 18. Russell argues that reading biblical narratives through feminist and liberation perspectives can transform previously marginal roles, lending agency to female characters and, by extension, contemporary women in the church.

However, implementing inclusive language is merely one step. If men still hold dominant control over finances, property use, or pastoral appointments, then symbolic equality remains fragile. Therefore, it is crucial that the cultural changes reflected in worship, teaching, and public statements mirror real policy reforms. In synergy, feminist theology reminds us that interpretive paradigms must value women's stories as integral, while gawani theology emphasizes that economic resources must be openly and managed. By doing so, congregations reinforce ethical consistency and empower women to shape not only the conversation but also the financial and organizational frameworks.

Prospects for a Holistic Approach

Bringing together feminist and gawani theologies offers a thorough strategy for congregations seeking to address patriarchy and economic inequity. This shared vision accentuates that structural reform, language revisions, and pastoral care should interact in ways that uphold the dignity of all believers. Churches that successfully integrate these viewpoints are likelier to create programs aimed at supporting survivors of domestic violence—ensuring that assistance includes both spiritual guidance and direct financial intervention. They are also poised to reexamine wage practices, bridging the gap between stated commitments to equality and actual compensation policies.

Moreover, a consistent, long-term effort to educate both clergy and lay members becomes fundamental. If leadership teams do not understand how patriarchal assumptions can resurface—even in apparently progressive settings—then well-meaning initiatives risk reproducing historical patterns of exclusion. Intentional training fosters awareness of how certain terminologies or roles perpetuate gender biases, while gawani theology frames these conversations within the broader realm of budgetary management. Ultimately, this holistic approach positions the church as a place where women play decisive roles in shaping policy, interpreting Scripture, and guiding community life.

Conclusion

Feminist theology has uncovered how patriarchal assumptions shaped Christian thought and practice, frequently hindering women's full

TOWARD A GAWANI-FEMINIST-BLACK LIBERATION ETHOS 199

participation in ecclesial life.[107] Gawani theology, rooted in the Acts paradigm of solidarity, likewise challenges believers to share resources equitably and adopt mutual responsibility for community welfare. Together, these perspectives present a vision of the church as a fellowship of equals, unmarried by gender-based hierarchy or economic exploitation. Where one tradition emphasizes the necessity of dismantling patriarchy in language, leadership, and ritual, the other focuses on the reordering of communal assets. The result is a comprehensive liberation ethos that unite spiritual, social, and material dimensions.

Neither tradition aims to abandon the biblical text. Rather, both endeavors to reread Scripture in ways that unveil the divine call for just relationships. Feminist theology does so by analyzing how patriarchal norms infiltrated theological discourse, while gawani theology foregrounds the biblical witness to shared stewardship. The synergy of these insights reveals that an authentic gospel message challenges all forms of exclusion—whether rooted in male-centered authority or inequitable wealth distribution. Such a church fosters new forms of worship where female voices and leadership are not peripheral, as well as new institutional practices that ensure resources support those historically sidelined.

In practice, this alignment means congregations may adopt inclusive language for God, promote women to the highest leadership roles, and institute coowned funds for community members at risk. They may reevaluate theological curricula, integrating feminist critiques so that future ministers appreciate how gender-based oppression overlaps with class-based injustices. They might also revise membership covenants to commit believers to active solidarity with women facing domestic violence or legal discrimination. Although such measures can be unsettling to those wedded to traditional hierarchies, both feminist and gawani theologies insist that the gospel requires daring steps toward equality.[108]

Ultimately, this combined framework stands as an invitation for the universal church to actualize its confessions of unity and love. It urges believers to examine how paternal structures impede genuine communion and how economic disparities perpetuate hidden injustices. By affirming

---

107. Ruether, *Sexism*, 66. Ruether emphasizes how patriarchal assumptions have distorted Christian thought, making women's full participation in ecclesial life difficult or impossible.

108. Johnson, *She Who Is*, 141. Johnson concludes that theological renewal necessitates courageous strides toward gender equality and inclusive language, reinforcing the biblical vision of justice for all.

that biblical liberation embraces every dimension of community—gender roles, economic relations, worship language, and moral responsibility—feminist and gawani perspectives together reaffirm the abiding potency of the Christian story. They speak not of abstract ideals but of living transformations, calling each church to embody tangibly the image of a God who rejects all dominance and fosters a fellowship where each person's dignity flourishes under a just and merciful Creator.

8.4. DIVERGENCES AND SYNERGIES: TOWARD A HOLISTIC LIBERATION

In contemporary theological discourse, the interplay among race, gender, and class remains a central concern for those who seek the liberation of marginalized communities. Scholars and activists in Black theology, feminist theology, and gawani theology each highlight a specific dimension of structural oppression—racism, patriarchy, or economic exploitation—and offer corresponding strategies of resistance. Yet these emphases are not meant to negate one another; rather, the challenge is to understand that struggles for human dignity intersect and overlap. When these movements listen and learn across their respective focal points, they open possibilities for a more holistic vision of justice that can transform both ecclesial and societal structures.

Distinct Emphases: Race, Gender, and Class

Black theology has historically emphasized the urgency of confronting racial injustice and retrieving Black dignity in a world that has systematically devalued African-descended peoples. Early proponents drew from the biblical narrative of the exodus to affirm that God stands on the side of those in bondage and leads them toward liberation. Such an emphasis proved essential to many Black churches in North America, where the memory of enslaved ancestors resonated powerfully with Israel's deliverance from Egypt.[109] Meanwhile, feminist theology has insisted that struggles against patriarchy are integral to any project of liberation, arguing that God's redemptive plan must ensure the well-being of women and

---

109. Cf. Cone, *God*, 11. Cone argues that the exodus narrative provided hope for enslaved Africans, reinforcing the belief that divine intervention on behalf of the oppressed is historically grounded.

other marginalized genders in ecclesial life and beyond.[110] In a parallel yet intersecting way, gawani theology focuses on socioeconomic justice, advocating for resource sharing and small-scale communities that embody mutual support and resist predatory capitalist systems.

The distinctiveness of these three movements does not indicate mutual exclusivity. Indeed, many womanist theologians and Latina theologians stress that dismantling racism cannot be done apart from dismantling patriarchy and that any project aiming to distribute resources more justly must also recognize how racial hierarchies shape economic inequalities. Feminist theologian Rosemary Radford Ruether argues that theological movements must guard against addressing one form of subjugation while leaving other forms of exclusion intact.[111] Likewise, scholars such as Mercy Amba Oduyoye point out that African women face a convergence of gender bias, racial discrimination, and neocolonial economic structures, requiring a multidirectional approach that addresses all these dimensions simultaneously.[112] When movements such as Black theology, gawani theology, and feminist theology engage one another, they can build a shared framework that acknowledges the interplay of race, gender, and class—rather than insisting on a hierarchy of oppressions.

Moreover, by acknowledging intersectionality, these theologians demonstrate that lived experiences do not fit neat categorization. A Black woman who struggles with both racism and sexism, for instance, may also face economic precariousness that magnifies her vulnerability.[113] Recognition of these intersecting burdens requires a theologically grounded praxis that encompasses community organizing, advocacy for political reform, and sustained critique of cultural ideologies that perpetuate dominance. Consequently, each of the three theological movements offers distinct insights: Black theology contributes a perspective

---

110. See Oduyoye, *Daughters of Anowa*, 200. Oduyoye highlights how patriarchal oppression intersects with racial and economic factors, intensifying burdens for African women.

111. Ruether, *Sexism*, 204. Ruether maintains that isolating one dimension of injustice can unintentionally reinforce other hierarchies, necessitating a broad liberative approach.

112. Ruether, *Sexism*, 205–6. Here, Ruether addresses how feminist base communities might engage challenges that also involve race and economic factors, suggesting that multiple forms of structural injustice are interwoven.

113. Townes, *Womanist Ethics*, 131. Townes argues that Black women must navigate oppressive forces on multiple fronts, including racism, sexism, and class-based discrimination.

on racial solidarity and cultural affirmation; feminist theology shapes a rethinking of ecclesial authority and gender equality; and gawani theology foregrounds economic justice and resource sharing practices that challenge exploitative market logics. When these streams converge, they form a broader liberative tapestry capable of addressing multiple levels of oppression without sidelining any demographic.

Ecclesiology and Community Practices

A second area where these movements diverge yet also converge is ecclesiology. Gawani theology is especially drawn to the Acts 2 model of believers pooling their resources, sharing meals, and resisting the commodification of essentials like food, shelter, and healthcare. According to this perspective, the church functions best in small, interdependent communities, where members consciously detach themselves from exploitative market forces, striving to embody what Leonardo and Clodovis Boff describe as "the social context of the message"—one that challenges the inequalities found in broader society.[114] Such small-scale models seek to transform everyday life into an ongoing witness to God's economic justice.

Black theology, by contrast, often emerges from a different ecclesial context. Historically, Black churches in the United States have occupied a central place in their neighborhoods, providing refuge, social services, political leadership, and spiritual guidance. These were not typically small intentional communities set apart from broader society; rather, they were community anchors in a segregated nation, creating spheres of empowerment where racial solidarity could flourish. Yet the emphasis on collective responsibility and local leadership echoes certain principles found in gawani theology, underscoring the church as a body tasked with communal uplift. Building on the biblical affirmation that God stands with the oppressed, many Black congregations became catalysts for civil rights activism and broader social movements.[115]

Feminist theology has often centered its ecclesiological critique on institutional structures and language practices within established

---

114. Boff and Boff, *Introducing Liberation Theology*, 34. The authors underline that liberation theology must always interpret the biblical message within the concrete social realities of communities struggling under injustice.

115. Cone, *God*, 90. Cone contends that Black churches become agents of social transformation precisely because they derive their mission from a liberation-centered reading of the gospel.

churches. Feminist scholars challenge hierarchical governance, exclusively male clerical authority, and the use of male-dominant language for God, asserting that inclusive language and women's ordination are non-negotiable for authentic Christian community. In this way, feminist theology seeks to reshape not merely how local congregations function but also how denominational and global ecclesial body's structure leadership and ministry. As Elisabeth Schüssler Fiorenza and others have argued, the liturgical and doctrinal portrayal of the divine intimately impacts whether women are viewed as fully empowered subjects or peripheral participants.[116] Hence, whether the reform is undertaken through gawani theology's small-scale communities, Black theology's strong congregational foundations, or feminist theology's institutional critique, each approach shares a commitment to crafting spaces in which historically silenced groups are heard, valued, and integrated into decision-making.

Despite these varied approaches, synergy emerges when each movement reflects on how to build inclusive, liberative ecclesial practices. Even if gawani theology stresses a more radical break from mainstream economic systems, it can still engage Feminist voices to ensure that women's economic roles are not overlooked or relegated to secondary status within resource sharing communities. Meanwhile, Black churches that draw on the legacy of resistance to racism can also incorporate feminist critiques of patriarchy and gawani critiques of capitalist exploitation, forging a more comprehensive approach to empowerment. Such mutual enrichment fosters a theological vision that extends beyond denominational lines to advocate systemic transformation at every level.

Retrieval of Lukan Imagery: The Role of Exodus

A unifying biblical motif across these theologies is the exodus narrative, reinterpreted through the lens of Luke's Pentecost account. The book of Acts depicts an eschatological community, united by the Spirit, that transcends ethnic, linguistic, and socioeconomic barriers. The reference to Jesus' exodus (Luke 9:31) on the Mount of Transfiguration signals that his death, resurrection, and ascension form a new covenant people, recalling Israel's journey out of Egypt.[117] For gawani theology, this motif grounds the im-

---

116. Ruether, *Sexism*, 206. Ruether emphasizes that language for God and structures of authority deeply affect how women are valued and recognized within church life.

117. Cf. Moltmann, *Theology of Hope*, 129. Moltmann discusses the eschatological

perative to break away from oppressive economic structures, paralleling how Israel was delivered from Egypt's forced labor system. Such deliverance, in gawani thought, necessitates building alternative communities of economic solidarity that mirror the Acts fellowship.

In Black theology, the exodus narrative has long served as a source of hope for African Americans and other peoples of African descent who faced enslavement and legal segregation.[118] James Cone, for example, underscores how the promise of liberation in the exodus resonated with Black communities yearning for deliverance from systems of racial bondage. Cone maintains that the God revealed in the exodus stands decisively with those who suffer, challenging every societal form of racial subjugation. This conviction resonates with the earliest spirituals sung by enslaved peoples in the Americas, in which the desire for liberation and the assurance of divine solidarity were intimately woven.[119] Such an interpretation reaffirms that the exodus event is neither a relic of the ancient Near East nor a purely spiritual symbol, but a living testament that liberation in history is possible through God's active involvement.

Feminist theology also interprets the exodus motif as a movement out of patriarchal captivity.[120] Here, the central analogy is that those social structures limiting women's agency and leadership must be cast aside much like the oppressive forces faced by Israel. According to Rosemary Radford Ruether, an exodus-informed feminist theology prompts Christian communities to take concrete steps to ensure women's full participation in ministry and to resist cultural norms that perpetuate gender discrimination.[121] This liberative thrust challenges ecclesial and societal patterns that reduce women's roles or exploit their labor, insisting that the biblical call to freedom extends to all facets of human life,

---

significance of Israel's historic exodus, which influences Christian hope for communal liberation.

118. Cone, *God*, 11. Cone details how Black communities found parallels between their condition and ancient Israel's servitude, reinforcing the conviction that God hears the cry of the oppressed.

119. Cone, *God*, 233. Cone underscores that early spirituals and worship practices among enslaved Africans in America testify to a profound hope in divine deliverance, rooted in exodus imagery.

120. Oduyoye, *Daughters of Anowa*, 175. Oduyoye connects the exodus symbol to African women's journey out of patriarchal constraints, tying the motif to broader movements for liberation.

121. Ruether, *Sexism*, 205. Ruether states that genuine exodus from patriarchal captivity includes reforming the structures and language that have historically marginalized women.

TOWARD A GAWANI-FEMINIST-BLACK LIBERATION ETHOS 205

including the reformation of traditional religious language, structures, and power dynamics.

Despite applying the exodus motif to different aspects of oppression, these three theological strands converge around the biblical testimony that divine liberation necessitates a concrete departure from oppressive situations. In their reading of Luke-Acts, many liberation theologians argue that the early Christian community embodied this departure by sharing possessions, welcoming diverse believers, and proclaiming God's sovereignty in ways that upset dominant sociopolitical hierarchies.[122] Gawani theology views such acts of economic solidarity as essential for resisting capitalism's exploitative tendencies, Black theology sees them as continuous with the biblical story of God's special regard for those historically relegated to society's margins, and feminist theology insists that these acts must be interpreted in ways that break patriarchal power structures.

By retrieving the Lukan image of a Spirit-driven, barrier-transcending community, modern theologians craft a shared framework that affirms the exodus as a living paradigm for diverse groups facing subjugation. In so doing, they remind the church universal that redemption is not an abstract promise but a summons to forsake entrenched systems of injustice. Here, the exodus transforms from a single-horizon metaphor to a multilayered lens that reveals new dimensions of God's liberating activity.[123] Consequently, whether one speaks of racism, patriarchy, or class exploitation, the invitation remains to participate in God's ongoing deliverance and to pursue a future where justice is tangibly realized.

8.5. CONTEMPORARY IMPLICATIONS AND FUTURE DIRECTIONS

Gawani theology emerges in response to a pressing reality: many Christian communities find themselves challenged by persistent social inequalities, gender-based violence, and structural racism. These conditions call for a faith-based framework that addresses economic disparities in meaningful, community-centered ways. Advocates of gawani theology propose

---

122. Boff and Boff, *Introducing Liberation Theology*, 50. The Boffs highlight Acts 2 as a prototype for the church's social and economic reorganization, fueled by the Spirit's transformative power.

123. Russell, *Feminist Interpretation*, 16. Russell proposes that the exodus paradigm can be viewed as a flexible lens that illuminates present struggles, encouraging Christians to seek tangible acts of liberation rather than purely theological abstractions.

that early Christian practices of communal resource sharing offer a model for transforming contemporary church life, encouraging congregations to embody tangible forms of solidarity. Their approach confronts the widespread perception that churches often remain distant from real-world issues, emphasizing communal action over abstract ideals.

Within this conversation, there is a growing recognition that economic justice must be expanded to incorporate the concerns of feminist theology. Gawani theology's commitment to shared responsibility resonates with feminist efforts to contest patriarchal power structures and inequitable labor practices. This overlap encourages congregations to think seriously about who benefits from current economic systems and whose voices are silenced. By combining a communal approach with feminist attention to women's leadership and undervalued caregiving labor, churches can begin to dismantle practices that exclude or disadvantage women.

Discussions also intersect with Black liberation theology, which highlights the interlocking factors of racism, exploitation, and social marginalization. Gawani theology's emphasis on practical collective action provides avenues for congregations to challenge economic systems that perpetuate racial inequalities. Advocates propose that the Acts 2 and 4 narratives—where believers share possessions and support one another—carry implications for confronting ongoing legacies of segregation and the structural barriers faced by racial minorities. In that sense, gawani theologians argue that financial sharing and intentional communal structures can be tools for both spiritual and societal renewal.

A related theme involves examining the intersection of consumer culture with Christian witness. Church members in postindustrial societies often absorb market-driven norms, prioritizing individual gain and private consumption. Gawani theology calls for an alternative: a practice-based understanding of discipleship that reorients believers toward collective responsibility and communal engagement. Yet advocates caution that attempts to apply these principles risk romanticizing or oversimplifying the challenges faced by real congregations, especially in urban contexts marked by gentrification, insufficient resources, and ongoing racial tension.

Feminist, womanist, and mujerista perspectives enrich these efforts by directing attention to how economic sharing intersects with everyday struggles, from single parenting to cultural bias and immigration-related obstacles. Such perspectives challenge faith communities to avoid narrow definitions of oppression and to address multiple layers of social inequality simultaneously. Consequently, advocates from various theological backgrounds promote a broader alliance of churches, grassroots movements, and advocacy organizations capable of advancing policy changes and rethinking ownership models in ways that uphold human dignity.

Another important aspect is the call to reenvision church structures themselves. Established leadership systems, budgeting processes, and property ownership patterns may unintentionally maintain hierarchies that run counter to a gawani ethic. A willingness to reform governance and integrate diverse leadership helps congregations model inclusivity rather than merely talk about it. In doing so, churches can become communities where the distribution of resources reflects compassion and mutual accountability, rather than concentration of power in the hands of a few.

These discussions, spanning gawani commitments, feminist concerns, and Black liberation viewpoints, converge on the conviction that economic sharing is inseparable from social justice. Church-based experiments in cooperative living, policy advocacy, and transnational solidarity networks can serve as touchpoints for rethinking how Christians embody their faith. By weaving these strands together, faith communities are better positioned to engage the realities of late capitalist societies, offering examples of alternative economic structures and leadership patterns that honor the worth of every individual.

Economic Justice and Institutional Witness

Contemporary Christian communities, particularly those located in postindustrial contexts, frequently face scrutiny regarding their capacity to mount credible responses to widespread economic inequalities, entrenched racial disparities, and systemic gender-based violence. Observers, including sociologists of religion and public theologians, have argued that ecclesial bodies may lose legitimacy if they fail to address such critical challenges in a direct and collaborative manner. Against this background, proponents of gawani theology emphasize that Christians should not merely espouse ideals of justice but also practice tangible modes of economic sharing in their day-to-day lives. These scholars contend that forming cooperatives, pooling financial resources, and fostering neighborhood-based communities constitute powerful demonstrations of collective responsibility—initiatives designed to counter isolationist practices shaped by market-driven competition. Such communal funds and policy engagements could potentially regenerate the church's public credibility, as the earliest Christian congregations distinguished themselves from the surrounding Greco-Roman culture through demonstrable generosity and inclusion.[124]

Nevertheless, a critical dimension of this discussion involves avoiding overly romantic portrayals of communal economics, since failing to account for contextual factors can lead to unintended consequences. For instance, urban congregations may encounter rising housing costs and precarious job markets, conditions that not only influence how members experience community life but also exacerbate disparities along lines of class, race, and gender. If gawani-based interventions or experiments operate in ignorance of these structural realities, they risk reproducing inequities such as racial bias or patriarchal norms—thus undermining their stated goals of inclusion and economic justice.[125] Indeed, some theologians argue that strategies of resource sharing must incorporate ongoing analyses of political dynamics, land use policies, and the historical legacies of segregation that persist in many modern urban centers. A gawani-oriented community that neglects discussions of entrenched racial marginalization or gender-based asymmetries may appear grounded in benevolence but ultimately reinforce existing hierarchies, a phenomenon Mercy Amba Oduyoye highlights in her critique of communal endeavors that sidestep the complexities of patriarchal influences in many African contexts.[126]

Furthermore, any attempt to implement economic alternatives requires partnerships across diverse theological and social movements. Feminist, womanist, Black liberation, and other activist-theological perspectives offer complementary insights, reminding gawani practitioners

---

124. Kang emphasizes that the communal economy described in Acts is not merely symbolic but constitutes a tangible witness to gawani love. This sharing of food, shelter, and economic resources becomes a theological act, embodying the eschatological ethic of Jesus's teachings. Kang, *Theology of Gawani*, 11–13.

125. Gutiérrez maintains that liberation theology must be grounded in the concrete historical realities of the poor and oppressed. Without context-sensitive engagement, communal sharing models risk collapsing into abstraction or utopianism. Gutiérrez, *Theology of Liberation*, 20.

126. Oduyoye highlights how traditional communal practices can unintentionally replicate patriarchal structures unless the embedded gender assumptions are addressed explicitly. Her African feminist critique cautions against cultural idealization that silences women's agency. See Oduyoye, *Daughters of Anowa*, 98.

that social formations cannot be reduced to a single axis of oppression. According to Emilie Townes, systemic evil often functions through overlapping mechanisms of cultural exclusion, class exploitation, and racial discrimination, necessitating a broad-based coalition that operates in solidarity with multiple marginalized groups.[127] Collaboration of this scope pushes congregations to build relationships with grassroots movements, community organizations, and professional advocacy networks that are capable of framing and advancing policy initiatives. In turn, these alliances enrich the moral imagination of church leaders, making it more likely that economic sharing practices—wage transparency, investment in communal infrastructure, or intentional cohousing projects—are informed by a thorough understanding of the sociopolitical environment.

An additional point to consider is how churches can strategically engage the public sphere. While some gawani advocates prioritize local initiatives, others argue for a broader approach that involves legislative advocacy or participation in municipal planning forums. Such engagement might include promoting living wage ordinances, demanding equitable zoning laws, and supporting measures that safeguard tenants from exploitative rent hikes. By pursuing these policy reforms, a gawani-inspired church signals that its economic solidarity practices extend beyond internal fellowship and seek the common good. In this manner, the church's communal efforts could evolve into a transformative force within civil society. Over time, these activities could help reshape cultural assumptions about ownership, merit, and social responsibility, thereby resisting the hyperindividualistic inclinations that dominate many late capitalist settings.

Finally, one might inquire whether the growth of gawani theology and related communal practices would provoke external resistance. Critics may charge that Christian communities, in espousing cooperative and redistributive models, are naive about global market forces or limited in scale. Yet proponents counter that the Acts 2 and 4 narratives represent not only an ethos of care but also a historically grounded instance where small groups meaningfully influenced the broader society by modeling egalitarian forms of living. They claim that although small communities cannot single-handedly overturn entrenched economic structures, they

---

127. Townes introduces the concept of "countermemory" to describe the ethical and theological importance of remembering historical suffering from the standpoint of the oppressed. She argues for intersectional analysis as a necessary method for any liberative practice. See Townes, *Womanist Ethics*, 8.

can symbolically disrupt hegemonic norms and embolden broader coalitions for transformation. By consistently bearing witness to gawani principles, churches cultivate a practice-based theology that upholds human dignity, fosters collaboration with various social actors, and offers a sign of hope amidst widespread disenchantment with dominant economic logics.

Expanding Feminist Concerns to Economic Solidarity

Feminist theology has long sought to unveil and challenge the patriarchal foundations that deform ecclesiastical language, leadership patterns, and scriptural hermeneutics, thereby generating significant debates over the theological and social place of women. Rosemary Radford Ruether's classic critique of exclusively male God language underscores the intimate link between conceptions of the divine and the allocation of religious authority.[128] However, despite remarkable achievements, some critics of mainstream feminist theology caution that insufficient attention to economic dimensions may leave women in precarious living situations. In many contexts, women experience a compounding effect of patriarchal subordination and market-driven exploitation, especially when they are responsible for caregiving and domestic labor without adequate compensation or social security.

Gawani theology holds potential to enlarge feminist theological discussions by situating gender-based oppression within wider frameworks of socioeconomic justice. At its core, gawani theology advocates for mutual care, solidarity, and the dismantling of economic hierarchies—a vision that resonates powerfully with feminist goals of dismantling patriarchal power structures. Yet, as Kang remarks, churches must ensure that gawani praxis does not remain gender-blind.[129] Adopting communal resource sharing or Acts 2 style living arrangements might inadvertently replicate male leadership if decisions regarding property, finances, and child-rearing remain in the hands of men. Consequently, implementing

---

128. Ruether underscores that any authentic theological transformation must begin with deconstructing patriarchal language and symbols, especially those that link male identity with divinity and authority. Without such reform, feminist inclusion remains superficial. Ruether, *Sexism*, 101.

129. Kang observes that the early church's economic model in Acts, often invoked in gawani theology, must be reinterpreted through a gender lens, noting that without deliberate inclusion of women in leadership and resource allocation, such communities risk reproducing patriarchy. Kang, *Theology of Gawani*, 17–19.

TOWARD A GAWANI-FEMINIST-BLACK LIBERATION ETHOS 211

wage transparency within church institutions, instituting inclusive budgeting processes, and formally structuring communal funds for childcare can all serve as practical expressions of a fully integrated gawani-feminist perspective.

Such measures could also remedy the persistent undervaluation of domestic labor, which typically falls upon women, especially in socioeconomically marginalized communities. By recognizing unpaid caregiving work as an indispensable contribution to the community, congregations could develop economic models that reward and uphold women's efforts, whether through a shared childcare cooperative or subsidized training for women reentering the workforce. In the spirit of gawani theology, these interventions remind us that love and mercy must manifest concretely in areas such as wage parity, access to health services, educational support, and genuine power-sharing structures. Without these elements, theological declarations about female empowerment risk being perceived as symbolic gestures rather than substantive transformations.

From a mujerista standpoint, Ada María Isasi-Díaz underscores the complexity faced by Latina women, who grapple with overlapping challenges related to poverty, immigration, cultural bias, and the duties of caring for extended kin networks.[130] Within such settings, a vision of gawani must adopt multifaceted tactics, bridging theological reflection and practical economic strategies. This might entail, for instance, forging alliances with local immigrant advocacy groups, setting up scholarship funds for mothers who aspire to advance their education, or facilitating cooperative ventures where women can share resources and reduce family expenses. By merging feminist perspectives that highlight women's voices with gawani commitments to equitable economic practices, believers can shape communities that are not only more inclusive but also explicitly resistant to patriarchal power structures.

Moreover, the synergy between feminist theology and gawani principles raises fundamental questions about ecclesiology and leadership. In many denominations, hierarchical models persist, relegating women to subordinate roles even when female membership is numerically dominant. A gawani-feminist approach would affirm that women's theological interpretations and administrative insights are indispensable for the

---

130. Isasi-Díaz introduces *lo cotidiano* as a critical theological category, arguing that daily life struggles, especially those faced by Latina women, must inform both theological reflection and social action. Solidarity must therefore integrate economic, cultural, and spiritual dimensions. See Isasi-Díaz, *La Lucha Continues*, 96.

church's integrity and for the health of its communal economy. Thus, women should be central participants in pastoral decision-making councils, finance committees, and teaching bodies, ensuring that financial commitments are aligned with the needs of women and children. Over time, such policies could revitalize older ecclesial structures and usher in a renewed moral imagination that validates women as coequal contributors to theological reflection and economic innovation.

Finally, one can envision the broader implications of such a gawani-feminist approach. If women are empowered to lead and shape the church's ethical commitments, the congregation may find itself more adept at developing inclusive outreach programs that benefit a diverse demographic. By integrating lived experiences of single mothers, immigrants, widows, survivors of violence, and other vulnerable individuals, the church positions itself as a vehicle for meaningful social transformation. In turn, feminist theologies would be enriched by reflecting on how collective ownership strategies, mutual aid funds, and reconfigured leadership practices might tangibly disrupt patriarchal norms. Such a convergence holds the promise of igniting a deeper reflection on the intersection of theology and praxis, fostering communities that actively confront economic and gender-based injustices rather than offering distant theoretical critiques.

Challenging Capitalist Culture and Celebrating Diversity

In the twenty-first century, capitalist expansion extends into nearly every realm of human life, shaping global markets, national priorities, and even individual aspirations.[131] From early childhood, many encounter the pervasive drive to consume and succeed under the metrics of profit and efficiency, often at the expense of collective well-being. Within Christian discourse, gawani theology stands out as an approach that calls for an economic ethic rooted in mutual care and shared responsibility, grounded in principles that question the morality of unregulated profit-making.[132]

---

131. In critiquing the alignment of Christian institutions with predominant capitalist interests, James Cone emphasizes that authentic theological witness must stand in opposition to systems of racial and class oppression. See Cone, *God*, 95.

132. Kang contends that sharing resources is integral to gawani communities' social witness, highlighting that this practice critiques the individualism characteristic of consumer culture. See Kang, *Theology of Gawani*, 4–5. Here Kang speaks of the community that forgoes individualism by pooling resources into a shared life that critiques

This perspective resonates with the biblical invitation to care for the least of these, urging congregations to see economic justice as more than a mere philanthropic endeavor. Instead, gawani theology frames it as an outgrowth of genuine discipleship, wherein the resources of the faith community are arranged and distributed in ways that confront greed and consumerist ideals.

Black theology likewise addresses economic injustice but insists that it cannot be examined in isolation from race, class, and historical oppression.[133] By linking current economic disparities to the legacy of colonialism and racial hierarchy, it challenges the church to reject neutrality and instead align itself explicitly with those suffering under systemic exploitation.[134] In this view, the legacy of the exodus narrative serves as a potent symbol for liberation, reminding believers that God's redemptive work includes emancipation from structural bondage.[135] Feminist theology extends this critique further by illuminating the ways patriarchal norms intersect with capitalist structures. When the voices of women are minimized or ignored in congregational settings, it becomes nearly impossible to actualize holistic liberation that addresses both economic and gender-based forms of marginalization.[136]

Yet confronting capitalism is not just about resisting market excesses; it involves cultivating partnerships and strengthening grassroots movements. Smaller gawani communities, for instance, have the capacity to deepen their social impact by forging alliances with anti-racist initiatives, women's cooperatives, labor unions, and ecological advocacy organizations.[137] This collective action echoes the narrative in Acts, where diverse

---

consumer culture.

133. Cone examines how institutional Christianity in the United States historically aligned with exploitative structures, arguing that the church must decisively reject and dismantle racial hierarchies if it wishes to remain faithful to the biblical witness. Cone, *God*, 148.

134. According to Cone, those involved in upholding oppressive frameworks are often unaware of how violence is perpetuated through structural means, underscoring the necessity of conscious resistance. Cone, *God*, 151.

135. Cone draws on the exodus narrative to highlight God's consistent movement toward liberating the oppressed, serving as a paradigm for modern struggles for racial and economic justice. Cone, *God*, 219.

136. Ruether asserts that relegating women's concerns to the periphery effectively undermines the comprehensive scope of liberation, rendering any social progress partial at best. Ruether, *Sexism*, 101.

137. Kang notes that gawani congregations can amplify their liberative message by participating in broader coalitions, thereby extending the reach of their theological and

groups unify for the common good despite myriad cultural or linguistic boundaries.[138] In that narrative, unity in the Spirit is never equated with homogeneity; rather, it is depicted as a genuine interweaving of varied gifts and perspectives working toward a shared goal. According to the Boffs, such collaborations can uphold core commitments while simultaneously celebrating differences of language and background.[139] Gawani theology, with its stress on interconnectedness, dovetails naturally with these endeavors, underscoring that neither women's voices nor the experiences of marginalized racial groups can remain peripheral if true economic justice is to be realized.

Moreover, some theologians emphasize that the church itself must undergo a process of decolonization to embody a credible alternative to capitalist culture.[140] In many instances, ecclesial structures inadvertently reinforce the same patterns of consumerism and profit orientation that they claim to critique. By adopting more transparent and egalitarian models of governance, congregations can begin to address internal contradictions that impede their public witness.[141] Such efforts involve not merely reforming organizational policies, but also transforming underlying assumptions about wealth, power, and moral responsibility.

Expanding Partnerships and Embodying Solidarity

Looking forward, one of the most pressing questions is how smaller and often resource limited gawani communities can magnify their influence for social transformation.[142] Partnering with various movements—anti-

---

social commitments. See Kang, *Theology of Gawani*, 8.

138. Boff and Boff examine the communal ethos in early Christian communities, arguing that unity arises precisely through the Spirit's capacity to transcend cultural barriers. Boff and Boff, *Introducing Liberation Theology*, 55.

139. The Boffs also observe that celebrating diversity of culture and language does not dilute core commitments to economic justice but strengthens the church's potential for transformative engagement. Boff and Boff, *Introducing Liberation Theology*, 56.

140. Decolonizing ecclesial practices involves unmasking how colonial mindsets persist in church governance, liturgy, and theology, with the goal of recentering marginalized perspectives. Cone, *God*, 148.

141. In his critique of capitalism's infiltration into church structures, Cone highlights the ways in which faith communities sometimes mirror the patterns of domination they profess to challenge. Cone, *God*, 95.

142. Collaboration with local labor unions or ecological advocacy can strengthen the moral and spiritual arguments for dismantling exploitative practices, aligning the church's mission with the pursuit of social equality. Boff and Boff, *Introducing Liberation*

TOWARD A GAWANI-FEMINIST-BLACK LIBERATION ETHOS 215

racist networks, cooperatives led by women, labor unions advocating fair wages, and environmental groups working for sustainability—amplifies their liberative message. While these alliances may present logistical challenges, they yield more comprehensive strategies for resisting exploitation and building social structures that honor human dignity.[143] In Acts, diverse believers transcended barriers of language and culture, illustrating that the Spirit's work naturally drives communities to collaborate in pursuit of the common good. Although differences in race, gender, culture, or class can generate tension, the Acts account also demonstrates that diversity can flourish within a shared commitment to dismantling oppressive frameworks.

Notably, Christian communities seeking such collaborations cannot merely remain in a posture of theoretical endorsement. They must develop concrete mechanisms—joint community centers, shared liturgies that highlight diverse voices, rotating leadership structures, and mutual accountability committees—to enact collective decision-making and resource sharing in real-life contexts.[144] Feminist theology reminds us that these initiatives will fall short if they fail to integrate women's leadership at every level, rather than confining women to supportive or peripheral roles.[145] Similarly, Black theology cautions that any coalition lacking an explicit stance against systemic racism risks perpetuating the very injustices it aspires to overcome.[146]

Embracing a unity in diversity model is not an optional add-on, but rather central to the biblical vision of the Spirit's activity among believers.[147] To that end, forming connections across organizations

---

Theology, 69.

143. Boff and Boff emphasize that unity in the Spirit is both spiritual and practical, urging churches to engage in social reforms as a natural outgrowth of Christian witness. Boff and Boff, *Introducing Liberation Theology*, 74.

144. Cone underscores that real transformation demands both institutional and personal involvement, cautioning against superficial attempts that only rearrange appearances. Cone, *God*, 219.

145. Ruether addresses how ecclesial structures frequently mirror patriarchal norms, thereby undercutting the radical call to liberation found in Scripture. Ruether, *Sexism*, 217.

146. Cone warns that churches which ignore the reality of systemic racism risk colluding with the status quo, perpetuating inequity. Cone, *God*, 151.

147. By insisting that the Holy Spirit unites people through shared commitments rather than uniformity, the Boffs illustrate how early Christian models of fellowship can inspire modern practices of inclusion. Boff and Boff, *Introducing Liberation Theology*, 56.

and marginalized groups enriches the collective witness of the church. Such practices challenge a hyperindividualistic culture that prioritizes personal gain over community well-being. By refusing to accept the fragmentation encouraged by profit-driven ideologies, gawani congregations demonstrate that economic solidarity can thrive even in a world where consumerism dominates social values.

A Holistic Vision of Liberation: Where Do We Go from Here?

Ultimately, the conversation among Pentecost-gawani communities, Black theology, and feminist theology converges on a broad vision of liberation that does not remain abstract but is instead lived out in local contexts.[148] Rather than viewing liberation as a distant hope or a purely spiritual concept, these traditions assert that freedom must be tangible, involving concrete engagement against oppressive realities.[149] Gawani theology's emphasis on shared resources ensures that concerns about hunger, economic exploitation, and social exclusion are addressed directly, preventing liberation from being relegated to the realm of theoretical ideals. Black theology's focus on racial justice, meanwhile, confronts the sin of racism without ambiguity, underscoring that no lasting transformation can occur while entire racial communities remain systematically marginalized.[150] Feminist theology, for its part, insists that patriarchal assumptions be dismantled, ensuring that women's experiences and leadership are integral to every layer of ecclesial life.[151]

---

148. Kang's framework for gawani theology posits that liberation should manifest in the concrete realities of everyday life, rather than remaining confined to doctrinal formulations. Kang, *Theology of Gawani*, 4–5. "Beyond contemporary progressive theological endeavors' emphasis on solidarity and identification with victims and the marginalized, the theology of gawani focuses on building trust, offering hope, and sharing in the suffering and despair, individually and communally. Above all, the theology of gawani focuses on sharing love." Here Kang lets the cry of Exod 3:7 echo in every parish ledger, reminding us that soteriology which stays aloft in doctrinal cumulus forfeits its claim to be gospel.

149. Kang specifically calls on churches to direct material resources toward marginalized groups, ensuring that liberation is experienced as something more than symbolic. Kang, *Theology of Gawani*, 8.

150. Cone identifies the sin of racism as fundamentally incompatible with a liberating gospel, necessitating deliberate confrontation within and beyond church contexts. Cone, *God*, 233.

151. Ruether champions a vision in which full participation of women in leadership, theology, and community life is indispensable to the authentic expression of

By merging these theological standpoints, the church recovers a more comprehensive understanding of witness, mission, and community. This reenvisioning resonates with Luke's portrayal in Acts: a faith collective that lives in the present reality of God's reign, thereby rejecting the normalization of injustice or dehumanization. As Kang observes, gawani congregations embrace shared goods and a collaborative spirit, working to overturn unjust frameworks rather than adjusting to them.[152] In so doing, they adopt both material and interpersonal dimensions of transformation—material, by restructuring economic priorities and alleviating inequality; interpersonal, by fostering genuine reconciliation across racial, gender, and cultural lines.[153] Cone highlights how the exodus narrative is not restricted to a distant past but signifies God's continuous intention to liberate oppressed people here and now.[154] Feminist perspectives add that such liberation must include the dismantling of all forms of patriarchy, ensuring that the pursuit of freedom does not bypass half the population.[155]

This holistic approach to liberation entails more than a singular focus on economics or political reform; it involves the formation of a new humanity. Kang articulates that the gawani practice of resource sharing is intimately linked with a renewed way of being, one that identifies with the marginalized from below, echoing the biblical motif of the worm's eye view, which centers the experiences of the oppressed rather than the powerful.[156] Here, transformation is not relegated to a future eschato-

---

Christian faith. Ruether, *Sexism*, 100.

152. Kang suggests that the identification of gawani theology with the worms' eye view underscores the church's solidarity with those who experience the most acute forms of marginalization. Kang, *Theology of Gawani*, 11.

153. Ruether stresses that a thorough commitment to liberation must involve interpersonal transformation that addresses sexism, racism, and classism at once. Ruether, *Sexism*, 217.

154. Cone's treatment of the exodus story as a paradigm for modern liberation underscores that divine salvation intervenes in historical and social contexts, not merely individual spirituality. Cone, *God*, 207.

155. Ruether highlights how partial forms of liberation lose credibility if they overlook women's ongoing struggles against patriarchy, emphasizing that ecclesial renewal must be inclusive. Ruether, *Sexism*, 100.

156. By situating Jesus' ministry within an apocalyptic framework, Kang illustrates how the gawani emphasis on new humanity speaks to a collective identity that transcends oppressive norms. Kang, *Theology of Gawani*, 11. Reading the Son of a Human Being logia through the apocalyptic lens of Dan 7 and the worm's-eye optics of Ps 8 and Ezekiel, Kang contends that Jesus' self-designation signals the irruption of a new humanity whose life is already enacted whenever the church relinquishes possessive

logical horizon but is actively enacted through communal practices of justice, empathy, and advocacy.

Toward a Gawani-Feminist-Black Liberation Ethos

By interweaving gawani theology, Black theology, and feminist theology, contemporary Christian communities can aspire to what might be termed a gawani-feminist-Black liberation ethos, firmly grounded in Scripture and enlivened by the Spirit.[157] Such an ethos urges believers to move beyond passive agreement into sustained reflection, robust critique of existing structures, and steadfast commitment to reforms that reflect God's compassionate reign in the here and now.[158] As Cone explains, genuine theological engagement cannot simply align with dominant economic or political interests; it must actively challenge the conditions that deny life and wholeness to the oppressed.[159] This directive finds parallels in feminist theologians like Ruether, who contends that no community can claim to be free if women are relegated to secondary status or if sexual violence and harassment remain unaddressed.[160]

Indeed, the mandate to pursue reconciliation across race, gender, culture, and class flows from the logic of Pentecost itself, which unites diverse voices and communities in pursuit of mutual flourishing. In that

---

isolation and elects mutual sharing. Such kenotic community, he writes, stands as a present sign of the coming judgment that topples oppressive orders, raising the small and silencing the self-secure (cf. Luke 1:52; Mark 10:45). The generosity of gawani is therefore not social ornament but eschatological obedience.

157. This ethos builds upon the incarnational principle that Christ's mission was not abstract but engaged social realities, challenging believers to incarnate God's compassionate reign in everyday structures. Cone, *God*, 219.

158. Kang explains that this commitment requires ongoing dialogue, practical forms of accountability, and the willingness to share resources across cultural and theological boundaries. Kang, *Theology of Gawani*, 8. Kang recalls the church to that costly vigilance by which koinonia remains alive: ceaseless conversation across every cultural fence, structures of transparent accounting, and the concrete renunciation of surplus so that no sister or brother begs bread while another stores grain. Only in such continuous self-expenditure, he argues, does liberation break free from rhetoric and become the recognisable activity of the living God (cf. Acts 4:32–35).

159. Cone links the credibility of Christian witness to its capacity to resist alliances with unjust power, pointing to the biblical narrative in which prophets often stood in direct opposition to reigning monarchs. Cone, *God*, 95.

160. Ruether observes that an authentic liberation theology must address every manifestation of oppression, including sexual exploitation, domestic violence, and the denial of reproductive rights. Ruether, *Sexism*, 217.

sense, the radical spirit displayed in Acts demonstrates that the church need not—and should not—replicate the unjust hierarchies of the surrounding world. Rather, faith communities can adopt new practices that epitomize God's invitation to inclusive fellowship. As Boff and Boff argue, such a stance testifies to the dynamic operation of the Holy Spirit, who empowers believers to "take history into their own hands" for the transformation of society.[161] In a capitalist milieu where individualism reigns, a gawani-feminist-Black liberation ethos announces that authenticity is to be found not in endless acquisition but in radical sharing, solidarity with the marginalized, and mutual accountability aimed at the common good.

Moving forward, fostering this ethos requires deliberate self-examination within ecclesial communities, as well as meaningful participation in the broader struggle for social justice. Churches must evaluate whether their own structures, language, and resource allocations inadvertently perpetuate gender and racial biases, or whether they indeed exemplify an alternative community of equality and compassion.[162] New alliances should be formed with secular and interfaith groups committed to social and economic equity. This collaborative work can bridge the gap between theological affirmations and lived reality, mirroring the earliest examples of the church's resolve to bear witness to God's liberating activity in real time.

Although the path requires clear analysis of societal power dynamics, structural critiques, and unwavering commitment, it remains faithful to centuries of biblical testimony and to the lived example of believers who have risked livelihoods and lives in the pursuit of righteousness.[163] The Acts narrative underlines that such a quest for unity

---

161. Boff and Boff underscore that the Holy Spirit's transformative power becomes visible when marginalized communities "decide to take history into their own hands," thereby driving social change. Boff and Boff, *Introducing Liberation Theology*, 56.

162. Kang's portrayal of gawani communities underscores the necessity of continual self-assessment, warning that even well-intentioned congregations can inadvertently replicate unjust patterns. Kang, *Theology of Gawani*, 11. Writing from the worm's-eye vantage, Kang warns that even the most earnest congregation may drift back into the quiet tyranny of possessive selfhood unless it subjects itself to regular, unsparing examination. Gawani, therefore, is not an achievement to be possessed but a posture to be rehearsed: a perpetual self-emptying whereby the community lets go of its own safety that the crucified poor may rise with it into freedom.

163. Cone emphasizes that biblical faith has always involved a risk-laden journey toward justice, as seen in the countless believers who have sacrificed personal security to confront entrenched systems. Cone, *God*, 207.

in diversity and collective well-being is not only achievable but vital, standing as a guiding light to the world. It points to the possibility that God's kingdom genuinely draws near, reshaping hearts and societies in truly transformative ways.

Shaping a Collaborative Future: Integrating Gawani, Feminist, and Black Liberation Perspectives

The church's commitment to economic justice can become far more holistic when gawani, feminist, and Black liberation frameworks engage each other. By centering shared responsibility, these perspectives challenge narrowly defined models of charity and create a more unified approach to community transformation. Emphasizing care for marginalized persons, such as those burdened by racial discrimination or patriarchal systems, encourages congregations to examine whether their current structures actively uplift or inadvertently exclude certain groups.

A focus on practical economic changes is vital in these discussions. Gawani theology contributes a call to communal sharing, urging churches to invest in cooperative ventures, transparent budgeting, and inclusive funds for childcare or healthcare. Feminist voices enrich this approach by highlighting how resource allocation must address the underpaid or unpaid labor often undertaken by women. Black liberation thought compels reflection on how historical segregation and institutional racism continue to create barriers for communities of color. Integrating these perspectives helps dismantle multiple layers of exclusion, ensuring that grassroots initiatives address the realities of economic and social inequality.

Collaborative strategies require more than occasional dialogues. Churches can form alliances with neighborhood associations, advocacy groups, and governmental bodies to secure policy changes related to equitable zoning, fair wages, and affordable housing. Drawing on these external partnerships allows faith communities to expand their impact, transcending traditional boundaries of ecclesial influence. In turn, shared actions can draw broader society's attention to the need for transformed structures that uphold human dignity and equality.

Central to this project is the necessity of participatory leadership, especially from those who have experienced marginalization. Feminist theology underlines the importance of women not only as caregivers but also as key decision-makers. Black liberation perspectives show how positions of leadership can challenge entrenched racial stereotypes. Gawani theology supports these efforts by encouraging mutual ownership of resources, making congregational governance an active expression of collective accountability rather than a top-down administration.

Resisting consumer-driven culture also requires reimagining the church's role in public life. By bridging internal resource sharing with outward-facing advocacy, congregations can become agents for change in policy forums, urban planning, and legislative debates. Such initiatives enlarge the moral and spiritual imagination of communities, reminding both church members and wider society that economic models founded on mutual care are not only possible but also deeply connected to scriptural visions of fellowship.

Grounding these pursuits in concrete, locally-based experiments helps congregations learn from missteps and context-specific factors. Whether establishing neighborhood cooperatives or supporting mothers pursuing education, practical steps illustrate how theological commitments translate into shared well-being. In this way, gawani, feminist, and Black liberation approaches come together to advance a vision of the church that evolves with changing social realities while maintaining a consistent focus on human dignity.

As congregations persist in bridging theological understanding with tangible action, they embody a deeper awareness of how oppression intersects across gender, race, class, and other markers of identity. By acknowledging these overlapping factors, churches can respond in ways that honor the lives of those most affected by economic and social barriers. This approach avoids simplistic solutions and fosters a sense of community ownership, in which everyone's voice and effort contribute to a renewed moral witness.

Ultimately, a gawani-feminist-Black liberation ethos calls for both an internal recalibration of church structures and an external commitment to societal change. By applying biblical themes of unity and neighborly care to complex social issues, believers demonstrate that faith communities can serve as catalysts for more equitable forms of existence. Although challenges remain, adopting a posture of solidarity, transparent leadership, and engaged advocacy brings congregations closer to the transformative fellowship envisioned in Acts: a collective that not only proclaims a hopeful message but also embodies it through ongoing and inclusive economic practices.

8.6. CONCLUSION: ENVISIONING SHARED TRANSFORMATION THROUGH GAWANI, FEMINIST, AND BLACK LIBERATION PERSPECTIVES

Christian communities that embrace a gawani-feminist-Black liberation ethos step beyond passive reflection and into thoughtful communal reform. Emphasizing responsibility for shared resources, this ethos challenges congregations to rethink entrenched hierarchies and commit wholeheartedly to the work of equality. Churches that integrate these overlapping frameworks of social renewal often find themselves developing programs and policies that honor cultural diversity, expand economic cooperation, and ensure gender-inclusive decision-making.

Feminist theology draws attention to the varied ways patriarchal assumptions have shaped biblical interpretation, worship language, and ministerial structures. By countering male-focused norms, congregations can promote inclusive leadership, revise worship materials to highlight women's experiences, and institute budgeting that reflects equitable resource distribution. Gawani theology echoes this call for equality but centers on economic transformations, especially in contexts where capitalist competition has overshadowed the communal sharing envisioned in Acts. Black liberation perspectives, in turn, foreground the significance of race in shaping economic and ecclesial realities, underscoring the interconnected nature of systems that marginalize communities of color.

Synthesizing these perspectives encourages a church that recognizes justice across multiple dimensions. Gawani theology's emphasis on collective goods aligns with feminist attention to unpaid caregiving labor and with the Black liberation focus on redressing centuries of racial exclusion. A congregation following this synergy would not only share finances transparently but also evaluate whether policies promote racial inclusion and champion women's leadership. Such efforts undermine compartmentalized approaches to ministry by insisting on a unified path toward communal life that respects all voices.

Local congregations often find tangible ways to enact these convictions. Some form cooperatives that challenge hyperindividualism; others establish rotating leadership councils, ensuring that women, Black congregants, and other marginalized members have real authority. When guided by gawani values, these organizational shifts are not restricted to superficial acts of charity but represent a blueprint for structural change. Practical measures might include coowned childcare initiatives, wage transparency in church staffing, and collaborative investments in under-resourced neighborhoods.

A significant theme emerging from these movements is the reminder that spiritual life cannot be separated from political and economic frameworks. Feminist theology highlights the prevalence of patriarchal assumptions in theological training and denominational governance, urging believers to see how these assumptions intersect with church finances and policymaking. Meanwhile, gawani theology pushes congregations to address more than individual generosity, calling for a shared approach to property, budgeting, and leadership. Black liberation priorities interweave with these actions by showing how segregated living patterns and systemic racism impede the possibility of authentic fellowship.

Calls for policy advocacy resonate powerfully across all three theological streams. Whether protesting unfair wage laws, opposing racially biased housing practices, or demanding protections for immigrants, congregations that endorse a holistic liberation view public engagement as central to their calling. Legislative advocacy offers a way to extend the ethos of communal care from the church into wider society. Far from being apolitical, such communities align personal devotion with collective action, translating worship into campaigns for broader economic and social equity.

Participatory leadership stands at the heart of these reform efforts. Feminist reflections show that women's representation often remains symbolic unless church structures explicitly affirm women's authority. Gawani theology fosters such affirmation by insisting that resource decisions be made communally, not by a small core of officials. Black liberation traditions have likewise emphasized how racially diverse leadership fosters unity and models the church's identity as a people called out of societal divisions. Together, these perspectives shape an environment in which leading roles are not defined by inherited privileges but by a shared commitment to restoring dignity for all.

Another recurring element is the recognition that local experiments can generate new paths toward transformation. Though small in scale, local gawani cooperatives or feminist-led ministries can inspire larger shifts, particularly when they form alliances across denominations and social movements. These linkages magnify their impact, challenging standardized assumptions about economics, family roles, and racial identity. Instead of remaining confined to isolated parishes, communal models of resource sharing, inclusive liturgies, and anti-racist organizing offer a glimpse of the church's potential to embody unity amidst difference.

Cultural shifts at the congregational level often reveal deeper questions about inherited traditions. Gawani theology exposes how unchecked authority structures can suppress lay voices, particularly the voices of women or marginalized ethnic groups. Feminist convictions affirm that interpretive power must be redistributed so that scriptural readings embrace the lived realities of diverse believers. Black liberation insights remind congregations of ongoing racial biases that compromise genuine fellowship. Through active listening and dialogue, these churches learn that reconfiguring leadership patterns, worship language, and communal budgets is a faithful response to the biblical call for reconciliation.

In academic and pastoral training, these integrated approaches can lead to revised curricular models. Seminaries might pair textual studies of Acts with courses exploring economic justice and intersectional feminism, highlighting how gawani ideals can transform local ministries. Black liberation theology could inform teaching on racial justice, fostering an understanding of how systemic oppression emerges in both theological discourse and everyday church life. Such comprehensive education prepares leaders who are ready to guide congregations in practicing communal stewardship, resisting patriarchal structures, and addressing racial inequalities.

Another key aspect lies in reevaluating worship practices. Liturgies can celebrate the experiences of women, immigrants, single parents, and low-wage workers who form the backbone of many communities yet are often minimized. Music, prayer, and biblical reflection are retooled to recognize not only personal faith but also collective commitments to social engagement. This cultivated awareness shapes a fellowship in which each person's story is viewed as integral to the church's shared identity. Black liberation hymnody or feminist reimagining of scriptural narratives can blend seamlessly into gawani-inspired eucharistic sharing.

In multicultural or postcolonial contexts, these issues become more complex. Churches that inherited hierarchical governance from missionary institutions face the challenge of integrating feminist, gawani, and Black liberation frameworks into local traditions. Past entanglements with colonial powers or racially biased policies often create obstacles for congregational renewal. Yet precisely in these zones of tension, the synergy of the three perspectives can birth innovative forms of ministry that harmonize local culture with shared Christian values of equity and compassion.

Movement toward shared responsibility reveals a church that refuses to isolate personal holiness from corporate life. Feminist convictions show that language for God shapes how believers perceive themselves and others, while gawani teaching stresses that finances and property must be subject to ongoing communal scrutiny. By listening to Black liberation thinkers, congregations wake up to the fact that racial justice is not a side project but a defining element of liberation for everyone. The result is a worshiping community poised to address overlapping injustices in a manner that resonates with the biblical call to love one's neighbor actively.

Overhauling institutional habits remains challenging. Congregations that embrace open governance, shared economics, and intersectional advocacy may encounter skepticism from those worried about tradition or financial security. Still, a gawani-feminist-Black liberation ethos offers an alternative to preserving the status quo. In that ethos, church members collaborate intentionally, forging a shared vision where spiritual values and social responsibilities align. The emphasis on supportive relationships counters the fragmentation imposed by consumerist ideals, inviting believers to look beyond personal ambition toward collective well-being.

Dedicated efforts to empower women, especially in leadership and theological interpretation, further cultivate mutual trust. When women occupy central roles—copastors, elders, budget directors—the entire congregation benefits. In parallel, adopting fair wage standards and comprehensive property management supports families in crisis, including those affected by domestic violence or income inequality. Likewise, when racial disparities are openly confronted—through scholarship funds, housing partnerships, and anti-racism training—the church embodies a cohesive witness that addresses multiple layers of oppression.

A collective sense of responsibility emerges, tying together spiritual growth with advocacy work. Biblical passages—once read as purely personal encouragement—take on new vibrancy when framed within a community that redistributes resources, values inclusive language, and amplifies marginalized voices. Sermons, fellowship groups, and Sunday schools thus integrate faithful study with practical reforms, grounding biblical teachings in everyday experiences. Congregational members come to see that speaking of God's reign demands addressing who has access to decision-making, land use, education, and worship leadership.

Engaging in local and global partnerships becomes part of the church's mission. Alliances might involve environmental collectives, immigrant support networks, or local labor unions, all seeking overlapping goals of fairness. Such partnerships enrich theological conversation by reminding believers that faith claims should bear relevance in pressing social challenges. Gawani communities that previously focused only on internal resource sharing discover that collaborations with feminist or Black liberation organizations can broaden their social reach, building a strong witness for justice.

Challenges persist, particularly the risk of fragmentation among those who prioritize different aspects, might focus more on racial justice, others on women's leadership, and still others on the economic dimension. Yet the gawani-feminist-Black liberation framework recognizes that race, gender, and class are interconnected. Churches aiming for integrity cannot address one form of exclusion while ignoring others. Only through regular dialogue and consistent reflection can communities maintain a shared path forward that encompasses multiple concerns without losing momentum.

Such a collective witness may also face external criticism: some claim these reforms dilute the gospel message, or that shared ownership models are unsustainable. Proponents respond that small-scale experiments in resource sharing, inclusive language, and anti-racist engagement have proven viable throughout Christian history—whether in early monastic communities, the civil rights activism of Black churches, or feminist congregational transformations worldwide. By recalling these precedents, contemporary believers anchor their experiments in a larger narrative of faith and solidarity.

Over time, these evolving models can transform broader cultural assumptions about individual success, hierarchy, and property. Members of gawani-based groups learn that ownership can be a collective matter, fostering communal stewardship and interdependence. Feminist convictions inspire reevaluation of how leadership is defined, ensuring that those previously silenced gain an equitable voice. Black liberation concerns keep the church vigilant against racial bias, reminding believers that solidarity with marginalized groups is not optional but central to following Christ's example.

The sum of these interactions lays the groundwork for a revitalized mission in which the church actively questions existing social structures. Instead of rendering the gospel a purely private affair, congregations translate their faith into real-world interventions—cooperatives, fairness-oriented finance, inclusive worship, and anti-racist alliances. Feminist and Black liberation theologies align with gawani convictions in insisting that shared spiritual formation goes hand in hand with systemic change. Each approach reveals that love of neighbor must be as tangible as collective bread breaking and communal budgeting.

As a result, Christian communities committed to this ethos become spaces where members nurture one another's growth in both spiritual and societal dimensions. Support for single mothers, health clinics for uninsured neighbors, or legal counseling for immigrants are no longer seen as extracurricular endeavors but as outgrowths of the biblical call to love one another. The creativity unleashed in these settings can ripple outward, encouraging neighboring churches and community organizations to adopt similar cooperative models or to explore new ways of demonstrating compassion on a structural scale.

This chapter's vision, then, rests upon a unified claim: that the gawani-feminist-Black liberation dialogue yields a comprehensive perspective of faith where resource sharing, anti-racist engagement, and inclusive leadership define Christian witness. By grounding these commitments in the biblical narrative—particularly the Acts imagery of shared goods—believers find a cohesive mandate to realign their ministries with God's reconciling work. This alignment is neither purely conceptual nor exclusively focused on personal piety. Rather, it calls for thorough communal involvement, fostering multilayered responses that touch on both immediate and systemic matters.

The possibilities for transformation extend far beyond church walls. Municipal governments, educational institutions, and civil society groups may all be influenced by a church that proactively pursues policy reforms, cultivates diverse leadership, and invests in grassroots empowerment. Over time, such witness can reshape the broader cultural imagination regarding ownership, worth, and human interdependence. In a society too often defined by consumerism and competition, gawani, feminist, and Black liberation frameworks together paint an alternative portrait of mutual care, grounded in the Christian call to love our neighbors as ourselves.

Though the journey poses real challenges, it offers constructive pathways for the church to reclaim its place as a voice of healing and unity. By crafting solutions that engage multiple layers of oppression, Christians discover that the biblical call to compassion is wide enough to include wage transparency, inclusive worship, and efforts to dismantle racist structures. These concrete actions, supported by theological reflection, ensure that faith remains vibrant, relevant, and responsive to human needs.

In conclusion, a gawani-feminist-Black liberation approach challenges believers to embody collective responsibility and radical hospitality. Faith communities that practice shared economics, inclusive leadership, and race-conscious solidarity display a resilient fellowship that can address contemporary social ills with tangible strategies. This holistic pathway resonates with the earliest Christian witness in Acts, where unity, service, and shared goods pointed to a world transformed by love. Such a vision, woven through theological reflection and daily practice, continues to offer a dynamic framework for the church's ministry in the modern era.

9.

Shared Horizons

A Thematic Conclusion on Community, Resource Sharing, and Transformative Faith

Faith-based communities often seek meaningful ways to align their spiritual convictions with tangible, real-world activities. At the outset, this study observed that congregations benefit when worship is not narrowly confined to private rituals but interacts with political, social, and economic realities. By moving beyond abstract spirituality, believers discover methods of collaborative organization that mirror biblical mandates to care for one another. The message running through this text is that neighborly care, practiced in deliberate and cooperative ways, offers a far-reaching framework for building communities that address everyday challenges. This communal ethic connects material distribution, whether in the form of food, shelter, or economic support, with the heart of worship, ensuring that faith-based commitments bear directly on social well-being.

Simultaneously, the argument has highlighted how these communal impulses receive support from diverse intellectual and cultural streams. Malawian customs illuminate daily rituals of sharing and interdependence, providing a lived model of neighborly accountability. Liberation theologians have likewise contended that faith communities must confront broader structures of power, advocating active solidarity with those overlooked or oppressed. Meanwhile, feminist scholarship critiques hierarchical norms that disregard women's leadership, urging equitable participation in decision-making and resource allocation. Black liberation thought adds another dimension by pointing to systems of racial exclusion, explaining why a just community ethic must tackle racial discrimination head-on. By weaving these perspectives together, congregations can enrich their shared life with a more comprehensive view of both local struggles and global injustices.

In examining how resource sharing and faith intertwine, the text underscores the need for more than occasional charity. Instead of ad hoc acts of assistance, the chapters propose that thoughtful distribution practices should become intrinsic to a congregation's structure. These practices entail rotating economic responsibilities, open budgeting, and the inclusion of all voices—especially those commonly sidelined—when forming collective goals. Through such sustained processes, members gain an expanded sense of moral accountability, viewing support for others not as a discretionary favor but as a communal priority. In turn, worship services evolve from purely ceremonial events into occasions for renewed dedication to mutual care.

A vital dimension here is the recognition that these principles apply across varying cultural contexts. While Malawian communities might exemplify specific resource sharing traditions, the broader argument is that faith-based groups worldwide can adopt, adapt, and refine similar patterns. In the United States, for example, local churches can initiate microfinance programs or housing co-ops, guided by theological commitments to equity and unity. Latin American ecclesial communities, as another illustration, tie bible study directly to grassroots development. In each context, believers reinforce the idea that worship aligns with tangible forms of neighborly support. This structural commitment challenges the assumption that religion remains detached from public life, revealing instead that congregations can tackle pressing needs through collective planning.

Crucially, the text also addresses the merger of theology with cultural knowledge. Rather than positioning Western academic frameworks as superior or exclusive, it advocates learning from local wisdom, specifically from communities that have managed adversity through collaborative survival strategies. For instance, Malawian practices—ranging from rotating meal schedules to seed loan networks—serve as applied examples of distributing goods in ways that resonate with biblical commands to love one's neighbor. This cultural-theological dialogue underscores that scriptural ideals become more robust when grounded in the lived experiences of marginalized or rural populations. The synergy between local practices and biblical teachings leads to renewed interpretations, where faith is not a detached belief system but a catalyst for ongoing transformation in communal life.

Intertwined with this cultural focus is the sustained critique of top-down approaches to mission or development. Historically, outside organizations have sometimes overlooked the agency of local participants, reducing them to passive recipients. By contrast, the chapters show that robust theology and durable social change emerge when frontline experiences direct resource allocation and shape common goals. Local leadership gains legitimacy through direct engagement with everyday hardships, offering insights into how faith communities can coordinate effectively. Moreover, this bottom-up orientation fosters trust and accountability, as members learn to value each other's contributions and recognize that theological reflection includes listening to those most affected by economic or social upheaval.

The conversation broadens through feminist insights, highlighting that resource sharing efforts risk falling short if they fail to account for gender dynamics. In many parts of the world, women shoulder the brunt of caregiving and domestic work, a reality often overlooked in ecclesial budgets or community planning. By unearthing these imbalances, feminist theologians encourage faith communities to ensure women's voices and labor are not simply acknowledged but actively prioritized. This perspective insists on reconfiguring leadership structures, introducing equitable wage systems, and removing barriers that keep women from meaningful participation in liturgy, decision-making, and organizational oversight. Through these measures, communities solidify the notion that genuine resource sharing must address hidden inequalities that stem from patriarchal assumptions.

At the same time, feminist perspectives offer methodological guidance for interpreting scripture and tradition. Rather than reading biblical texts in ways that implicitly endorse male-dominated structures, scholars propose that careful exegesis can uncover moments where women's experiences shaped communal survival. Narratives of female leadership, hospitality, and resilience often furnish scriptural anchors for inclusive practices in modern congregations. This academic rigor grounds feminist theology in a well-established historical and literary foundation, while the real-world examples illustrate how these findings can translate into new policies in local parishes. Ultimately, communities that integrate feminist insights discover that they are better equipped to foster equity in practical arenas, from child-rearing responsibilities to property management.

Black liberation approaches introduce another layer, exposing how racial prejudice and economic deprivation frequently intersect. Building on foundational critiques that racism is embedded in many societal institutions, these interpretations urge churches to stand unequivocally with those most harmed by racist policies. Resource sharing, from this vantage, cannot be separated from advocacy for racial justice. Allocating funds to assist marginalized families, restructuring hiring protocols, and lobbying for fair housing are among the concrete steps congregations might undertake. Such measures flow naturally from biblical imperatives to care for strangers, welcome outsiders, and challenge oppressive norms.

In practice, Black liberation thought shows how faith-based movements can transform local environments through persistent efforts against systemic discrimination. Congregations sponsor educational scholarships for minority youth, coordinate voter registration drives, and cultivate entrepreneurial support networks within historically underserved communities. These collective endeavors demonstrate that racial equality is not an abstract concept but a tangible element of communal stewardship. The combination of theological study and localized activism helps break down entrenched divides, offering a template for how worship and justice can converge. By recognizing systemic racism as an affront to community well-being, believers can better align their moral commitments with their institutional practices, ensuring that resource sharing includes those consistently denied equal opportunities.

Beyond the specifics of gender and race, the text underscores a broader principle: a congregation's commitment to justice should incorporate every sphere of life, from ecological stewardship to the distribution of farmland. This holistic viewpoint finds consistent affirmation throughout scriptural narratives, especially where care for the oppressed is woven together with care for the earth. Within gawani theology, for example, distributing leftover seeds or produce exemplifies how ecological resources become instruments of solidarity. Rather than treating environmental issues as peripheral, communities learn to see that soil erosion, water scarcity, and biodiversity loss can all intersect with poverty and displacement, demanding shared solutions. Linking these topics in a unified framework helps believers envision the common good as involving both human welfare and the earth's vitality.

When such ecological commitments are woven into the daily rhythms of congregational life, worship itself resonates more fully with biblical teachings. Sermons on creation care prompt practical measures such as community gardening, tree planting, or sustainable agricultural training. Likewise, prayers for global peace may extend to local efforts to reduce pollution or fund greener technologies. By integrating ecological consciousness into resource sharing, believers affirm that true fellowship cannot exist apart from the responsible management of God-given environments. This dual focus on neighborly care and environmental stewardship exemplifies an interconnected ethic, grounded in a scriptural call to honor both human dignity and the natural world.

Critical throughout the text is the worm's eye perspective, wherein theological reflection and historical analysis begin with those often considered insignificant by mainstream society. By placing laborers, peasants, or marginalized urban families at the center of the narrative, faith communities uncover patterns of resilience that might otherwise remain undocumented. This vantage champions the claim that community organization and moral clarity often originate from the ground up. Rather than waiting for elites to lead, congregations invest energy in smaller, direct partnerships, ensuring the experiences of vulnerable neighbors drive collective priorities. In these contexts, theology transcends academic speculation, grounding itself in the everyday realities of families facing eviction, land appropriation, or wage theft.

Such an approach also reshapes how worship communities view power. The text observes that leadership ceases to be exclusively the domain of those with formal titles; instead, moral authority emerges when individuals stand alongside those who struggle. This realignment is especially valuable for congregations seeking to avoid paternalistic patterns or disinterested theological arguments. Instead, members gather testimonies from the worm's eye vantage—stories of local adaptation to harsh climates, creative ways of financing children's education, or discreet resistance to authoritarian controls—and incorporate these experiences into liturgy and policy. Consequently, theology evolves as a collaborative enterprise, refined by dialogue with those whose voices were previously muted or dismissed.

Several discussions highlight the link between scriptural interpretation and social ethics, reminding readers that biblical texts are read differently when communities consider how Jesus and the prophets interacted with marginalized people. Parables of banquets or stories of debt forgiveness become more than metaphors; they become invitations to rethink how goods, debt, and land should be shared today. Churches that incorporate these biblical dimensions into their planning processes not only affirm cherished doctrines but also practice them through deliberate economic structures. Community kitchens, job training programs, and rotating savings clubs, for instance, reflect a tangible response to Jesus's command that believers build a fellowship inclusive of the needy and excluded.

Such biblically-grounded efforts address the reality that spiritual maturity must align with ethical engagement. Indeed, the text cautions that private piety can inadvertently endorse injustice if it neglects the material needs of neighbors. To avoid this disconnect, the chapters propose that preaching, small group study, and pastoral counseling all incorporate reflections on society's distribution of resources. Rather than confining salvation to an afterlife promise, the argument insists on situating redemption within the present world, where daily interactions around land, money, and labor reveal whether communities embody or forsake biblical commands to love and protect. This orientation prevents theology from becoming stagnant, consistently reminding believers that faith calls them to push boundaries and care for those left behind by dominant economic frameworks.

An essential element of the text involves describing how small-scale actions can eventually lead to more significant shifts. Organizing seed exchanges, for instance, might seem modest at first. Yet the sense of collective responsibility fostered in such a project can inspire broader commitments, such as forming credit unions or microfinance institutions. As shared experiences accumulate, congregations develop networks of trust, enabling them to confront larger-scale social problems like forced relocations or exploitative taxation. This chain reaction exemplifies how practical fellowship builds capacity for deeper engagement with systemic challenges. By the time a crisis unfolds, these trusting relationships can rapidly mobilize resources and volunteer efforts, avoiding the delays and suspicion that plague top-down interventions.

Equally important is the text's observation that no single project or theological viewpoint can address all injustices at once. Instead, progress emerges as communities weave multiple strands—liberationist calls for social justice, feminist challenges to patriarchal norms, ecological safeguards, and localized knowledge—into a cohesive framework. When each dimension is recognized, the outcome is a more resilient community ethic that endures shifting political circumstances or economic pressures. Over time, these incremental successes lead believers to recognize that seemingly minor acts, such as collectively storing leftover produce, point toward larger transformations in the way the church envisions mission and mutual care.

A recurring motif is worship as a space of renewal, where believers can practice and celebrate resource sharing within a liturgical context. The text asserts that acts of giving, open confession of failures, and mutual recognition of dignity can all find expression in communal gatherings. Rather than relegating such endeavors to separate outreach programs, worship itself embodies these values, binding the spiritual and material together. Congregations that learn to embed these rituals of solidarity into their services may find that participants experience worship less as a solitary exercise and more as a dynamic rehearsal of neighborly responsibility.

This liturgical focus also offers an opportunity for instructing newer generations. Children and young adults who witness communal sharing in worship are more likely to adopt these values as standard practice. Over time, the church fosters a culture where generosity, accountability, and attentiveness to marginalized voices become second nature. In an era where consumer-driven attitudes often dominate, these sacred rites counter prevailing norms by showing that genuine community thrives when resources are shared equitably, and status is not linked solely to individual wealth or achievement. By centering communal well-being within religious observances, the congregation exemplifies a model of faith committed to unity and cooperation.

One of the text's most practical outcomes is the encouragement to establish institutional frameworks that reflect gawani, feminist, and Black liberation teachings. Rather than relying on short bursts of goodwill, congregations can formalize equitable decision-making structures. For instance, they might create rotating leadership councils, mandate gender parity in committees, or adopt transparent accounting processes that enable members to see precisely how funds are used. These systems help maintain accountability over time, guaranteeing that resource sharing remains more than a buzzword. Coupled with ongoing theological study, these structural shifts create a community environment where every individual's perspective informs policy and spiritual growth.

In concert with such internal reforms, the text advocates for strategic external partnerships. Local faith communities can join broader coalitions to address housing shortages, environmental degradation, or discriminatory lending. By collaborating with civic groups, nonprofits, and even government agencies aligned with fairness-driven aims, congregations magnify their collective influence. Partnerships, however, also involve risks, as external entities may have diverging agendas or power imbalances that undermine community aims. Consequently, the text recommends that churches remain vigilant, ensuring that any alliance fortifies, rather than dilutes, their theological commitments to equity and compassion.

Throughout all of these discussions, hope emerges as an indispensable element. The study does not suggest that confronting injustice is simple or that communal cooperation always runs smoothly. On the contrary, disagreements, resource limitations, and external political barriers can pose ongoing challenges. Yet this hope is anchored in a theological conviction that acting in solidarity with marginalized neighbors aligns with fundamental scriptural teachings about compassion and shared responsibility. Because of this alignment, even modest results become occasions for renewed commitment, knowing that persistent, smaller efforts often accumulate into a broader social movement.

Moreover, the text reframes the typical narrative of despair that can overshadow discussions of poverty, racism, or environmental harm. While acknowledging these crises' severity, it highlights how genuine collective engagement can mitigate their damaging effects and restore a sense of communal fortitude. Whether describing families supporting each other through political intimidation or churches establishing childcare cooperatives for working parents, the text consistently affirms that local alliances can foster surprising resilience. This foundation of hope is not unrealistic optimism; it is a recognition that small-scale acts of solidarity, rooted in carefully considered theological reflection, carry forward a legacy of meaningful change.

Concluding these reflections, the study envisions a model of faith that is neither exclusively personal nor overwhelmingly institutional. It conceives of congregations as interlinked networks of commitment, where theological concepts gain traction in everyday practices of sharing land, money, time, and moral support. This understanding dismantles the notion of religion as a purely private affair, exposing instead how theological convictions translate into public witness. By establishing transparent structures for giving, involving women and marginalized groups in leadership, and collaborating with broader social movements, churches become catalysts for more equitable societies.

These transformations do not happen instantly. As the text underscores, genuine change typically unfolds through patient, iterative processes, shaped by the uniqueness of local environments. One community might start with agricultural cooperatives, while another focuses on addressing gender disparities. Over time, these local endeavors become steppingstones for expansive coalitions, broadening the scope of communal transformation. In each instance, theological dialogue remains central, reminding participants that justice-oriented faith is not an optional add-on but a direct outworking of biblical imperatives.

Extending this trajectory further, the study encourages ongoing research, experimentation, and mutual learning. Faith leaders, academics, and community organizers can benefit from consistent exchanges, sharing lessons from successful projects as well as cautionary tales. This cumulative knowledge fosters an adaptive communal ethic that can respond to emerging issues like climate disruption, new economic models, or shifting demographic patterns. Ultimately, such adaptability reflects a commitment to weaving theology, culture, and social engagement into a coherent vision—one that tackles real-world problems without sacrificing its core moral convictions.

On a broader level, embracing adaptability also highlights the importance of humility. While the text offers a comprehensive framework, it does not claim that every congregation must replicate the same set of strategies. Instead, it suggests that listening to diverse contexts, whether urban, rural, wealthy, or impoverished, is crucial in shaping relevant responses. What remains constant, however, is the principle that congregations flourish most when they anchor their spiritual lives in demonstrable solidarity. By maintaining a posture of openness to continuous learning and adjustment, they carry forward the scriptural call to love neighbors in continually evolving circumstances.

Looking beyond the congregational sphere, the text envisions that these faith-driven approaches can radiate outward, influencing entire societies. By fostering a spirit of cooperation, churches can help reorient popular ideas about individualism, resource accumulation, and inequality. Educational programs, advocacy campaigns, and public events become conduits for expanding local efforts into larger regional or even national transformations. In some cases, alliances formed around water rights or wage justice have already proven that faith communities can enact policies protecting the vulnerable. The study holds that such policy-level engagement, if grounded in communal practices of sharing, can gradually reshape cultural norms about distribution and equity.

To sustain this expanded role, the text highlights the importance of maintaining theological depth and collective accountability. Without an ongoing ethical framework, activism can drift from its moral center, pursuing short-term successes that do not ultimately serve shared well-being. Therefore, communities are encouraged to keep reflecting on scriptural insights, historical lessons, and interdisciplinary research. Engaging with a range of viewpoints helps them remain flexible yet committed to the fundamental calling to care for one another. In turn, this balance preserves an ethos that is both creative and anchored, capable of addressing contemporary ills without losing sight of longstanding commitments to unity, empathy, and shared responsibility.

In the final analysis, the study offers a comprehensive arrangement of ideas and practical possibilities. By drawing on gawani theology, feminist critiques, Black liberation approaches, and other contextual streams, it provides a robust lens to perceive how faith, economics, and social ethics are intertwined. While acknowledging that obstacles persist, it underscores that repeated, structured acts of resource sharing can reshape communities over time, building trust and empowering marginalized voices. Through worship, policy advocacy, and alliances with various social movements, congregations are positioned to bridge personal devotion with public engagement. This integrated approach stands against superficial forms of charity, calling instead for deeper commitments to changing institutional structures.

One underlying message is that theological reflection remains indispensable, especially when it arises from grassroots experiences of solidarity. Whether gleaned from Malawian farming communities, urban Black churches, feminist reading circles, or any other sphere, local knowledge breathes life into faith traditions. By listening carefully to these voices, believers refine their priorities, ensuring that the church remains an environment where people collaborate for genuine social and economic healing. Far from existing in an isolated domain, faith communities can thus contribute to broader movements seeking a world shaped by collective well-being.

In an era defined by considerable global uncertainty—manifested in political instability, environmental crises, and economic volatility—this text's central themes resonate especially strongly. The emphasis on continuous, practical sharing, supported by scriptural traditions and diverse cultural insights, offers a measure of stability grounded in moral commitments. Communities that devote themselves to neighborly care, transparent leadership, and the honest acknowledgement of injustices forge relationships capable of withstanding external threats. They do so by creating inclusive networks in which resources, responsibilities, and decision-making power circulate rather than concentrate in the hands of a few.

The broader aspiration remains the cultivation of a faith-based environment where spiritual practices, communal ties, and advocacy efforts reinforce one another. Instead of regarding each domain as separate, congregations learn to see their worship and justice work as mutually enriching. In this sense, the text culminates in a vision of church life that actively counters alienation, fosters cross-boundary partnerships, and demonstrates compassion in action. By making these commitments explicit, the faithful show that their gatherings aim to do more than comfort individual souls—they also set out to transform social realities in alignment with longstanding biblical imperatives.

Finally, the study points toward an enduring principle: the integrity of religious devotion grows when congregations embrace solidarity as both a guiding ethic and a lived routine. Even as believers confront internal disagreements or external pressures, a shared focus on distributing goods, knowledge, and support remains a unifying factor. This ethic, affirmed through liturgical moments and community-based practices, testifies that faith cannot be restricted to words alone. Rather, it manifests in consistent, deliberate acts that uphold human dignity across race, gender, class, and nationality. By continuing to refine these practices and learn from one another, congregations cultivate a broader sense of kinship, one aligned with the scriptural call to love one's neighbor fully.

In this arrangement, the pursuit of justice is no longer a fringe activity. Instead, it becomes the natural extension of the church's core identity. Families and individuals, in sharing resources freely, illustrate that living in mutual support is both feasible and theologically resonant. What might start as a grassroots effort in a single locale eventually gains momentum, linking with parallel endeavors worldwide. By taking on these responsibilities consistently and thoughtfully, faith communities fulfill an essential role: they stand as beacons of cooperation and care, determined to practice a vision of collective life where no one is forgotten, and every neighbor is included.

FIVE ADDITIONAL REFLECTIONS FOR ONGOING INQUIRY

A crucial avenue for further research lies in studying how newly emerging digital tools might facilitate and expand these resource sharing frameworks. As technology reshapes communication, networking, and economic exchange, congregations could integrate digital platforms to organize donations, monitor transparency, and establish translocal partnerships. In doing so, they could extend the ethical precepts of gawani or feminist theology into virtual spheres, ensuring that digital innovations serve rather than undermine community well-being. Faith leaders, academics, and activists might collaborate to design platforms that encourage communal accountability and real-time reciprocity, revealing novel horizons for theological engagement in the digital age.

Another promising domain involves the intersection of health advocacy with resource sharing practices. Because health inequalities—evident in disparities in insurance access, hospital proximity, and preventive care—often mirror broader social inequities, congregations are well-suited to address them. By organizing cooperative health funds, advocating mobile clinics, or partnering with community health workers, faith communities can integrate local knowledge about medical needs with broader theological imperatives for healing. This convergence offers a tangible way to demonstrate love of neighbor, reminding believers that caring for bodies, like sharing material goods, is a collective moral priority.

Examining how these efforts interact with governmental policies and institutions constitutes another layer of exploration. While the text highlights the potential of grassroots movements, larger administrative structures inevitably shape the scope of what local groups can accomplish. Some governments may welcome faith-based coalitions, offering grants or legal support, whereas others could be hostile or indifferent, complicating the push for social reform. Future researchers and congregations can analyze these political contexts, determining the most effective ways to balance cooperation with healthy scrutiny of bureaucratic interests. Understanding these institutional contexts empowers believers to engage with public officials while still preserving their core theological commitments to communal equity.

There is also a growing need to investigate how resource sharing models intersect with religious pluralism and interfaith collaboration.

Many global cities house diverse religious communities that might share common values regarding social equity, gender justice, or ecological stewardship. Fostering interreligious dialogue on these topics could create broader alliances, amplifying the impact of local congregations. Shared service projects—such as food banks, refugee assistance, or environmental cleanups—can become catalysts for deeper mutual understanding, transcending doctrinal differences without diluting each tradition's identity. This path requires skillful leadership attuned to potential tensions but also holds promises for more extensive and inclusive community renewal.

Finally, future discussions could delve into the psychology of communal generosity, examining how daily exposure to cooperative practices reshapes individual attitudes. While the text shows that these initiatives collectively strengthen communities, it would be instructive to explore in detail how participants alter their personal outlooks over time. Such research might reveal that repeated participation in shared ownership and economic distribution fosters sustained empathy, heightened moral sensitivity, and a broader inclination to contribute to civic life. By documenting such transformations, theologians and social scientists alike could build a stronger case for why faith-informed resource sharing not only meets immediate needs but also cultivates healthier, more compassionate citizens and institutions for future generations.

Epilogue

Where Seeds of Mercy Take Root

There are moments when a quiet community meal, shared beneath the same roof, can speak of far more than an empty stomach. In these pages, that unspoken language has guided us through fields of leftover maize, through hushed evenings when neighbors pass along whatever they can spare, and through the long shadows cast by forces too large to resist alone. Gawani theology was never simply a formal theory or distant principle—it was the way people lived and breathed their compassion, how they steadied each other's spirits on days when oppression loomed like a storm cloud refusing to move on. By its rhythms of giving and receiving, ordinary families in Malawi discovered that the humblest of gestures can mend more than physical hunger; it can also restore the dignity that an austere world threatens to take away.

In each neighborhood and across many seasons, distributing seeds or harvest wasn't just about practicality. Sometimes, it was about a mother pressing into another's hand a handful of corn kernels at dusk, believing that dawn might bring the promise of survival for both their families. Sometimes, it was about congregations that turned Sunday prayer into a vow, a promise that no one in the village would face hunger or eviction alone. In that gentle light, the local church was no longer a building to be visited but a circle of extended arms, offering safety and companionship. Gawani theology breathed in these protective gestures, insisting that no outside authority could ever fully crush a tradition born from centuries of adversity and hope.

Through these stories, one glimpses how small streams of everyday kindness can flow together into a larger river. Even when crises—political or environmental—swept in, those droplets of compassion created invisible paths of resilience. Some might say each act of sharing was too modest to matter against the grand stage of systemic challenges. But in Malawi, a neighborly loan of seeds became a bright thread in a tapestry of mutual trust, weaving families together and sustaining them during seasons of lurking threats. Gawani theology, standing beside liberation perspectives, liberation theologies, and other movements, offers its own gentler but tenacious claim: that real faith doesn't drift above our daily struggles but walks among them, creating a legacy of communal care that can outlast repression.

It was never enough to speak of abstract theology or moral principles from a distance. Instead, a pastor learned from market vendors how to manage leftover produce, or a missionary quietly realized that the greatest teacher in the room was often the woman who had balanced farmland tasks with raising a dozen children. In these daily lessons, mutual discovery replaced one-sided instruction, guiding communities to the realization that their future lay in valuing each person's insight. Hand in hand, they transformed resource sharing into a form of unspoken worship, weaving biblical themes of neighborly love with local customs of clan-based support. No matter how austere the times, these unassuming steps etched out a path toward unity.

Within the simplest rituals—dividing harvest, comanaging livestock, rotating small loans—there grew a sense of covenant. Week by week, families who had little knew precisely how vital it was to sustain each other, especially under the long arm of an authoritarian presence. Seeds passed from household to household, and so did quiet affirmations of care. If the only real power people held was in their ability to stand shoulder to shoulder, then they transformed that power into a warm heartbeat of generosity. Gawani theology spoke into this reality like a familiar voice, reminding them that wherever two or three gather to share burdens, a holy bond takes shape.

Yet this narrative carries complexities. In times when intimidation seems to color every corner of life, collective trust can be fragile, subject to manipulation by those who want to bind communities under a single will. Even so, gawani theology repeatedly illustrated how local solidarity could slip through the fingers of oppressive authority, like seeds sowed in unexpected cracks of land. Quiet networks, clandestine gatherings, and the relentless vow that no one should be left behind became forms of defiance. Under such tension, even a little leftover produce or a discreetly offered place to sleep spoke volumes: the language of the people was woven with generosity, and no top-down rule could easily tear that fabric.

The reason these gestures carried such promise was not because anyone believed in an ideal, untainted tradition. Gawani theology acknowledges that its own cultural practices need constant examination. Some customs risk preserving imbalances—whether through patriarchy, undervalued female labor, or subtle social divisions. Yet the real strength of gawani lies in its openness to introspection, in the communal resolve to refine any habit that undermines fairness. Time and again, this approach has shown that living theology means being willing to discard practices that harm the vulnerable, even if doing so demands reshaping local norms. In that sense, gawani is neither frozen in the past nor wholly unsettled by the present; it is always poised at the intersection of memory and tomorrow.

For a church in Malawi, worship can take the shape of an entire evening spent working together under lamplight, packaging seeds for each household, discussing next season's planting strategy, or deciding how to support a distant neighbor. In these intervals, Scripture finds new life as people mirror the earliest believers who pooled resources, ensuring no one stood forsaken. The sermon is no longer confined to words from a pulpit, for the sermon is also in the roughened hands passing along sacks of grain and in the quiet gratitude of those receiving them. Far from being a separate domain, theology manifests when hearts and bodies come together for the common good, moment by moment.

There is also a light that flickers as more modern influences reach across Malawi, from mobile financial apps to sprawling urban job opportunities. Younger generations seek to balance ancient communal wisdom with the faster pace of technological possibilities. Gawani theology may adapt by endorsing new microfinance systems, reimagined cooperatives, or alternative trading structures, all the while remembering that at its core it remains an ethic of generosity: a vow not to let each other slip into isolation or despair. The frame shifts over time, an agricultural field might become a digital platform—but the impulse to share endures as the anchor.

Above all, these stories urge us to see that forging a communal future is less about grand programs than about the steady accumulation of heartfelt acts. Each bowl of shared porridge, each seed-lending arrangement, each child taught to pass their extra portion to a less fortunate friend—these are the seemingly minor threads that can stitch a more harmonious society. From the vantage point of gawani, each neighbor's well-being is already intricately tied to our own. In that sense, the theology illustrated here dares to say that caring is not a gift bestowed from the powerful to the weak but a commitment that we all shape, day after day.

When we gather all these pieces—day-to-day resource sharing, scriptural echoes, communal resilience, and the willingness to evolve—gawani theology stands before us as a living tapestry rather than a finished document. It mirrors the humility and perseverance of so many Malawian families who refuse to let intimidation or scarcity define their destiny. In small rooms, under candlelight, seeds of mercy and hope pass from one hand to another, and in that gentle act, we witness the simple truth that community can be both cradle and shield. If we look closer, we may see that this understanding extends far beyond Malawi's borders, suggesting that no matter where we call home, we can find paths to stand beside each other and live out our compassion in ways both tender and strong.

So let this serve as a final invitation. Let these accounts breathe into our awareness a gentler but enduring possibility: that theology, rightly lived, is an exchange of comfort and resolve, anchoring us to the people around us. Let it remind us that every shared handful of grain or shared place at the table carries the stories of our past and the seeds of what might yet come. And let it encourage us to recognize that every time we choose to see another's need as part of our own, something sacred resonates in the ordinary, and hope stands ready to shape tomorrow.

Bibliography

Ahn, Byung-Mu. *Draußen vor dem Tor: Kirche und Minjung in Korea*. Theologische Beiträge und Reflexionen. Göttingen: Vandenhoeck & Ruprecht, 1986.
Althaus-Reid, Marcella. *Indecent Theology: Theological Perversions in Sex, Gender and Politics*. London: Psychology Press, 2000.
Amosi, Mercy. "Ubuntu Liturgy and Social Ethics in Malawian Churches." *Journal of African Christian Thought* 10 (2020) 33–36.
Bantekas, Ilias, and Cephas Lumina, eds. *Sovereign Debt and Human Rights*. Oxford: Oxford University Press, 2018.
Boff, Leonardo, and Clodovis Boff. *Introducing Liberation Theology*. London: Burns & Oates, 1987.
———. *Introducing Liberation Theology*. Maryknoll, NY: Orbis Books, 2001.
Bonhoeffer, Dietrich, and Samuel Wells. *Life Together*. London: SCM, 2015.
Brueggemann, Walter. *Deliver Us: Salvation and the Liberating God of the Bible*. Louisville: Westminster John Knox, 2022.
———. *Genesis: Interpretation—A Bible Commentary for Teaching and Preaching*. Louisville: Westminster John Knox, 2010.
Buber, Martin. *I and Thou*. New York: Simon & Schuster, 2000.
Carmichael, Stokely, and Charles V. Hamilton. *Black Power: The Politics of Liberation in America*. New York: Random House, 1967.
Chopp, Rebecca S. *The Power to Speak: Feminism, Language, God*. Eugene, OR: Wipf & Stock, 2002.
Cone, James H. *A Black Theology of Liberation*. Maryknoll, NY: Orbis Books, 2010.
———. *God of the Oppressed*. Maryknoll, NY: Orbis Books, 1975.
———. *The Spirituals and the Blues: An Interpretation*. Maryknoll, NY: Orbis Books, 1991.
Davies, Anna R. *Urban Food Sharing: Rules, Tools, and Networks*. Bristol, UK: Policy Press, 2019.
Derrida, Jacques. *Of Grammatology*. Translated by Gayatri Chakravorty Spivak. Baltimore: Johns Hopkins University Press, 2016.
Dube, Musa W., et al., eds. *Postcolonial Perspectives in African Biblical Interpretations*. Atlanta: Society of Biblical Literature, 2012.

Dupont, Jacques. *Les Béatitudes: Le problème littéraire—Les deux versions du Sermon sur la montagne et des Béatitudes*. Bruges: Abbaye de Saint-André, 1958.
Ela, Jean-Marc. *Cri de l'homme africain*. Paris: Éditions L'Harmattan, 1980.
Engels, Friedrich. *The Origin of the Family, Private Property, and the State*. New York: International Publishers, 1972.
Fanon, Frantz. *Black Skin, White Masks*. New York: Grove Press, 2008.
Frankl, Viktor Emil. *Man's Search for Meaning*. Boston: Beacon, 2006.
Freire, Paulo. *Pedagogy of the Oppressed*. New York: Continuum, 2000.
———. *Pedagogy of the Oppressed*. 50th anniversary ed. London: Bloomsbury Academic, 2018.
Fretheim, Terence E. *Exodus: Interpretation: A Bible Commentary for Teaching and Preaching*. Louisville: Westminster John Knox, 2010.
Friesen, Steven J. *Imperial Cults and the Apocalypse of John: Reading Revelation in the Ruins*. Oxford: Oxford University Press, 2001.
———. "Poverty in Pauline Studies: Beyond the So-Called New Consensus." *Journal for the Study of the New Testament* 26 (2004) 323–61.
Gadamer, Hans-Georg. *Truth and Method*. 2nd rev. ed. London: Continuum, 2004.
Gutiérrez, Gustavo. *A Theology of Liberation*. Rev. ed. Maryknoll, NY: Orbis Books, 1988.
Herder, Johann Gottfried. *Philosophical Writings*. Cambridge: Cambridge University Press, 2002.
Hill, Christopher. *The World Turned Upside Down: Radical Ideas During the English Revolution*. London: Penguin Books, 2020.
Huizinga, Johan. *Homo Ludens: A Study of the Play Element in Culture*. Boston: Beacon, 1955.
Isasi-Díaz, Ada María. *La Lucha Continues: Mujerista Theology*. Maryknoll, NY: Orbis Books, 2004.
Johnson, Elizabeth A. *She Who Is: The Mystery of God in Feminist Theological Discourse*. New York: Crossroad, 1992.
Kang, Joseph. *Theology of Gawani: Toward Interconnectedness and Wholeness of Life—A Preliminary Survey of the Gospels and the Book of Acts*. Unpublished manuscript, 2023.
Kayange, Grivas M., and Charles Verharen, eds. *Ethics in Malawi*. Washington, DC: Council for Research in Values and Philosophy, 2021.
Kim, Yong Sung. *Theodizee als Problem der Philosophie und Theologie: Zur Frage nach dem Leiden und dem Bösen im Blick auf den allmächtigen und guten Gott*. Münster: Lit Verlag, 2002.
Kittel, Gerhard, et al., eds. *Theological Dictionary of the New Testament*. Vol. 5. Grand Rapids: Eerdmans, 1964.
Kröger, Wolfgang. *Die Befreiung des Minjung: Das Profil Einer Protestantischen Befreiungstheologie für Asien in Ökumenischer Perspektive*. Ökumenische Existenz Heute 10. Munich: Kaiser, 1992.
Kwok, Pui-lan. *Postcolonial Imagination and Feminist Theology*. Louisville: Westminster John Knox, 2005.
Lonergan, Bernard. *Method in Theology*. Toronto: University of Toronto Press, 1990.
Mbiti, John Samuel. *African Religions and Philosophy*. 2nd ed. London: Heinemann, 1990.
McCracken, John. *A History of Malawi, 1859–1966*. Woodbridge, UK: Boydell & Brewer, 2012.

Metz, Johann Baptist. *Faith in History and Society: Toward a Practical Fundamental Theology*. New York: Crossroad, 2007.
Moltmann, Jürgen. *The Church in the Power of the Spirit: A Contribution to Messianic Ecclesiology*. Philadelphia: Fortress, 1993.
———. *The Crucified God: The Cross of Christ as the Foundation and Criticism of Christian Theology: 40th Anniversary Edition*. Translated by R. A. Wilson and J. Bowden. Philadelphia: Fortress, 2015.
———. *Jesus Christ for Today's World*. London: SCM, 1994.
Moyo, Thokozile. "Naming Practices in Colonial and Postcolonial Malawi." *Inkanyiso: Journal of Humanities and Social Sciences* 4 (2012) 10–17.
———, ed. *Minjung Theologie des Volkes Gottes in Südkorea*. Neukirchen-Vluyn: Neukirchener Verlag, 1984.
———. *Theology of Hope: On the Ground and the Implications of a Christian Eschatology*. New York: Harper & Row, 1967.
Nasambu-Mulongo, Emily. "Bosadi: Madipoane (Ngwana' Mphahlele) Masenya's Contribution to African Women's Biblical Hermeneutics." In *Postcolonial Perspectives in African Biblical Interpretations*, edited by Musa W. Dube et al., 43–62. Atlanta: Society of Biblical Literature, 2012.
Novak, Michael. *The Experience of Nothingness*. New York: Harper & Row, 1970.
Oduyoye, Mercy Amba. *Daughters of Anowa: African Women and Patriarchy*. Maryknoll, NY: Orbis Books, 1995.
Phiri, Isabel Apawo. *Women, Presbyterianism and Patriarchy: Religious Experience of Chewa Women in Central Malawi*. Blantyre, Malawi: CLAIM, 1997.
Pieris, Aloysius. *Asian Theology of Liberation*. London: Bloomsbury, 1988.
Ross, Kenneth R., and Wapulumuka O. Mulwafu, eds. *Politics, Christianity and Society in Malawi: Essays in Honour of John McCracken*. Mzuzu, Malawi: Mzuni Press, 2020.
Ruether, Rosemary Radford. *Sexism and God-Talk: Toward a Feminist Theology*. Boston: Beacon, 1983.
Russell, Letty M., ed. *Feminist Interpretation of the Bible*. Philadelphia: Westminster Press, 1985.
Schleiermacher, Friedrich. *On Religion: Speeches to Its Cultured Despisers*. Cambridge: Cambridge University Press, 1996.
Schüssler Fiorenza, Elisabeth. *In Memory of Her: A Feminist Theological Reconstruction of Christian Origins*. New York: Crossroad, 1984.
Sobrino, Jon. *Christology at the Crossroads*. Maryknoll, NY: Orbis Books, 1978.
Styron, William. *The Confessions of Nat Turner*. New York: Random House, 1966.
Townes, Emilie Maureen. *Womanist Ethics and the Cultural Production of Evil*. Cham, Switzerland: Springer, 2006.
Trible, Phyllis. *God and the Rhetoric of Sexuality*. Philadelphia: Fortress, 1978.
Trilling, Wolfgang. *Das Wahre Israel: Studien Zur Theologie des Matthäusevangeliums*. Liepzig: Benno, 1959.
Tutu, Desmond. *No Future Without Forgiveness*. New York: Doubleday, 1999.
Ucko, Hans. *The People and the People of God: Minjung and Dalit Theology in Interaction with Jewish-Christian Dialogue*. Münster: Lit Verlag, 2002.
van Breugel, Johannes W. M. *Chewa Traditional Religion*. Blantyre, Malawi: Christian Literature Association in Malawi, 2001.

Vermeullen, Jules. *Chinyanja (Chichewa)–English Dictionary*. Ndola, Zambia: Missionaries of Africa (White Fathers), 1979.

Waetjen, Herman C. *The Gospel of the Beloved Disciple: A Work in Two Editions*. London: Bloomsbury, 2005.

———. *Matthew's Theology of Fulfillment, Its Universality, and Its Ethnicity: God's New Israel as the Pioneer of God's New Humanity*. London: T&T Clark, 2017.

———. *A Reordering of Power: A Sociopolitical Reading of Mark's Gospel*. Philadelphia: Fortress Press, 1989.

Walton, Steve, and Hannah Swithinbank. *Poverty in the Early Church and Today: A Conversation*. London: Bloomsbury, 2019.

Willms, D. Glen, et al. "Malawi Faith Communities Responding to HIV/AIDS: Preliminary Findings of a Knowledge Translation and Participatory-Action Research (PAR) Project." *African Journal of AIDS Research* 3 (2004) 23–32.

Witherington, Ben, III. *The Acts of the Apostles: A Socio-Rhetorical Commentary*. Grand Rapids: Eerdmans, 1997.

Wright, N. T., et al. *Surprised by Hope Participant's Guide: Rethinking Heaven, the Resurrection, and the Mission of the Church*. Nashville: HarperChristian Resources, 2013.

www.ingramcontent.com/pod-product-compliance
Lightning Source LLC
Chambersburg PA
CBHW050343230426
43663CB00010B/1974